Performance Indicators in Higher Education

UK Universities

Jill Johnes and
Jim Taylor

The Society for Research into Higher Education
& Open University Press

Published by SRHE and
Open University Press
Celtic Court
22 Ballmoor
Buckingham
MK18 1XW

and
1900 Frost Road, Suite 101
Bristol, PA 19007, USA

First Published 1990

Copyright © Jill Johnes and Jim Taylor 1990

British Library Cataloguing in Publication Data

Johnes, Jill
    Performance indicators in higher education.
    1. Great Britain. Universities
    I. Title.   II. Taylor, Jim.
    III. Society for Research into Higher Education
    378.41

    ISBN 0–335–09455–4
    ISBN 0–335–09454–6 (pbk)

Library of Congress Cataloging in Publication Data

Johnes, Jill, 1962–
        Performance indicators in higher education: UK universities/
    Jill Johnes and Jim Taylor.
        p.   cm.
        Includes bibliographical references and index.
        ISBN 0–335–09455–4   ISBN 0–335–09454–6 (pbk.)
        1. Universities and colleges – Great Britain – Evaluation.
        2. Educational accountability – Great Britain.
        3. Federal aid to higher education – Great Britain.
    I. Taylor, Jim, 1941–
    II. Title.
    LA637.J64   1990
    379.1'54 – dc20   90–39316
                                                           CIP

ISBN 0–335–09455–4
ISBN 0–335–09454–6 pbk (Open University Press)

Typeset by Scarborough Typesetting Services
Printed in Great Britain by St Edmundsbury Press,
Bury St Edmunds, Suffolk

To our parents

Contents

Preface

Our interest in performance indicators in UK universities began by accident. One of the authors was asked by a colleague what he thought of Michael Dixon's annual league table (in the *Financial Times*) based upon the first destination of newly qualified graduates. It is sufficient to say that the reply to this question was not very complimentary. The perpetual appearance of this annual league table – and the accompanying self-congratulation or paranoia which it appears to generate – induced the authors to investigate whether the first destination record of each university's annual crop of graduates served any useful purpose as a performance indicator. After all, it is intuitively appealing to regard universities which have a high proportion of their graduates obtaining permanent jobs as being more successful than universities in which a much smaller proportion of their graduates manage to do so. The truth is more complicated, as we shall see.

While this work on the first destination of graduates was in progress, it became clear that the government was becoming increasingly keen on a more systematic evaluation of the higher education sector. This became clear with the publication of a Green Paper in 1985, *The Development of Higher Education into the 1990s*, and was reinforced in the subsequent White Paper on *Higher Education: Meeting the Challenge*. Both of these affirmed the government's commitment to making the higher education sector more accountable to the taxpayer. The Committee of Vice-Chancellors and Principals had anticipated these developments and as early as April 1984 had set up a committee chaired by Sir Alex Jarratt to inquire into the efficiency of the management of universities. The Jarratt Report argued strongly for an improved system of monitoring what universities do and how they do it so that their performance could be assessed. It was hardly surprising to find the government in complete agreement with Jarratt's proposals.

It is therefore the purpose of this book to explore the possibility of constructing performance indicators for the university sector. Given the inevitable resource constraints, we have focused attention on a limited range of variables which purport to measure the teaching and research outputs of universities. Furthermore, we made an early decision to concentrate our attention on the university sector as a whole rather than focus on any one part of it. We therefore set our sights on comparing the performance of *institutions*, using a range of variables which have been frequently mentioned as potentially useful performance indicators by policy-makers and university administrators. Initially we concentrated on what may be termed 'teaching indicators', namely the undergraduate non-completion rate, degree results and the first destination of newly qualified graduates. This list was subsequently extended to cover unit costs and research performance (following the Universities Funding Council's 1989 research selectivity exercise).

It needs to be stressed at the outset that our intention in this book is not to produce a set of ready-made, off-the-shelf performance indicators which those administering the university sector, either within institutions or at 'higher' levels, can use for resource allocation purposes. Our primary aim is to take a critical look at several variables which have been identified as potentially useful quantitative indicators of performance at the institutional level. It also needs to be stressed that the performance indicators investigated in this book provide only a very narrow and partial picture of the activities of the higher education sector. They provide very little information about the wider social, cultural and economic benefits accruing from higher education. We do not pretend that we are doing anything more than scratching the surface of what is, in effect, an immensely difficult (and perhaps ultimately impossible) task. Nevertheless, we feel that the issue of performance measurement in higher education is sufficiently important for serious questions to be asked about its usefulness and practicality. Whether those involved in academia like it or not, performance indicators are probably here to stay – at least for the foreseeable future. It is therefore essential to investigate thoroughly any so-called performance indicators which are likely to be used for resource allocation purposes. The main aim of this book is to do just that.

We should like to thank various people and organizations for making this book possible. The most credit goes to Michael Dixon of the *Financial Times* for his initial provocation and for suggesting that more detailed research into performance indicators would be an interesting avenue to pursue – and he was right. We are also grateful to Geraint Johnes and Gareth Williams for their encouragement and advice, as well as the many registrars who very kindly permitted us to use unpublished data stored at the Universities' Statistical Record (USR), Cheltenham.

This book would not have been written without financial help from the ESRC, the SERC (which funded Jill Johnes's PhD studentship) and the Nuffield Foundation. To all three funding bodies, we offer our sincere thanks. In addition, we relied to a very considerable extent on unpublished data obtained from the USR at Cheltenham. We thank the USR's staff for the efficient and cheerful way in which they dealt with our numerous requests for information. The research reported in this book would not have been possible without their help and co-operation. It goes without saying that the authors themselves are responsible for all errors, omissions, inaccuracies and views expressed in this book.

Last but by no means least, we thank Janet Parker for her excellent secretarial assistance and our respective spouses for their forbearance.

We hope that this book contributes in some way to the debate on the evaluation of the higher education sector.

1
The Clamour for Performance Indicators

Introduction

This book is concerned with the construction and evaluation of performance indicators in higher education. Not many years ago, any attempt to measure the performance of institutions of higher education would have been regarded with horror in academic circles. Attitudes have changed very rapidly during the 1980s, however, as a result of the government's determination to make the public sector more accountable to the taxpayer. This has inevitably led towards more careful scrutiny of the way in which the taxpayers' money is being used in order to discover whether the public sector's efficiency and effectiveness could be improved. All parts of the public sector – including higher education – are now expected to monitor and evaluate their activities more carefully than has hitherto been the case.

The government's interest in developing a more rigorous set of procedures for evaluating the higher education sector was first highlighted in the 1985 Green Paper on *The Development of Higher Education into the 1990s*. This pressed for fundamental improvements in the contribution of the higher education sector to national economic development. According to the Green Paper, the higher education sector's performance was below par and needed to be improved. In particular,

> there is continuing concern that higher education does not respond sufficiently to changing needs. This may be due in part to disincentives to change within higher education, including over-dependence on public funding, and to failures in communication between employers and institutions.
>
> (DES 1985: 6)

Moreover,

> The Government believes that it is vital for our higher education to contribute more effectively to the improvement of the performance of the economy.
>
> (DES 1985: 3)

According to the government, the higher education sector could improve its efficiency and effectiveness in several ways:

1. *Higher education should be more responsive to the needs of the economy.* This will require closer links to be forged between higher education and industry. In addition, it will also be necessary to switch the subject mix away from the arts and humanities towards technical and vocational courses.
2. *Higher education depends far too heavily on public funds* and greater efforts are needed to raise private funds through applied research, consultancy and continuing education.
3. *Greater selectivity is needed in the allocation of research funding* so that more resources are concentrated in the centres of excellence.
4. *The higher education sector needs to be more cost-conscious* and should manage its resources more efficiently and more effectively. This will require the construction and regular publication of a range of performance indicators. These will be used to aid the resource allocation process both within and between institutions.

These recommendations were reiterated in the White Paper (DES 1987b) on *Higher Education: Meeting the Challenge*, which provided a clear statement (in broad terms) of the government's main policies for higher education. The government's own summary statement of these policies is given in Table 1.1. The White Paper also announced that the University Grants Committee (UGC) was to be replaced by the Universities Funding Council (UFC) and that polytechnics and colleges were to be funded by the newly established Polytechnics and Colleges Funding Council (PCFC). These two new bodies became operational in April 1989.

The change from being a *grant* awarding body to a *funding* council (in the case of the replacement of the UGC by the UFC) is worth noting. The significance of this distinction between grants and funding was made crystal clear in a consultative document issued by the government in 1987 (DES 1987a). This document was important in so far as it gave advance warning of a change in the way the higher education sector was to be funded. It proposed that the method of allocating funds to universities should be changed from the block grant system to one based upon contractual agreements drawn up between each university and the UFC (and similarly for the polytechnics' and colleges' sector). According to this consultative document, universities would be expected to offer and deliver a clearly specified range of educational services in return for UFC funding. If implemented, this new method of funding would give the UFC and the government much greater control over the range and type of courses offered by each institution.

More recently the DES has released a further consultative document (DES 1989) which proposes an amendment to the existing method of funding by suggesting that higher education institutions should obtain a greater proportion of their income from student fees and correspondingly

Table 1.1   The government's policy towards higher education

Higher education has a crucial role in helping the nation meet the economic and social challenges of the final decade of this century and beyond. The main elements of the Government's policies for higher education and the major changes it intends to secure to improve the effectiveness of the system are:

Higher education should

serve the economy more effectively

pursue basic scientific research and scholarship in the arts and humanities

have closer links with industry and commerce, and promote enterprise.

To take greater account of the country's needs for highly qualified manpower, the Government will

plan for student numbers to increase in the next few years, to return to present levels in the mid-1990s and then grow again

study the needs of the economy so as to achieve the right number and balance of graduates in the 1990s

plan to increase participation rates among young people, particularly young women, and mature entrants – by building on improvements in schools and colleges, and in admission arrangements for those with non-traditional qualifications

further develop continuing education, particularly professional updating.

Quality will be enhanced by

improvements in the design and content of courses, and in validation procedures

better teaching through staff training, development and appraisal

more selectively funded research, targeted with attention to prospects for commercial exploitation.

Efficiency will be increased by

improvements in institutional management

changes in the management of the system

the development and use of performance indicators.

Source: DES 1987b; iv.

less from block grants. It is proposed that about 30 per cent of each university's income should come from student fees (by 1991/92) compared to only 8 per cent in 1989/90. This swing in the balance of funding away from block grants towards student fees is intended to make the university sector more responsive to the demand for higher education courses. This issue is discussed in more detail in Chapter 2.

The new funding arrangements announced in 1989 will therefore have mixed effects on the higher education sector. On the one hand, institutions of higher education are being required to bid for a slice of the block grant allocated by the two Funding Councils. This proportion of the funding will consequently be determined by the Funding Councils' views about the quality and cost of the educational services delivered by each institution. There will therefore be more control from the centre. On the other hand, the sharp increase in the proportion of funding emanating from student fees means that consumer demand will play an increasing role in determining the distribution of public funds between institutions and between courses. Consumer power will therefore become more important. The balance between these two opposing determinants of the way in which public funds are allocated between institutions (central control v. consumer power) will ultimately be decided by the government in the light of experience. (Chapter 3 discusses these new funding arrangements in more detail.)

The demand for evaluation

Growing discontent within government circles in the early 1980s about the effectiveness of the university sector and its contribution to the national economy led directly to the setting up of the Jarratt Committee by the Committee of Vice-Chancellors and Principals (Jarratt 1985). The purpose of this Committee was to inquire into the efficiency and effectiveness of universities. This involved an investigation into the general management structure and decision-making processes of institutions as well as reviewing the methods used by individual universities for monitoring the use of resources. Jarratt's main recommendations were that the management structure of universities needed to be overhauled and that each university should develop its own strategic plan.

One of the consequences of the recommendation that universities should be managed more efficiently and more effectively was the further recommendation that reliable and consistent performance indicators needed to be developed for evaluation purposes. Jarratt suggested that

> A range of performance indicators should be developed, covering both inputs and outputs and designed for use both within individual institutions and for making comparisons between institutions.
>
> (Jarratt 1985: 36)

The Jarratt Committee was not slow to respond to its own suggestion that performance indicators should be constructed. It proposed three groups of indicators: internal indicators, external indicators and operational indicators (see Table 1.2). *Internal indicators* relate to variables such as each university's market share of undergraduate applications, degree results, completion rates, teaching quality and attraction of research funds. *External indicators* are concerned with the external performance of a university as reflected by the employability of its graduates, its research record, the reputation of its staff and its success in producing inventions.

Table 1.2 Performance indicators proposed in the Jarratt
Report

Internal performance indicators include

– market share of undergraduate applications (by subject)
– graduation rates and classes of degrees
– attraction of masters and doctoral students
– success rate of higher degrees (and time taken)
– attraction of research funds
– teaching quality.

External performance indicators include

– acceptability of graduates (postgraduates) in employment
– first destination of graduates (postgraduates)
– reputation judged by external reviews
– publications by staff and citations
– patents, inventions, consultancies
– membership, prizes, medals of learned societies
– papers at conferences.

Operational performance indicators include

– unit costs
– staff/student ratios
– class sizes
– course options available
– staff workloads
– library stock availability
– computing availability.

Source: Jarratt 1985: 53.

Operational indicators relate more directly to the activities of individual
departments and include variables such as cost per student, student/staff
ratios, staff workloads, availability of library and computing facilities and
class sizes.

The DES responded immediately and warmly to the Jarratt Report's
recommendations on performance indicators:

> The Government believes there would be advantage in the regular
> publication of a range of unit cost and other performance indicators by
> institution and by department. It therefore welcomes the Jarratt
> Report's suggestions for developing reliable and consistent perform-
> ance indicators designed for use both within individual universities
> and for making comparisons between them. The development of such
> indicators will be important for the internal management of insti-
> tutions and for the development of a policy on the allocation of
> resources more generally.
>
> (DES 1985: 31)

The government was not content with simply supporting the Jarratt Committee's suggestion that a range of performance indicators should be constructed. It also expressed a clear view about how the performance of institutions should be measured:

> Academic standards and the quality of teaching in higher education need to be judged by reference mainly to students' achievements. The numbers and class distribution of degrees awarded provide some measure as, conversely, do non-completion rates. External examiners' reports offer a vital commentary, and effective scrutiny of these by institutions is essential.

Moreover,

> The subsequent employment patterns of students provide some indication of the value of higher education courses to working life. Evaluation of institutional performance also requires students' achievements to be set alongside their entry standards. Greater attention needs to be given to these questions both nationally and by institution; and the essential data on performance in each institution should be published so that its record can be evaluated by the funding agencies, governing bodies, students and employers.
>
> (DES 1987b: 18)

Hence it is the government's view that the regular publication of performance indicators will be useful to various agents. The UFC want information which will permit an evaluation of whether universities are achieving their objectives and at what cost. The governing bodies of universities need to know how their own university is performing compared to other institutions. Potential students want to know which institutions are performing well in the provision of teaching and in the success of graduates in the labour market.

But how should universities be evaluated? What kind of information is required in order to assess the performance of individual institutions and their constitutent parts? What methods are available for assessing an institution's performance? So far, very little attention has been paid to such questions. Attention has been focused almost entirely on the collection and publication of basic information which it is believed will be needed for assessing institutional performance. Very little thought has yet been given to exactly how performance indicators can be constructed from this information (Cave and Hanney 1990). It therefore seems appropriate to consider how the increasing amount of information relating to the activities of universities should be used in the evaluation process.

The response to the demand for performance indicators

The UGC and the Committee of Vice-Chancellors and Principals (CVCP) responded quickly to the Jarratt Report's recommendations on performance indicators by setting up a joint Working Group, which proposed a more detailed set of indicators than those suggested in the Jarratt Report. More importantly the UGC/CVCP Working Group proposed the publication of a set of performance indicators at the earliest possible date. The aim of the Working Group was to develop, construct and publish (annually) a range of *quantitative* indicators which would 'assist universities in the running of their affairs'. In addition, the flow of more information describing the activities of universities was intended to 'enhance greater public accountability and a better informed public involvement in university affairs' (CVCP 1988: 5).

The indicators produced by the Working Group are intended to have the following characteristics:

1. they should relate to the objectives of universities, especially those concerned with teaching and research;
2. they should be specific, quantifiable and standardized so that comparisons can be made within and between institutions;
3. they should be as simple as possible in order to aid understanding of the activities of universities about which they provide information;
4. they should be acceptable, credible and free from bias;
5. they should provide useful information about the operations and activities of institutions and they should be expected to provoke questions about these operations and activities.

Three broad types of indicators were identified by the Working Group:

1. input indicators: these are concerned with the resources and factors employed in order to produce each institution's outputs;
2. process indicators: these relate to the way in which resources and factors are combined and used in order to produce each institution's outputs;
3. output indicators: these describe the outputs produced by universities.

During the first three years of its operation, the Working Group concentrated mainly on producing indicators relating to inputs into the university system since this information has been the easiest to collate. There is very little information about processes and about outputs (see Table 1.3).

Hence, although a wide range of management statistics has been collated by the UGC/CVCP Working Group (CVCP 1987; 1988; 1989), it is still far from clear whether this information will be useful for evaluating the performance of institutions. Evaluation involves far more than simply providing information about a set of variables which relate to the activities of institutions. If institutions are to be evaluated, it is first necessary to establish each institution's objectives. Their objectives need to be clearly

Table 1.3 Management statistics and performance indicators published by the UGC/CVCP Working Group: summary table

Indicators (Numerator of each indicator)	(Denominator of each indicator)			
	Total general expenditure	Number of students[1]	Number of academic staff[1]	Available for cost centres
Expenditure indicators				
Total general expenditure		+	+	
Expenditure on				
support staff			+	
equipment			+	
central administration	+	+	+	
library – total	+	+	+	
– books	+	+		
– periodicals	+	+		
computer services	+	+		
premises	+	+		
heat, water, electricity	+	+		
cleaning, custodial services	+	+		
repairs, maintenance	+	+		
telephones	+	+		
careers		+		
student unions, societies		+		
Student input indicators[1]				
Students			+	+
Research postgraduates			+	+
Taught postgraduates			+	+
Research indicators				
Research income			+	
Other indicators				
Percentage of new graduates unemployed or in a short-term job				
Percentage successful leavers				+
Entry qualifications (A level scores and Scottish highers)				+

Note:
1. Full-time equivalents
Source: CVCP 1988.

specified so that an attempt can be made to measure the extent to which they are being achieved – and at what cost. Indeed, it is also necessary to evaluate the objectives themselves since it is important to establish whether what each university aims to achieve is worthy of public funding.

In practice, it is likely that the evaluation process will be limited to inter-departmental and inter-university comparisons between the variables produced by the Working Group. Whether such comparisons will serve any useful purpose is impossible to say, especially in the absence of an acceptable evaluation methodology. It is tempting, for example, to compare the performance of universities by using variables such as

– unit costs
– percentage of students not completing their degree course
– percentage of graduates with a first or upper second class honours degree
– percentage of graduates unemployed or in a short-term job (six months after graduation)
– research grants per full-time academic
– research rating (calculated from the UFC's research rating exercise).

Tables 1.4 and 1.5 provide information on each of these variables for all UK universities. It can be seen that some universities performed relatively well on several indicators while others performed relatively badly. The 'good performers' include Cambridge, Durham, Oxford, Southampton, Warwick and York; the 'poor performers' include Liverpool, Aberdeen, Glasgow, Heriot-Watt, Stirling, Wales and Ulster.

The information given in Tables 1.4 and 1.5 should not, however, be taken seriously even though the individual indicators may look plausible at first sight. The main problem is that the individual indicators do not compare like with like. For example, although it may be interesting to know that university *A* awards a higher proportion of first class degrees than university *B*, this information is of little use *per se* for evaluation purposes since we do not know whether the difference between *A* and *B* is a result of better teaching in *A* or a result of *A* attracting students with more innate ability. If indicators of output (or the quality of output) are to be used as performance measures it is essential to compare like with like. This can be done by taking differences in inputs into account before comparing outputs. The basic procedure is very simple. Instead of comparing each university's outputs with (say) the average for all universities, each university's outputs should be compared with the outputs that we would *expect* each university to produce given its particular mix of inputs. This procedure underlies the method used to construct performance indicators in this book.

In view of the potential importance of the increasing flow of information describing the inputs, processes and outputs of the university sector, especially the influence which such information may have on the allocation of resources within and between institutions, it is the purpose of this book to investigate the possibility of constructing an appropriate methodology for assessing the performance of institutions.

Table 1.4   Some popular performance indicators, 1986/87

University	Unit costs[1] (£ thousands)	% of students not completing their degree course	% of graduates with a first or upper second	% of graduates unemployed or in a short-term job[2]	Research grants per full-time academic (£ thousands)	UFC research rating (1984–88)[3]
Aston	2617	16.8	48.1	9.7	8.4	2.53
Bath	3002	14.1	57.7	8.6	8.3	2.86
Birmingham	3335	10.5	43.3	8.2	8.5	3.29
Bradford	2789	16.0	41.9	8.9	5.8	2.56
Bristol	3797	7.3	52.1	11.9	9.4	3.80
Brunel	2926	21.8	45.9	6.3	12.2	2.27
Cambridge	3201	3.4	66.2	9.3	11.2	4.77
City	3466	19.3	45.3	4.7	6.6	2.11
Durham	2641	5.2	47.8	6.5	6.4	3.20
East Anglia	2853	9.6	42.9	17.2	5.9	3.27
Essex	2372	14.6	43.5	13.5	6.5	3.69
Exeter	2661	8.8	45.1	10.2	3.8	3.07
Hull	2598	12.3	41.9	9.5	5.7	2.72
Keele	2580	16.3	42.5	13.9	6.0	2.14
Kent	2310	13.3	43.6	14.9	6.2	2.85
Lancaster	2927	8.7	43.5	9.3	5.2	3.28
Leeds	3613	10.9	37.8	14.7	7.0	3.12
Leicester	3132	9.7	42.4	10.6	8.4	2.87
Liverpool	3596	14.3	35.0	16.6	8.4	3.22
London	4293	16.5	43.2	11.8	14.9	3.44
Loughborough	3139	10.3	47.2	11.0	10.9	2.74
Manchester	3519	12.8	40.7	12.0	7.7	3.59
UMIST	3963	14.8	43.3	7.9	15.0	3.71
Newcastle	3430	16.9	35.2	7.5	8.3	3.50
Nottingham	3183	9.2	47.3	9.6	9.0	3.38
Oxford	3083	7.0	56.8	9.6	13.8	4.79
Reading	3172	12.0	51.1	9.3	7.6	2.89
Salford	2972	19.5	43.9	10.2	6.0	2.24
Sheffield	3162	9.9	41.4	12.9	7.2	3.31
Southampton	3436	9.1	43.4	9.6	12.3	3.72
Surrey	3454	14.7	43.6	9.2	11.7	3.28
Sussex	2827	12.2	44.1	16.1	9.2	3.42
Warwick	2749	11.5	47.7	10.3	9.8	4.24
York	2566	8.7	54.0	13.5	9.9	3.79
Aberdeen	3236	23.6	33.3	10.2	6.0	2.78
Dundee	3585	22.4	31.8	8.0	11.5	2.70
Edinburgh	3695	14.0	37.7	12.4	10.7	3.31
Glasgow	3512	20.8	29.8	10.6	10.2	3.32
Heriot-Watt	3154	21.5	28.2	11.4	11.5	2.27
St Andrews	2590	11.8	47.8	8.9	6.2	3.14
Stirling	2420	14.9	32.5	16.9	5.7	2.43
Strathclyde	2795	21.6	39.1	9.6	9.7	2.85
Queen's	3044	11.5	33.4	11.7	4.8	2.56
Ulster	2176	15.9	33.3	19.9	2.6	2.19
Wales	2904	15.7	39.1	12.6	9.1	2.74

Notes:
1. Unit costs = general expenditure on academic departments per FTE student
2. Six months after graduation
3. All data for 1986/87 except for UFC research rating, which was based on the period 1984–88

Sources: University Statistics, vols 1 and 2; Universities' Statistical Record, Cheltenham, for data on first destination of new graduates; 'Research Selectivity Exercise 1989: The Outcome', Universities Funding Council, Circular letter 27/89 for research rating data.

Table 1.5 Rank of each university on several indicators

University	Rank of each university (1 = 'best')						
	Unit costs	% of students not completing their degree course	% of graduates with a first or upper second	% of graduates unemployed or in a short-term job	Research grants per full-time academic	UFC research rating	Overall rank (rank of average rank)
Aston	9	36	7	20	22	38	21
Bath	21	25	2	8	25	28	10
Birmingham	32	14	23	7	20	17	12
Bradford	13	33	30	10	39	37	31
Bristol	43	4	5	31	16	4	9
Brunel	18	43	13	2	5	41	18
Cambridge	30	1	1	13	9	2	2
City	36	38	14	1	30	45	33
Durham	10	2	9	3	32	22	4
East Anglia	16	10	26	44	38	20	29
Essex	3	27	21	37	31	8	20
Exeter	11	7	15	22	44	25	19
Hull	8	21	30	15	41	34	26
Keele	6	34	27	38	36	44	39
Kent	2	23	19	40	34	30	24
Lancaster	19	6	21	13	42	19	14
Leeds	41	15	35	39	29	24	38
Leicester	24	11	28	26	22	27	22
Liverpool	40	26	38	42	22	21	42
London	45	35	25	30	2	11	26
Loughborough	25	13	12	27	10	33	16
Manchester	38	22	32	32	26	9	30
UMIST	44	29	23	5	1	7	11
Newcastle	33	37	37	4	25	10	23
Nottingham	29	9	11	18	19	13	7
Oxford	23	3	3	18	3	1	1
Reading	28	19	6	13	27	26	15
Salford	20	39	17	22	36	42	37
Sheffield	27	12	31	35	28	16	27
Southampton	34	8	22	18	4	6	6
Surrey	35	28	19	11	6	19	13
Sussex	15	20	16	41	17	12	17
Warwick	12	17	10	24	14	3	5
York	5	6	4	37	13	5	3
Aberdeen	31	45	41	22	36	31	44
Dundee	39	44	43	6	8	35	36
Edinburgh	42	24	36	33	11	16	32
Glasgow	37	40	44	26	12	14	35
Heriot-Watt	26	41	45	28	8	41	41
St Andrews	7	18	9	10	34	23	8
Stirling	4	30	42	43	41	39	43
Strathclyde	14	42	34	18	15	30	28
Queen's	22	17	39	29	43	37	40
Ulster	1	32	41	45	45	43	45
Wales	17	31	34	34	18	33	34

Note: See notes to Table 1.4 for more details of variables.

Conclusion

Government policy towards higher education has been changing rapidly in the 1980s. The government has made it crystal clear in various publications that it expects higher education to make a greater contribution to the economy than it has done in the past and this will involve several fundamental changes in the activities of the higher education sector.

The main changes which the government would like to see are as follows. First, it expects the higher education sector to become more responsive to the needs of industry and commerce. Second, it expects higher education to become less dependent on public funding and more dependent on private sources of income. Third, it expects the higher education sector to provide wider access to its services so that a greater proportion of the population are able to reap the benefits of a university, polytechnic or college education. Finally, it expects higher education to become more cost effective and to allocate resources more efficiently between competing uses. This last objective will involve more careful monitoring and evaluation of the activities of individual institutions, which in turn will require the construction of performance indicators.

It is the purpose of this book to address the question of whether performance indicators which will be useful in evaluating the activities of the higher education sector can be constructed.

2
The UK University Sector: Recent Trends in Size and Structure

Introduction

This chapter describes some of the main longer-term trends in the size and structure of the UK university sector. The intention is simply to provide some background information which will help to put the later chapters of this book into a broader context. Attention is focused in the present chapter on just two variables: student and staff numbers. Changes in the *size* of the university sector are measured by trends in staff and student numbers over the period 1965/66 to 1988/89. Changes in the *structure* of the university sector are indicated by the distribution of staff and students between institutions.

The growth of the university sector

The university sector experienced very rapid growth between 1965 and 1980. The number of full-time students increased from 173,000 to 307,000 during this period. This compares to an increase of 92,000 in the public sector of higher education (see Table 2.1). Academic staff who were wholly financed from general university funds increased from 22,000 to 34,000 over the same period.

This rapid growth in students and staff came to an abrupt halt in the 1980s (see Table 2.2 and Figure 2.1). After growing at an average annual rate of 5.1 per cent during 1965–80, the average student growth rate fell to 1.1 per cent per annum during 1980–88. The corresponding average annual growth rates for the number of full-time staff (wholly financed from university funds) were 3.6 per cent and −1.3 per cent. The reasons for this sudden change in the fortunes of the university sector are discussed in Chapter 3. More recently the growth in the student numbers has picked up sharply and seems set to continue to grow rapidly during the 1990s. This will be achieved by increasing the proportion of 18- and 19-year-olds who proceed to higher education and by attracting older people back into the educational system who missed out on higher education.

Table 2.1   Total number of full-time students in
higher education: 1965/66 to 1987/88

Year	Total number of full-time students in higher education (thousands)	
	Universities	*Public sector¹*
1965/66	173	136
1970/71	235	221
1975/76	269	246
1980/81	307	228
1985/86	310	290
1987/88	321	305

Note:
1. The public sector includes polytechnics, Scottish central institutions and colleges of education

Source: Education Statistics for the United Kingdom, 1988 edn, Table 27,
p. 32.

It is useful to distinguish between two categories of academic staff when
measuring changes in staff numbers. Total full-time academic staff can be
divided into (1) those who are wholly financed from university general
funds (provided mainly by the Universities Funding Council) and (2) those
who are *not* wholly financed from university general funds. The latter
group are financed from 'specific' sources such as research grants and
contracts, and income from short courses and overseas students. Thus,
although the number of staff wholly financed from university general
funds has declined during the 1980s, the *total* number of staff has increased
strongly since 1983.

The growth in total academic staff during the 1980s has therefore been
entirely due to the rapid growth in the number of staff *not* wholly financed
from general funds. Table 2.2 shows that this latter category of staff has
increased steadily since 1970 without any evidence of slackening growth
during the early 1980s. This section of academic staff was apparently
immune from the financial adversities affecting the university sector in the
early 1980s. By contrast, the number of staff wholly financed from general
university funds has remained virtually static since 1982 (see Figure 2.2).
The consequence of the more rapid growth of staff *not* wholly financed
from general university funds has been a steady decline in the proportion
of staff who *are* financed from general funds – from 84 per cent in 1970 to
64 per cent in 1988 (see Table 2.3). The university sector has therefore
become relatively much less dependent on central funding during the past
two decades.

Since the number of students has been increasing at a faster rate than the
number of academic staff, it is not surprising to find a steady upward trend

Table 2.2 Students and staff in the UK university sector: 1965/66 to 1988/89

Year	Students (thousands)		Staff (thousands)				Student/staff ratio	
	1	2	3	4	5	6	7	8
1965/66	173	—	—	22.2	—	—	7.8	—
1966/67	189	—	—	24.0	—	—	7.9	—
1967/68	206	—	—	25.8	—	—	8.0	—
1968/69	217	—	—	26.7	—	—	8.1	—
1969/70	226	—	—	27.5	—	—	8.2	—
1970/71	235	237	34.1	28.7	5.4	—	8.2	—
1971/72	242	243	35.1	29.7	5.4	—	8.1	—
1972/73	247	249	36.5	30.7	5.8	—	8.0	—
1973/74	251	254	37.1	31.5	5.6	—	8.0	—
1974/75	258	262	37.9	32.1	5.8	—	8.0	—
1975/76	269	273	39.1	32.2	6.9	—	8.4	—
1976/77	279	284	40.2	32.7	7.5	33.4	8.5	8.4
1977/78	288	292	40.6	33.0	7.6	33.7	8.7	8.5
1978/79	296	302	41.9	33.7	8.2	34.4	8.8	8.6
1979/80	301	307	43.4	34.3	9.1	35.0	8.8	8.6
1980/81	306	312	44.1	34.3	9.8	35.1	8.9	8.7
1981/82	309	314	43.9	33.7	10.2	34.7	9.2	8.9
1982/83	304	309	43.1	31.6	11.5	32.8	9.6	9.3
1983/84	300	305	43.1	31.1	12.0	32.4	9.6	9.3
1984/85	305	304	44.2	31.0	13.2	32.7	9.8	9.3
1985/86	310	308	45.7	31.4	14.3	33.3	9.9	9.3
1986/87	316	313	47.0	31.4	15.6	32.5	10.1	9.7
1987/88	321	318	47.7	31.3	16.4	33.4	10.3	9.6
1988/89	334	—	48.1	30.6	17.4	33.0	10.9	10.1

Notes:
1 = Total full-time students
2 = Full-time equivalent students
3 = Total full-time staff
4 = Full-time staff wholly financed from university general funds
5 = Full-time staff *not* wholly financed from university general funds
6 = Full-time teaching and research staff (excluding 'research only')
7 = Student/staff ratio (col. 1/col. 4)
8 = Student/staff ratio (col. 1/col. 6)

Source: University Statistics, vols 1 and 3, various issues.

in the student/staff ratio (see Figure 2.3). Using staff wholly financed from general university funds as the denominator, the student/staff ratio can be seen to have risen from 8:1 in the late 1960s to nearly 11:1 in 1988/89. Whether this represents a deterioration or an improvement is not clear. Staff and students have presumably witnessed a deterioration in their working and learning environment while the taxpayer is presumably

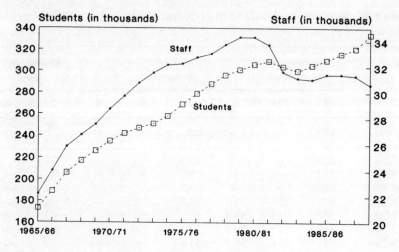

Figure 2.1   Full-time students and full-time academic staff in UK universities: 1965/66 to 1988/89

Source: University Statistics: Students and Staff, vol. 1, various issues.

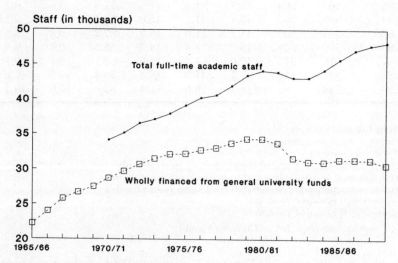

Figure 2.2   Full-time academic staff in UK universities: 1965/66 to 1988/89

Source: University Statistics: Students and Staff, vol. 1, various issues.

Table 2.3 Full-time academic staff wholly financed and not wholly financed from general university funds: UK universities, 1970/71 to 1988/89

Year	Full-time staff					
	Wholly university financed		Not wholly university financed		Total	
	(thousands)	%	(thousands)	%	(thousands)	%
1970/71	28.7	84.2	5.4	15.8	34.1	100
1971/72	29.7	84.6	5.4	15.4	35.1	100
1972/73	30.7	84.1	5.8	15.9	36.5	100
1973/74	31.5	84.9	5.6	15.1	37.1	100
1974/75	32.1	84.7	5.8	15.3	37.9	100
1975/76	32.2	82.4	6.9	17.6	39.1	100
1976/77	32.7	81.3	7.5	18.7	40.2	100
1977/78	33.0	81.3	7.6	18.7	40.6	100
1978/79	33.7	80.4	8.2	19.6	41.9	100
1979/80	34.3	79.0	9.1	21.0	43.4	100
1980/81	34.3	77.8	9.8	22.2	44.1	100
1981/82	33.7	76.8	10.2	23.2	43.9	100
1982/83	31.6	73.3	11.4	26.7	43.1	100
1983/84	31.1	72.2	12.1	27.8	43.1	100
1984/85	31.0	70.1	13.2	29.9	44.2	100
1985/86	31.4	68.7	14.3	31.3	45.7	100
1986/87	31.4	66.8	15.6	33.2	47.0	100
1987/88	31.3	65.6	16.4	34.4	47.7	100
1988/89	30.6	63.7	17.4	36.6	48.1	100

Note: Errors in summation due to rounding

Source: University Statistics: Students and Staff, vol. 1, various issues.

getting better value for money. Both presumptions are, of course, debatable. Using an alternative measure of staff in the denominator (i.e. total full-time staff engaged in teaching and research but not including those engaged *only* in research), the student/staff ratio can be seen to have risen somewhat less quickly than in the case of the former measure.

Hence, the main long-term trends in the university sector as a whole since the mid-1960s have been: first, a rapid growth in the total number of staff and students (except for a brief period of decline in the early 1980s); second, a steadily increasing proportion of staff not wholly financed from general university funds; and third, a steady increase in the student/staff ratio since 1974. These changes to the UK university sector as a whole, however, conceal far greater changes which have been occurring in individual institutions. The next section investigates inter-university differences in these longer-term trends.

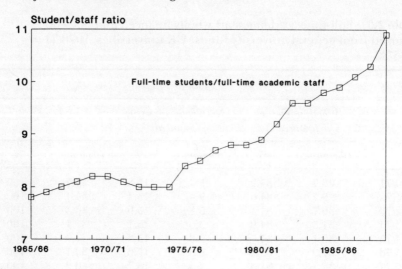

Figure 2.3   Student/staff ratio in UK universities: 1965/66 to 1988/89

Note: Full-time academic staff includes only those financed from university general funds (see Table 2.2)
Source: University Statistics: Students and Staff, vol. 1, various issues.

The structure of the university sector

The average size of universities, measured in terms of students and staff, has increased considerably during the past two decades. The average number of students, for example, increased from 4,200 per institution in 1970 to almost 6,000 in 1988 (see Table 2.4). These averages conceal considerable changes, however, in individual institutions. They also conceal the very wide variation in size between institutions. Seven institutions, for example, had over 10,000 students in 1988 while twenty-three had under 5,000. Changes in the size distribution of UK universities between 1970 and 1988 are shown in Figure 2.4.

Closer scrutiny of the change in student numbers in each institution between 1970 and 1988 reveals wide variations in growth between institutions during this period (see Table 2.5). This variation in the growth of student numbers has meant that several institutions have experienced a considerable change in their rank size position, the most noticeable being Aston, which fell from 22nd to 39th position as a result of a sharp fall in its student numbers between 1980 and 1988. By contrast, Warwick, Swansea and Herriot-Watt all moved up significantly in the size rankings during the 1980s.

Although different universities were growing at vastly different rates during the 1970s, it was not until the 1980s that inter-institutional

Table 2.4 Average size of UK universities

Year	Full-time staff			Full-time students		
	$\bar{x}$	s.d.	c.v.	$\bar{x}$	s.d.	c.v.
1970	571	377	66	4196	2487	59
1975	663	404	61	4819	2530	53
1980	745	413	55	5504	2619	48
1988	807	455	56	5992	2824	47

Notes:
London and Lampeter are excluded from the above calculations

$\bar{x}$ = mean
s.d. = standard deviation
c.v. = coefficient of variation (%)

Sources: Statistics of Education: Universities and *University Statistics: Students and Staff*, vol. 1
(various).

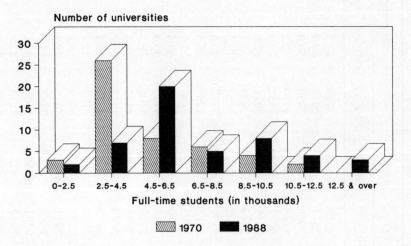

Figure 2.4 Size distribution of UK universities in 1970 and 1988

Note: London University is excluded
Sources: University Statistics: Students and Staff; Statistics of Education.

differences in the growth of student numbers became the cause of considerable concern amongst the academic community. The reason for this heightened concern about differential growth rates during the 1980s was the sharp decline in student numbers in several universities. Differential growth rates between institutions appear to be acceptable provided no institutions actually shrink in size. This was not the case in the 1980s

Table 2.5 Full-time students by university: 1970/71 to 1988/89

University	Full-time students				% change		Rank (1 = largest)			Change in rank
	1970/71	1975/76	1980/81	1988/89	1970–80	1980–88	1970/71	1980/81	1988/89	1980–88
Aston	3226	4529	5306	3729	64.5	−29.7	29	22	39	17
Bath	2187	3351	3581	3945	63.7	10.2	42	35	36	1
Birmingham	6785	7980	8884	9580	30.9	7.8	8	8	8	0
Bradford	3461	4175	5060	4470	46.2	−11.7	23	24	30	6
Bristol	6238	6637	7010	7452	12.4	6.3	10	14	17	3
Brunel	1744	2375	2826	3016	62.0	6.7	46	45	47	2
Cambridge	10720	10849	11479	12893	7.1	12.3	3	3	2	−1
City	2383	2202	2825	3484	18.5	23.3	39	46	42	−4
Durham	3394	4192	4770	5177	40.5	8.5	25	27	24	−3
East Anglia	2700	3472	4206	4266	55.8	1.4	31	31	33	2
Essex	1934	2294	2970	3283	53.6	10.5	44	42	44	2
Exeter	3387	4076	5064	5436	49.5	7.3	26	23	22	−1
Hull	3943	4174	5498	5143	39.4	−6.5	20	20	25	5
Keele	1863	2320	2801	3102	50.3	10.7	45	47	46	−1
Kent	2251	2008	3956	4347	75.7	9.9	41	34	31	−3
Lancaster	2784	3828	4627	4943	66.2	6.9	30	29	27	−1
Leeds	9126	9480	10885	10611	19.3	−2.5	5	5	6	0
Leicester	3364	3774	4789	5121	42.4	6.9	27	26	26	0
Liverpool	6613	7151	7859	8019	18.8	2.0	9	11	13	2
London	33161	35941	40538	44612	22.2	10.0	1	1	1	0
Loughborough	2538	3684	5399	5347	112.7	−1.0	34	21	23	2
Manchester	8320	10381	11327	11601	36.1	2.4	6	4	4	0
UMIST	3340	3540	4137	4275	23.9	3.3	28	32	32	0
Newcastle	5869	6682	7805	8134	33.0	4.2	12	12	12	0

Nottingham	5199	5988	7053	6502	35.7	6.4	17	13	16	3
Oxford	11073	11591	11802	12533	6.6	6.2	2	2	3	1
Reading	4917	5329	5819	6032	18.3	3.7	18	18	20	2
Salford	3412	3968	5449	4111	33.3	−9.6	24	29	34	5
Sheffield	5744	7121	8369	8663	45.7	3.5	13	10	9	−1
Southampton	4381	5437	6168	6772	40.8	9.8	19	17	18	1
Surrey	2383	2770	3255	3708	36.6	13.9	39	38	40	2
Sussex	3629	4191	4463	4588	23.0	2.8	21	30	29	−1
Warwick	2038	3944	5002	6639	145.4	32.7	43	25	19	−6
York	2411	2814	3357	3894	39.2	16.0	37	36	37	1
Aberystwyth	2587	2974	3224	3299	24.6	2.3	32	39	43	4
Bangor	2450	2720	2962	2999	20.9	1.2	36	43	48	5
Cardiff/UWIST	5525	7098	8685	8139	57.2	−6.3	14	9	11	2
Lampeter	354	536	767	793	116.7	3.4	49	49	49	0
Swansea	3475	3221	4022	4721	15.7	17.4	22	33	28	−5
Aberdeen	5360	5325	5590	5681	4.3	1.6	15	19	21	2
Dundee	2527	2758	3060	3613	21.1	18.1	35	41	41	0
Edinburgh	9368	9337	9783	10403	4.4	6.3	4	7	7	0
Glasgow	7969	9241	9830	11049	23.4	12.4	7	6	5	−1
Heriot-Watt	2285	2792	3205	4108	40.3	28.2	40	40	35	−5
St Andrews	2577	3037	3348	3782	29.9	13.0	33	37	38	1
Stirling	1137	2075	2925	3207	157.3	9.6	48	44	45	1
Strathclyde	5356	5983	6707	7936	25.2	18.3	16	15	14	−1
Queen's	6046	5735	6248	7682	3.3	23.0	11	16	15	−1
Ulster	1379	1721	1686	8293	22.3	391.0	47	48	10	−38
All universities	235556	268714	306614	333547	30.2	8.8	—	—	—	—

Note: The New University of Ulster merged with Ulster Polytechnic in October 1984

Sources: Statistics of Education: Universities (1970, 1975); *University Statistics: Students and Staff,* vol. 1 (various).

Table 2.6 Full-time academic staff by university: 1970/71 to 1988/89

University	Full-time academic staff				% change	
	1970/71	*1975/76*	*1980/81*	*1988/89*	*1970–80*	*1980–88*
Aston	436	490	644	326	47.7	−49.4
Bath	260	359	453	511	74.2	12.8
Birmingham	1265	1451	1505	1490	19.0	−1.0
Bradford	415	520	590	518	42.2	−12.2
Bristol	895	909	1127	1247	25.9	10.6
Brunel	243	320	366	367	50.6	0.3
Cambridge	1232	1179	1200	1970	−2.6	64.2
City	308	329	355	371	15.3	4.5
Durham	417	484	580	620	39.1	6.9
East Anglia	298	328	461	509	54.7	10.4
Essex	205	307	340	370	65.9	8.8
Exeter	390	492	603	581	54.6	−3.6
Hull	484	524	582	467	20.2	−19.8
Keele	284	336	348	330	22.5	−5.2
Kent	311	423	475	510	52.7	7.4
Lancaster	364	491	557	594	53.0	6.6
Leeds	1266	1364	1395	1459	10.2	4.6
Leicester	359	566	622	750	73.3	20.6
Liverpool	886	1005	1148	1222	29.6	6.4
London	6414	6963	7891	9104	23.0	15.4
Loughborough	302	456	590	758	95.4	28.5
Manchester	1416	1704	1655	1808	16.9	9.2
UMIST	465	536	622	641	33.8	3.1
Newcastle	935	1053	1140	1233	21.9	8.2
Nottingham	698	888	948	1115	35.8	17.6
Oxford	1544	1777	1994	1961	29.1	−1.7
Reading	649	703	753	796	16.0	5.7
Salford	444	503	508	420	14.4	−17.3
Sheffield	725	866	1088	1117	50.1	2.7
Southampton	524	657	1020	1192	94.7	16.9
Surrey	285	318	498	544	74.7	9.2
Sussex	507	641	660	587	30.2	−11.1
Warwick	284	442	637	875	124.3	37.4
York	293	284	407	500	38.9	22.9
Aberystwyth	353	407	451	365	27.8	−19.1
Bangor	375	365	414	397	10.4	−4.1
Cardiff/UWIST	747	857	1076	868	44.0	−19.3
Lampeter	42	64	71	72	69.0	1.4
Swansea	456	485	508	499	11.4	−1.8
Aberdeen	704	832	887	754	26.0	−15.0
Dundee	438	492	533	517	21.7	−3.0
Edinburgh	1389	1419	1529	1757	10.1	14.9
Glasgow	1341	1460	1501	1505	11.9	0.3

Table 2.6 Continued

University	Full-time academic staff				% change	
	1970/71	*1975/76*	*1980/81*	*1988/89*	*1970–80*	*1980–88*
Heriot-Watt	200	273	372	419	86.0	12.6
St Andrews	274	358	381	419	39.1	10.0
Stirling	174	281	302	353	73.6	16.9
Strathclyde	717	838	900	997	25.5	10.8
Queen's	667	820	830	913	24.4	10.0
Ulster	171	239	245	862	43.3	251.8
All universities	34103	39126	44092	48057	29.3	9.0

Notes:
1. Full-time academic staff includes those not wholly financed from university general funds
2. The large increase in academic staff experienced by Ulster was due to the merger between the New University of Ulster and Ulster Polytechnic in October 1984

Sources: Statistics of Education: Universities, 1975; University Statistics: Students and Staff, vol. 1 (various).

(see Table 2.5). The universities experiencing the fastest growth or decline in student numbers during 1980–88 were as follows:

Fastest growers	% change in students 1980–88	Fastest decliners	% change in students 1980–88
Warwick	32.7	Aston	−29.7
Heriot-Watt	28.2	Bradford	−11.7
City	23.3	Salford	−9.6
Queen's	23.0	Hull	−6.5
Strathclyde	18.3	Cardiff/UWIST	−6.3
Dundee	18.1		
Swansea	17.4		
York	16.0		

Similarly wide disparities in growth rates between universities occur for academic staff (see Table 2.6). The reasons for these very wide inter-institutional differences in growth (and decline) are discussed in Chapter 3, which is concerned with the funding of the university sector.

We turn finally to inter-institutional differences in the student/staff ratio. (Note that this can be measured in different ways.) These are shown in Table 2.7 for 1980/81 and 1988/89. Comparing these ratios between institutions for any given year is not very helpful since each university's student/staff ratio is strongly influenced by its subject mix. The importance of subject mix in determining each university's student/staff ratio is demonstrated in Figure 2.5, which shows a high correlation between the

Table 2.7   Student/staff ratios by university: 1980/81 and 1988/89

University	Student/staff ratios		Change 1980–88
	1980/81	*1988/89*	
Aston	10.0	15.4	5.4
Bath	10.0	11.1	1.1
Birmingham	5.9	9.4	3.5
Bradford	9.8	11.0	1.2
Bristol	8.5	9.6	1.2
Brunel	9.8	11.6	1.8
Cambridge	9.6	11.3	1.7
City	8.9	11.0	2.2
Durham	10.5	11.6	1.1
East Anglia	10.9	10.9	−0.0
Essex	10.9	11.7	0.8
Exeter	10.0	11.3	1.3
Hull	10.7	13.3	2.6
Keele	9.3	11.4	2.1
Kent	10.4	11.6	1.2
Lancaster	9.6	11.1	1.4
Leeds	9.8	9.9	0.1
Leicester	9.9	10.0	0.0
Liverpool	8.3	8.9	0.6
London	7.1	7.9	0.8
Loughborough	10.5	10.2	−0.2
Manchester	8.3	8.7	0.3
UMIST	9.4	10.3	0.9
Newcastle	8.7	9.4	0.8
Nottingham	9.7	9.9	0.2
Oxford	9.0	10.5	1.5
Reading	9.5	10.5	1.0
Salford	9.5	11.8	2.4
Sheffield	9.1	10.7	1.7
Southampton	8.8	9.6	0.7
Surrey	7.5	11.9	4.4
Sussex	9.7	11.6	1.9
Warwick	10.0	10.9	0.9
York	11.0	11.8	0.8
Aberystwyth	8.8	11.9	3.1
Bangor	9.1	10.3	1.2
Cardiff/UWIST	10.0	12.2	2.2
Lampeter	11.1	11.2	0.1
Swansea	9.7	11.6	2.0
Aberdeen	8.2	10.5	2.4
Dundee	7.1	10.5	3.4
Edinburgh	8.0	8.7	0.7
Glasgow	8.3	10.7	2.4

Table 2.7 continued

University	Student/staff ratios		Change 1980–88
	1980/81	*1988/89*	
Heriot-Watt	11.8	14.4	2.6
St Andrews	9.9	11.7	1.8
Stirling	11.0	11.6	0.7
Strathclyde	9.4	11.7	2.2
Queen's	8.4	11.2	2.9
Ulster	7.9	10.9	3.0
All universities	8.7	10.1	1.4

Note:
Students = total full-time students
Staff = total teaching and research staff but *excluding* 'research only' staff
Source: University Statistics: Students and Staff, vol. 1 (1980/81, 1988/89).

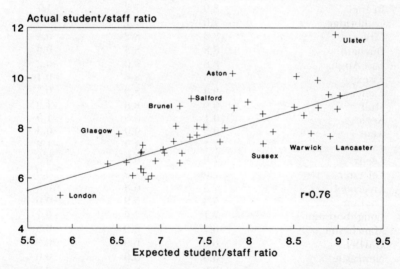

Figure 2.5 Student/staff ratio in UK universities: actual v. expected 1986/87
Note: See Table 2.8 for the definition of student/staff ratio used in this figure
Source: University Statistics, Finance, 1986/87.

actual student/staff ratio and the student/staff ratio that each university could have been expected to have *given its cost centre mix*. The *expected* student/staff ratio is obtained by applying UK student/staff ratios in each cost centre to each university's cost centre mix. The method is described in the appendix to this chapter (p. 28). It is also interesting to note, however, that the actual student/staff ratio in several universities is substantially different from that which could have been expected. It can be seen from

Table 2.8 that Lancaster, Warwick, Sussex and Glasgow all had student/
staff ratios substantially lower than could have been expected given their
respective cost centre mixes. The opposite is the case for Wales, Aston,
Salford, Brunel, Keele, Heriot-Watt, Hull, Bradford and Stirling, all of
which had substantially higher than expected student/staff ratios.

Table 2.8   Student/staff ratios in UK universities: actual v.
expected 1986/87

University	Student/staff ratio[1]		
	Actual	*Expected*[2]	*Difference*[3]
Aston	10.2	7.8	2.4
Bath	7.7	7.4	0.3
Birmingham	6.2	6.8	−0.6
Bradford	9.0	8.0	1.1
Bristol	6.1	6.7	−0.6
Brunel	8.9	7.2	1.7
Cambridge	7.0	7.2	−0.3
City	8.6	8.2	0.4
Durham	8.8	8.5	0.3
East Anglia	8.8	9.0	−0.2
Essex	8.5	8.6	−0.1
Exeter	9.4	8.9	0.5
Hull	9.9	8.8	1.2
Keele	10.1	8.5	1.5
Kent	9.3	9.0	0.3
Lancaster	7.7	8.9	−1.2
Leeds	7.0	6.8	0.3
Leicester	7.0	7.0	0.0
Liverpool	7.3	6.8	0.5
London	5.3	5.9	−0.6
Loughborough	7.1	7.0	0.1
Manchester	6.7	6.9	−0.3
UMIST	6.0	6.9	−0.9
Newcastle	6.6	6.6	0.0
Nottingham	7.0	6.8	0.2
Oxford	6.6	7.2	−0.6
Reading	7.5	7.7	−0.2
Salford	9.2	7.3	1.8
Sheffield	8.1	7.2	0.9
Southampton	6.4	6.8	−0.4
Surrey	6.4	6.8	−0.4
Sussex	7.4	8.2	−0.8
Warwick	7.8	8.7	−0.9
York	7.9	8.3	−0.4
Aberdeen	7.5	7.1	0.3
Dundee	6.6	6.4	0.2

Table 2.8 continued

University	Student/staff ratio[1]		
	Actual	Expected[2]	Difference[3]
Edinburgh	6.1	6.9	−0.8
Glasgow	7.8	6.5	1.2
Heriot-Watt	7.6	7.3	0.3
St Andrews	8.8	7.8	1.0
Stirling	8.8	8.8	0.0
Strathclyde	8.0	7.7	0.3
Queen's	8.1	7.4	0.7
Ulster	11.7	9.0	2.8
Wales	8.0	7.5	0.5

Notes:
1. Students = total full-time equivalent student load
   Staff = total full-time academic staff
2. The expected student/staff ratio was calculated by applying the UK
   student/staff ratio in each cost centre to each university's cost centre mix
   (see appendix to chapter for details)
3. Errors in differencing are due to rounding

Source: Data for calculations obtained from *University Statistics: Finance*,
1986/87, Table 9.

Changes in the student/staff ratio over time are interesting since they
vary considerably between institutions. The universities experiencing the
largest and smallest increases in their student/staff ratios during 1980–88
were as follows (see Table 2.7):

Change in student/staff ratio (1980–88)

Aston	5.4	Loughborough	−0.2
Surrey	4.4	East Anglia	0.0
Birmingham	3.5	Leicester	0.0
Dundee	3.4	Leeds	0.1
Aberystwyth	3.1	Nottingham	0.2
Ulster	3.0	Manchester	0.3
Queen's	2.9	Liverpool	0.6

Conclusion

The purpose of this chapter has been to describe some of the longer-term
trends in the size and structure of the UK university sector during the last
two decades. The main features of these longer-term trends are as follows.

First, after expanding very rapidly in the 1960s and 1970s, the growth of
the university sector as a whole went into reverse in the early 1980s but has
since recovered its earlier momentum. This growth is likely to be sustained

(and possibly increased) in the 1990s if the government follows through with its intention of substantially increasing the participation rate of 18- and 19-year-olds in higher education during the next decade.

Second, there has been a substantial switch in the proportion of staff financed wholly from general university funds compared to those *not* financed from general university funds. Thus in 1970/71 under 16 per cent of full-time academic staff were *not* financed from general university funds. This had risen to over 36 per cent by 1988/89. This clearly implies that the university sector has become increasingly less dependent upon the public purse since the early 1970s (a topic to be taken up in the next chapter).

Third, the student/staff ratio has risen strongly since the mid-1970s and seems likely to continue its upward trend into the 1990s in view of the government's determination to reduce unit costs in the higher education sector. This is discussed in detail in Chapter 3.

Finally, substantial changes have been taking place in the broad structure of the university sector, as reflected by changes in the size of individual institutions. Inter-institutional differences in the growth of staff and student numbers have been viewed with particular concern during the 1980s since several institutions have experienced substantial decline – an entirely unprecedented (though not unpremeditated) situation. The reasons for the substantial differences in growth (and decline) between individual institutions are discussed in the next chapter, which examines the funding of the higher education sector.

Appendix to Chapter 2

Calculation of the expected student/staff ratio for each university

$$
\text{Expected student/staff ratio in university } i = \sum_{j}^{m} \left(\frac{\text{STAFF}_{ij}}{\text{STAFF}_i} \right) \left(\frac{\text{STUD}_j}{\text{STAFF}_j} \right)
$$

where

$j = 1, \ldots m$ (cost centres)

STAFF_{ij} = full-time academic staff in university i, cost centre j

STAFF_i = full-time academic staff in university i

STUD_j = full-time equivalent student load in cost centre j in all UK universities

STAFF_j = full-time staff in cost centre j in all UK universities.

3

Government Funding of the University Sector

Introduction

The UK university sector depends very heavily on public funding. In 1987/88, for example, nearly three-quarters of university recurrent income was provided by the Treasury. It is this high dependence on the taxpayer which has motivated the government to insist on a more thorough evaluation of what universities do and whether they are doing it effectively and efficiently. The purpose of this chapter is to provide some background information about the extent of public funding and how this has changed since the first grant was made to UK universities over a century ago, in 1889. It is important to review the funding process (and how it has changed over time) since the ultimate purpose of developing more thorough methods of appraising and evaluating universities is to help the funding agencies to allocate funds more efficiently.

This chapter is in five sections. The first section discusses the early development of public funding and the creation of institutional arrangements for allocating funds between universities. The rapid growth of the university sector which culminated in the establishment of twenty-one new universities in the mid-1960s is discussed in the second section. The third section reviews the restructuring process initiated in the early 1980s when severe financial constraints were imposed on the university sector. The fourth section discusses how the university sector responded to those financial constraints by switching to other sources of income. The fifth section discusses the prospects for the 1990s in the light of new policy proposals emanating from the Department of Education and Science (DES) in 1989 and 1990. The appendix to this chapter (pp. 48–9) chronicles the main events in the history of the public funding of universities since 1889.

Early developments: the creation of the University Grants Committee

The first government grant to universities was made in 1889. The universities asked for £50,000 and received £15,000 (equivalent to around half a million pounds at 1988 prices). Since there was no formal mechanism for distributing this money to individual institutions, the Treasury set up an *ad hoc* committee. This procedure continued until the University Grants Committee (UGC) was established under the jurisdiction of the Treasury in 1919 after the universities had requested substantial public funding. Inflation and a large fall in student numbers during and immediately after the First World War had led to severe financial problems for the universities. The UGC was created in order to act as a buffer between the universities and the government since the universities were determined to maintain their autonomy in spite of their increased dependence on public funding. The UGC was consequently charged

> to enquire into the financial needs of university education and to advise government as to the application of any grants that may be made by Parliament to meet them.
>
> (DES 1987c: 20)

It was not until 1925, however, that the UGC introduced the *quinquennial* system of funding, which was to last until national economic problems eventually brought about its downfall over half a century later in 1977. The quinquennial system required each university to submit a plan of student and staff numbers by subject at five-yearly intervals. On the basis of these plans and the expected income from other sources, the UGC advised the government (in confidence) on the appropriate size of the *total* grant which should be made available. The allocation between universities was then decided by the UGC on the basis of the original plan and a *block grant* was then made available to each institution accompanied by advice on how it should be spent. The incentive to follow the UGC's advice was a strong one since the next quinquennium was always lurking on the horizon.

The post-war expansion of universities: demand-led growth

Throughout the inter-war period, exchequer grants to universities accounted for only about one-third of their total recurrent income. This dependence on public funds increased sharply in the immediate post-war years. The Education Act 1944 promised an increase in the number of students who would qualify for university entrance and this was followed in

1945 by a joint proposal from the UGC and the Committee of Vice-Chancellors and Principals (CVCP) that the university sector should be substantially expanded. Needless to say, this expansion required a vast increase in public funding and by 1946–47 exchequer grants accounted for approximately half of the university sector's total income (Berdahl 1983).

The direct consequence of the increase in public funding of universities was an enhanced role for the UGC (Shattock and Berdahl 1984). In 1946 its terms of reference were extended so that in addition to inquiring into the financial needs of universities and advising the government about these needs, the UGC had also

> to collect, examine and make available information relating to university education throughout the UK; and to assist in . . . the preparation and execution of such plans for the development of the universities as may from time to time be required in order to ensure that they are fully adequate to national needs.
>
> (DES 1987c: 20)

The most rapid expansion in the history of the UK university sector, however, did not occur until after the Robbins Report (1963) which had argued that sustained economic growth would require a significant expansion of the university sector. Robbins argued that

> progress – and particularly the maintenance of a competitive position – depends to a much greater extent than ever before on skills demanding special training. A good education, valuable though it may be, is frequently less than we need to solve many of our most pressing problems.
>
> (Robbins 1963: 6)

This set the scene for what has become known as the Robbins principle, which stated that

> courses of higher education should be available for all those who are qualified by ability and attainment to pursue them and who wish to do so.
>
> (Robbins 1963: 8)

The acceptance of the Robbins principle meant that total expenditure on universities became demand-driven in the mid-1960s. Together with the Anderson Report (1960), which recommended the award of a maintenance grant to all students able to get a university place, the Robbins principle inevitably led to a rapid expansion of the university sector. Nine new greenfield universities were established in 1964 and twelve colleges of advanced technology were converted into universities. The sharp increase in the size of the university sector is clearly indicated by the rapid increase in the number of students and staff after 1965 (see Figure 2.1, p. 16).

Financial constraints on the growth of universities

Not surprisingly, the rapid expansion of government expenditure on higher education in the 1960s led to greater control from the centre. This was signalled in 1967 when the UGC started issuing *written* as opposed to *oral* guidelines on how block grants to the universities should be spent. In addition, the Comptroller and Auditor-General gained access to UGC and university records for the first time in 1968.

It was the world economic crisis of 1974/75 following the trebling of oil prices, however, which made it crystal clear just how dependent the universities were on public funding. In the face of over 20 per cent inflation and sharply rising student numbers the expenditure plans for the 1972/77 quinquennium began to look hopelessly inadequate. The financial problems of individual institutions were made worse by the increasing delay in deciding on the allocation of funds between universities, which made financial planning far more difficult. The quinquennial system was consequently abandoned (since inflation was undermining financial planning) and was replaced by a rolling triennial system. Allocations were fixed for one year and provisional allocations were decided for the following two years.

The effect of the tightening of the government's purse strings on the university sector during the 1970s is vividly illustrated in Figure 3.1. The real value of both recurrent income and exchequer grants failed to grow

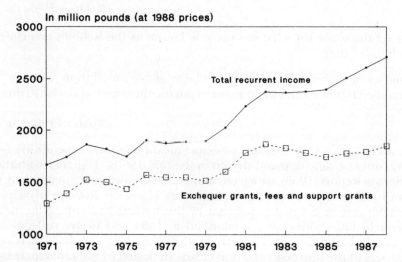

Figure 3.1   Recurrent income of GB universities at 1988 prices: 1971–88

Sources: University Statistics, Finance, vol. 8; Economic Trends.

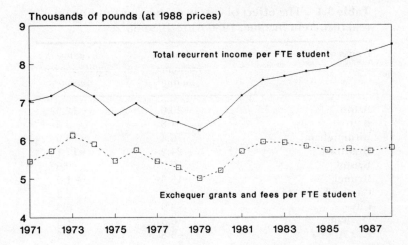

Figure 3.2 Recurrent income per full-time equivalent student in GB universities

Sources: University Statistics, Finance, vol. 3; *Economic Trends.*

during 1973–79 before rising strongly again during 1979–82 in the wake of the substantial pay increase won by university staff following the Clegg Commission's inquiry into public sector pay. A similar picture is obtained from Figure 3.2, which shows recurrent income and exchequer grants per student. The sharp fall in exchequer funding per student is particularly evident during 1973–79. The imposition of much tighter controls over public spending in the mid-1970s (particularly after the national economic crisis in 1976 when the government had to arrange a substantial loan from the International Monetary Fund to finance a large current account deficit in the balance of payments) signalled the beginning of financial constraints being imposed on universities. The university sector suddenly switched from being demand-led to being finance-constrained. This policy was reinforced with a change of government in 1979 when the DES asked the UGC to estimate the effect of reductions in funding on the university sector (Moore 1987).

The UGC responded to the DES's request for its views about the effect of cuts in funding by reporting that any reductions in excess of 2.5 per cent *in real terms* would lead to a serious reduction in efficiency. The government's response was the announcement of level funding for home students and full-cost fees for overseas students. Level funding did not, however, materialize and a *real* cut of 8.7 per cent in exchequer funding occurred between 1980/1 and 1984/5 (see Table 3.1).

These funding changes had far-reaching effects on the structure of the university sector and its future operations. One of the most notable effects resulted from the UGC's decision not to apply the cut in exchequer funding proportionally across institutions. The cuts were, in fact, highly selective

Table 3.1 The effect of cuts in exchequer funding on real recurrent income, 1980/81 to 1984/85[1]

University	% change in exchequer funding[2]	% change in total recurrent income
Aston	−20.0	−17.3
Bath	−1.8	3.5
Birmingham	−6.4	3.9
Bradford	−24.2	−17.1
Bristol	−9.9	0.6
Brunel	−15.3	−1.5
Cambridge	−6.0	2.3
City	−8.9	6.3
Durham	−6.5	1.5
East Anglia	−3.8	3.5
Essex	−13.3	4.2
Exeter	−6.8	1.4
Hull	−15.1	−8.3
Keele	−26.3	−14.7
Kent	−12.0	3.9
Lancaster	−9.9	−1.2
Leeds	−10.6	−0.9
Leicester	−4.8	8.3
Liverpool	−8.7	2.1
London	−11.4	1.6
Loughborough	−5.1	5.5
Manchester	−10.9	−0.5
UMIST	−22.4	−8.7
Newcastle	−4.5	4.6
Nottingham	−7.5	2.4
Oxford	−7.4	4.5
Reading	−12.5	2.0
Salford	−36.4	−9.9
Sheffield	−7.5	−2.8
Southampton	−7.3	4.4
Surrey	−18.6	9.8
Sussex	−11.7	−5.4
Warwick	−5.5	8.2
York	8.0	15.5
Aberystwyth	−14.5	13.2
Bangor	−6.5	−1.0
Cardiff	3.7	5.1
Lampeter	−3.7	−0.6
Swansea	−12.7	−5.9
UWIST	−15.9	−1.9
Aberdeen	−15.9	−6.7
Dundee	−8.5	−0.5
Edinburgh	−3.5	5.6

Table 3.1   Continued

University	% change in exchequer funding[2]	% change in total recurrent income
Glasgow	−4.3	10.2
Heriot-Watt	−6.0	13.5
St Andrews	−11.9	−2.1
Stirling	−9.3	2.8
Strathclyde	−2.9	9.1
Queen's	−4.1	0.4
Ulster[3]	—	—
All universities	−8.7	2.4

Notes:
1. The index of university costs was used to convert recurrent income to 1980 prices (see *University Statistics: Finance*, 1985/86, Table 2)
2. Exchequer funding is defined here to include: exchequer grants, home rate fees, part-time course fees, research training and other support grants
3. Ulster is omitted since it merged with Ulster Polytechnic in 1984

Source: University Statistics: Finance, vol. 3.

(see Table 3.1). This was achieved by persuading the government to finance an early retirement scheme to cut academic staff. The cuts were consequently not shared equally between institutions. Salford suffered the worst cut in exchequer funding, which fell by 36 per cent (in real terms) between 1980/1 and 1984/5. Other universities experiencing large cuts were Keele (−26 per cent), Bradford (−24 per cent), UMIST (−22 per cent) and Aston (−20 per cent). These cuts should be compared with the increase in exchequer funding at York (8 per cent) and Cardiff (4 per cent) and cuts of under 5 per cent at several other universities. It is also worth noting that the cut in exchequer funding was more than offset by a simultaneous increase in non-exchequer funding in the majority of universities, part of this coming from a sharp increase in income from overseas student fees. We return to this switch in funding sources in the next section.

Although the criteria used to decide how the cuts in UGC funding were to be allocated between institutions were not spelt out in detail, the UGC gave some idea of the factors which were taken into consideration in its annual report for 1980/81 (UGC 1982). These included

1. the views of the UGC sub-committees about the quality of individual institutions and their departments
2. the quality of student applicants
3. the stock of facilities and their intensity of use
4. staffing levels

5. the first destination of graduates
6. the strength of research activity

To what extent each of these criteria influenced the way in which the UGC allocated the cut in funding between institutions was not made clear. Indeed, exactly how these various measures of each institution's performance were constructed was left unexplained, thus reinforcing the view that the entire evaluation exercise was done with inadequate preparation. The inadequacy of the evaluation exercise is further reflected by the UGC's statement that

> for the best distribution of resources to the universities there is no substitute for judgement based on experience and repeated review of relevant information.
>
> (UGC 1982: 9)

It is this kind of bland statement which undermined confidence in the allocation process, especially since there was no evidence that a set of *relevant information* had been produced.

By 1984 the UGC was becoming more responsive to repeated criticisms about the way in which funding decisions were being made. Specifically the UGC said:

> We intend to be more open about decisions and advice than in the past. In particular we aim to give a rather more detailed explanation of the grants to individual institutions.
>
> (UGC 1984: 43)

The UGC realized that if more detailed information was to be provided to universities about its decisions, more effort would have to be devoted to measuring performance more systematically than had been the case in the past. The pressure for a more detailed explanation of funding decisions therefore steered the UGC in the direction of more systematic performance assessment. We return to this topic in Chapter 4.

The shift towards greater selectivity in the allocation of public funds within the university sector was supported, and indeed encouraged, by the government, which turned its attention to subject balance in the 1985 Green Paper (DES 1985). There had been growing doubts in government circles about the validity of the assumption that investment in all types of higher education would ultimately be 'good for growth'. The result was a clear signal from the government that more resources should be switched into the physical sciences, engineering, technology and mathematics. Inevitably the arts and humanities were to be the losers. Despite a shortage of candidates in the sciences, the government made it clear that 'the proportion of arts places in higher education as a whole can be expected to shrink' (DES 1985: 9).

Attempts to resist the cuts in government funding to universities in the early 1980s were made not only on the grounds that well-qualified students would have to be turned away but also because the research output of universities would be harmfully affected. Since university research is funded partly by the UGC and partly by the Research Councils, the UGC joined forces with the Advisory Board for the Research Councils (ABRC) in 1982 to examine the extent of the damage to research in the natural and social sciences which would result from the funding cuts. The findings were published in the Merrison Report (1982), which argued that

the rate of withdrawal of resources is such that whatever happens research will suffer to an unprecedented extent during the turmoil.

(ABRC/UGC 1982: 32)

Although the Merrison Report recommended the provision of more money for research, it also proposed that research funds would have to be concentrated in selected areas given that resources were likely to continue to be restricted. The UGC subsequently stated its intention 'to develop a more systematic and selective approach' to the allocation of research funds (UGC 1984: 15). This approach was backed by the government in its 1985 Green Paper: 'Effectiveness in research requires concentration in strong centres. At present our resources are too thinly spread' (DES 1985: 5).

Having accepted the principle of allocating the research component of its total grant to universities on the basis of a more selective approach, the UGC began its first selectivity exercise in 1985 and published the results in 1986. It was decided that the majority of the grant to individual universities would be determined by planned student numbers and that the funding would be based upon historical cost data. Subjects were grouped into thirty-nine cost centres so that costs could be calculated for individual cost centres and then aggregated for each institution. The criteria for distributing the research elements were more complex. The total for each university was based partly on student numbers in each cost centre and partly on each cost centre's research record. The total grant for each university was therefore based upon criteria used at the cost centre level. Each university was free to allocate its grant between cost centres in the way it thought best but had to take note of the UGC's research rating of individual departments.

The UGC was severely criticized in the wake of its research selectivity exercise. Criticisms were levelled against the methodology, the secrecy surrounding the exercise, the lack of evidence to support the ratings on which the allocation of funds was based, the apparent positive relationship between research rating and a department's size, and the apparent use of research income to reflect research quality (D. M. Smith 1986; T. Smith 1987; Bentham 1987; Gleave *et al.* 1987; Gillett 1987a; 1987b; Gillett and Aitkenhead 1987; Phillimore 1989). The 1986 research selectivity exercise is discussed in more detail in Chapter 9.

Table 3.2   The sources of recurrent income in UK universities

Income source[1]	1974/5	1982/3	1983/4	1984/5	1985/6	1986/7	1987/8
Exchequer							
Exchequer grants	77.7	64.4	62.1	59.8	57.8	55.6	55.3
Fees – home rates	2.9	8.1	7.7	7.6	7.3	7.1	6.8
– part-time courses	0.2	0.5	0.5	0.6	0.6	0.6	0.7
Other support grants	0.3	0.3	0.3	0.4	0.3	0.4	0.3
Computer Board	0.8	0.8	0.8	0.8	0.8	0.8	0.7
Research grants[2]	7.9	8.9	9.5	9.7	10.0	10.5	10.0
	89.8	83.0	80.9	78.9	76.8	75.0	73.8
Other government sources							
Government departments	0.3	0.3	0.3	0.3	0.4	0.3	0.4
Hospital authorities	1.3	1.5	1.6	1.7	1.8	1.9	2.0
	1.6	1.8	1.9	2.0	2.2	2.2	2.4
Other							
Fees – other rates	1.1	4.3	4.6	4.8	5.3	5.6	5.6
Endowments	1.1	1.0	1.1	1.0	1.2	1.3	1.3
Other recurrent income	1.7	3.3	3.6	4.1	3.7	3.6	3.5
Research contracts[2]	4.0	4.8	5.5	6.5	7.5	8.5	9.2
Other services rendered[2]	0.7	1.9	2.4	2.8	3.2	3.8	4.2
	8.6	15.3	17.2	19.2	21.1	22.8	23.8
Total	100	100	100	100	100	100	100

Notes:
1. The methods used to allocate income to each income source have changed over time: comparisons between years are likely to be less adversely affected by this problem for the 1980s due to greater consistency in the compilation of the income statistics in recent years.
2. Definition of various items (1982/83 to 1987/88):
   Research grants   = grants from research councils and UK government
   Research contracts   = grants from UK-based charitable bodies, UK industry, overseas and other sources
   Other services rendered = special and short courses and other.

Sources: Statistics of Education 1975: Universities, vol. 6, University Grants Committee, Table 34; *Universities Statistics*, vol. 3, Tables 1 and 3.

The response of the university sector to financial constraints on growth: the switch to non-government funding

The 1981 cuts in government funding had the effect of inducing universities to search more vigorously for alternative sources of funding.

The decreasing dependence of the university sector on public funds is shown in Table 3.2. Exchequer grants and home fee income declined from 81 per cent of the total recurrent income of universities in 1974/5 to 73 per cent in 1982/3 and then to 62 per cent in 1987/8. This was offset by the rapid increase in the relative contribution coming from three other income sources: overseas student fees, industry, and research foundations. Income from these 'other' sources increased from under 9 per cent to over 23 per cent of total recurrent income between 1974/5 and 1987/8, a truly remarkable increase over such a relatively short time.

Universities have therefore become increasingly dependent upon non-government sources of income since the mid-1970s, a process which was given the government's blessing in the 1985 Green Paper on *The Development of Higher Education into the 1990s*.

Greater financial independence could give institutions greater flexibility. Private finance already enriches the education provided by many universities. Although reliance on public finance is to a great extent unavoidable, the Government wishes to see it reduced. To encourage universities' efforts in this direction, the Government has confirmed that increases in income from outside sources will not lead to reductions in Government funding.

(DES 1985: 5)

This policy statement was reinforced in the 1987 White Paper on *Higher Education: Meeting the Challenge*:

Notable successes by higher education in partnership with industry and commerce are now frequent, leading to the provision of goods and services sold at a profit; they could become much commoner, given further determination on the part of academic staff and a more positive attitude by British industry.

(DES 1987b: 19)

Differences between universities

To complete the picture of changes which have been occurring in the funding of the university sector during the 1980s, it is useful to investigate how these funding changes have differed between institutions. As might be expected, the relative importance of individual sources of income has been changing at different rates in different universities. This is most easily demonstrated by comparing the relative contribution of exchequer grants and fees between institutions and by examining the major changes which have been occurring in the 1980s. It is particularly appropriate to examine changes in the exchequer grants' and fees' component in view of the Thatcher government's policy of reducing the university sector's dependence on exchequer funding.

Table 3.3   Exchequer funding as a percentage of total recurrent income, 1980/81 and 1987/88

University	Exchequer grants, home fees, research training and support grants as a percentage of total recurrent income		
	1980/81	*1987/88*	*change*
Aston	77.7	72.0	−5.7
Bath	76.4	67.7	−8.7
Birmingham	76.5	59.9	−16.6
Bradford	80.9	71.8	−9.1
Bristol	76.3	65.0	−11.3
Brunel	82.8	67.4	−15.4
Cambridge	71.0	60.4	−10.6
City	80.7	60.5	−20.2
Durham	84.9	70.0	−14.9
East Anglia	84.9	76.3	−8.6
Essex	74.9	62.4	−12.5
Exeter	85.3	76.8	−8.5
Hull	85.6	75.5	−10.1
Keele	86.6	67.3	−19.3
Kent	80.4	61.6	−18.8
Lancaster	83.0	71.1	−11.9
Leeds	79.4	68.5	−10.9
Leicester	83.2	66.2	−17.0
Liverpool	85.0	67.5	−17.5
London	70.6	55.3	−15.3
Loughborough	73.4	62.7	−10.7
Manchester	77.3	64.6	−12.7
UMIST	71.0	57.3	−13.7
Newcastle	77.0	65.4	−11.6
Nottingham	79.1	64.1	−15.0
Oxford	66.2	52.9	−13.3
Reading	78.4	61.4	−17.0
Salford	85.3	56.1	−29.2
Sheffield	82.5	72.0	−10.5
Southampton	69.3	59.2	−10.1
Surrey	81.3	54.4	−26.9
Sussex	71.5	67.0	−4.5
Warwick	80.5	56.8	−23.7
York	77.1	69.1	−8.0
Aberystwyth	87.1	74.3	−12.8
Bangor	81.4	70.0	−11.4
Cardiff	78.9	73.5	−5.4
Lampeter	93.1	80.7	−12.4
Swansea	81.5	72.0	−9.5
UWIST	78.4	68.9	−9.5
Aberdeen	79.7	64.7	−15.0

Table 3.3 Continued

University	Exchequer grants, home fees, research training and support grants as a percentage of total recurrent income		
	1980/81	*1987/88*	*change*
Dundee	82.0	68.4	−13.6
Edinburgh	74.3	63.1	−11.2
Glasgow	81.3	66.1	−15.2
Heriot-Watt	75.2	58.8	−16.4
St Andrews	86.7	72.1	−14.6
Stirling	88.2	64.6	−23.6
Strathclyde	78.1	65.2	−12.9
Queen's	86.0	76.3	−9.7
Ulster	93.4	87.6	−5.8
All universities	76.7	63.1	−13.6

Source: University Statistics: Finance, vol. 3, Tables 1 and 3.

The relative contribution of exchequer grants and home fees to each university's income is given in Table 3.3. This table indicates the existence of very substantial differences between universities in their exchequer dependency, the highest and lowest rates being in the following institutions:

	%		%
Ulster	87.6	Oxford	52.9
Exeter	76.8	Surrey	54.4
East Anglia	76.3	London	55.3
Queen's	76.3	Salford	56.1
Hull	75.5	Warwick	56.8
Aberystwyth	74.3	Heriot-Watt	58.8
Cardiff	73.5	Southampton	59.2
St Andrews	72.1	Birmingham	59.9

Changes in exchequer dependency during the 1980s are also shown in Table 3.3. Once again, variations in the *reduction* in exchequer dependency between universities were substantial:

	% point change		% point change
Salford	−29.2	Sussex	−4.5
Surrey	−26.9	Cardiff	−5.4
Warwick	−23.7	Aston	−5.7
Stirling	−23.6	Ulster	−5.8
City	−20.2	York	−8.0

Funding in the 1990s

Radical changes to the method of funding the university sector are to occur in the 1990s. The initial announcement of these changes came through a DES consultative document in April 1989 (DES 1989). This indicated a fundamental change in the government's attitude towards the higher education sector by turning away from the increasingly centralized control that occurred during the 1980s and towards a more decentralized system. Greater decentralization is to be achieved in two ways: first, by switching the balance of public funding away from the block grant system to one more responsive to student demand for higher education courses; and second, by making universities bid for UFC funding of students through the introduction of competitive tendering. These are discussed separately below.

Fee income v. the block grant

Public funding to support the recurrent costs of undergraduate higher education in Great Britain are channelled through (1) the block grant, and (2) student fees. In 1989/90 the block grant constituted about 92 per cent of the total public funding of undergraduate tuition in Great Britain, the remaining 8 per cent coming from publicly funded tuition fees. The allocation of the block grant element of public funding is determined by the UFC and the fee income is determined by student numbers. This division of public funding between the block grant and fee income is to be changed substantially during the early 1990s. The intention is to reduce the share of the block grant from 92 per cent to about 70 per cent of the public funding of undergraduates by 1991/92. This will be achieved by raising fee income and allocating a smaller proportion of total public funding to be distributed by the UFC.

The increase in the relative share of fee income in the total grant is to be achieved by increasing student fees from £607 per student in 1989/90 to £1,675 per student in 1990/91. A differential fee system will then be installed in 1991/92. This will comprise three bands: £1,675 for classroom-based subjects; £2,500 for laboratory-based subjects; and £4,500 for medicine, dentistry and veterinary science.

The purpose of this switch in public funding from block grants to fee income is to encourage universities to provide a better service. The government argues that:

> by making institutions' income dependent in larger measure on their ability to attract and satisfy student demand, this funding approach will both promote effectiveness in marketing and teaching, and enhance the scope of institutional independence.

Moreover

> to the extent that the higher fee income covers marginal costs, it will
> assist in encouraging institutions to exploit spare capacity by taking in
> additional students, so contributing to the objective of widening access
> to those able to benefit and wishing to do so, while in the process
> reducing unit costs.
>
> (DES 1989: 2)

The policy of changing the balance of public funding away from block
grants and towards student fees is therefore motivated by four main
objectives:

1. to make individual institutions more responsive to student demand for
   higher education courses
2. to make institutions less dependent on centralized control over the
   public funding of higher education
3. to widen access to higher education by encouraging universities to
   search more vigorously for non-conventional entrants (e.g. mature
   students without A levels but with other relevant qualifications or
   experience)
4. to reduce unit costs.

The latter objective was reinforced by the higher education minister who
stated: 'We believe there is considerable scope for low-cost expansion'
(*Financial Times*, 26 April 1989).

The government therefore aims to expand the student intake into
higher education but at lower unit costs than currently prevail. Lower unit
costs will be achieved since the extra fee income accruing to institutions
from admitting extra students is to be set lower than the average cost of
tuition per student. Institutions which have spare capacity in particular
courses can be expected to increase their admissions since the marginal
costs of doing so will be lower than the fee income. The danger is that the
new system of funding will induce higher education institutions to relieve
their short-term financial problems by admitting more students into
popular subjects but where there is no spare capacity (e.g. where
student/staff ratios are already high). The result of relieving financial
problems will therefore be higher student/staff ratios, which may be
expected to lead either to a fall in the quality of teaching or to lower
research output. Driving unit costs down by setting fee income well below
average costs can therefore be expected to have harmful longer-term
consequences on either teaching or research (or both). At the very least, it
can be expected to have a deleterious effect on the quality of tuition.

Although the switch in public funding from block grants towards student
fees marks a radical change of course in the government's higher education
policy, it is far too early to sound the death knell for centralization. Even
when differentiated fees are introduced for different subjects, the Universities Funding Council (which replaced the UGC in 1989) will still be

dispensing 70 per cent of total public funds in the form of block grants. Moreover, the government itself will ultimately set the fee structure and this can be devised such that it deliberately favours some subjects rather than others. In discussing the fee bands to be established for individual subjects, for example, the consultative document states that

> the main criterion for allocation of courses to particular fee bands should be the cost of the course, although other features may have a part to play in particular circumstances.
>
> (DES 1989: 12)

Exactly what these 'other features' may be is not clarified but it seems likely that the government will set the fee structure according to its own view of which subjects should be given the greatest encouragement to expand. If there is deemed to be an inadequate supply of places in engineering or technology, for example, student fees could be raised in order to encourage universities to expand the supply of places on such courses – and indeed to recruit more actively to achieve a greater input of students into such courses.

One of the more optimistic points to emerge from the proposed new system of funding is that total expenditure on higher education will become more responsive to demand. The Secretary of State for Education has clearly indicated the government's commitment to a substantial expansion of the higher education sector and this is expected to be achieved by widening access to it beyond the normal channels (i.e. A levels and Scottish highers). The promise of an increased level of funding came directly from the then Secretary of State, Kenneth Baker, who said that

> the Treasury had agreed that, in future years, extra fee-based spending generated by colleges recruiting additional students to courses would not necessarily be clawed back in the form of equivalent cuts in central grants. He pointed out that spending on tuition fees was not cash-limited.
>
> (*Financial Times*, 26 April 1989)

The sting in the tail, however, is that extra funding will be provided simultaneously with a reduction in unit costs. This is an inevitable outcome of setting student fees at well below average costs while encouraging universities to take on more students than they are funded for by the UFC. It should also be pointed out that the Treasury subsequently failed to back Mr Baker's statement that spending on tuition fees was not cash-limited. This came as no great surprise to the higher education sector.

The block grant: the funding of teaching and research

A new system of allocating the block grant element of public funding is to be introduced in 1991/92 (to cover the planning period 1991/92 to

1994/95). Two factors lie at the heart of the new system. First, universities are required to bid for funds to support their teaching activities by offering to take on a specific number of students in each degree subject at a specific price per student. This price must be at or below the 'guide' price determined by the UFC. This guide price, which varies between subjects, was constructed by estimating the total recurrent costs per student of providing the necessary teaching resources (for undergraduates and taught postgraduates). The guide price for each main subject area is given in Table 3.4. The second feature of the new system of funding concerns the distribution of the research funds element in the block grant. This is to be allocated selectively during 1990/91 to 1994/95 and the actual allocation will be strongly influenced by the 1989 research selectivity exercise. The main principles of the new arrangements for determining the allocation of the UFC funds to universities are summarized in Table 3.5.

From 1991/92 the funding of the teaching activities of universities will be based upon a new system of bidding for funded students. The new system will operate during the planning period 1991/92 to 1994/95. Universities

Table 3.4 The guide prices

Academic subject group	*Guide price (£)*
Politics, law and other social studies	2,200
Mathematics and statistics	2,700
Economics and sociology	2,700
Business and administration studies	2,800
Humanities	2,800
Mass communication and documentation	2,900
Languages and related disciplines	2,900
Creative arts	3,300
Applied social work	3,400
Archaeology	3,400
Computer studies	3,500
Education	3,500
Architecture, building and planning	3,700
Subjects allied to medicine	4,000
Agriculture	4,200
Biological sciences	4,300
Pre-clinical medicine	4,600
Physical science	4,600
Engineering and technology	4,600
Pre-clinical dentistry	5,200
Metallurgy	5,400
Veterinary science	8,100
Clinical medicine	8,500
Clinical dentistry	9,400

Source: UFC 1989a: Annex D (revised).

Table 3.5   The new funding principles as set out in 'Funding and planning, 1991/92 to 1994/95'

A   General principles

1. Funding will be determined on a competitive basis.
2. Funding will be flexible in so far as it will be adjusted during the planning period (to take account of each institution's performance and its success in achieving its stated objectives).
3. The funding of teaching, research and continuing education will be determined and indicated separately for each university.
4. Universities will be expected to restructure and rationalise themselves within the basic funds made available by the UFC (i.e. no extra funding is available for restructuring).

B   Teaching

1. Funding will be based upon a system of competitive bidding for student numbers based upon a guide price per full-time equivalent student determined by the UFC.
2. The allocation of funds will favour universities which submit low bids (other things being equal).
3. Funding decisions will not be made solely on the basis of the bid price. The UFC will take account of the extent to which each university's plans contribute towards achieving the UFC's aims.
4. Universities will be free to admit students in excess of the numbers for which they are funded by the UFC (e.g. self-financing and part-time students).

C   Research

Research funding will be strongly competitive, based on the quality of research output. A significant element of research funding, however, will reflect the basic research commitment required of academic staff.

D   Continuing education

Funds will be determined separately for these activities.

Source: UFC (1989b).

have been asked to bid for funded students for 1994/95 and the outcome of these bids will then determine the allocation of funds between institutions for the period 1991/92 to 1993/94 (through a process of interpolating from their 1990/91 position). Each university will bid against a maximum guide price set by the UFC for each main subject group. Although universities will be encouraged to bid at less than the guide price, the UFC will take account of the extent to which bids below the guide price will result in a loss of quality before such bids are accepted. The UFC is therefore interested in the quality of the product in relation to its price.

The primary purpose of asking universities to bid for public funds to support their teaching activities is (obviously) to encourage the provision of higher education at a lower cost to the public purse. It is expected that universities with spare capacity in specific subject areas will have an incentive to take on more students at less than the guide price, thereby reducing unit costs. The UFC is therefore reinforcing the government's policy of imposing the discipline of the market on universities by making them compete for public funds through the introduction of a system of tendering for funded students. How universities will respond to the new funding system is still unclear, but it seems unlikely that many bids will fall below the guide price given the existence of excess demand for places in most parts of the university sector.

Conclusion

Government funding of the higher education sector has changed radically in recent decades. After expanding steadily during the 1950s and early 1960s in response to the growing demand for higher education, the establishment of twenty-one new universities in the mid-1960s marked the beginning of a decade of extremely rapid growth in government funding. Since 1975, however, government funding has become less certain and more unstable. The national economic crisis of 1975/76 (following the first oil shock in 1973/74) led to the imposition of financial constraints right across the public sector, including higher education. Demand-led growth in higher education was consequently replaced by an extended period of financially constrained growth which continued throughout the 1980s.

Universities responded to the tight financial constraints on public funding after 1975 by seeking alternative sources of income. Between 1974/75 and 1987/88 UK universities as a whole reduced their exchequer funding from 90 per cent to 74 per cent of total recurrent income. This decline in the relative importance of exchequer funding was matched by a corresponding increase in income from overseas student fees, industry, and research foundations.

Radical changes to the funding of universities will occur in the 1990s as a result of initiatives taken by the DES and UFC. Both bodies have introduced new measures for funding which are likely to have a substantial impact on the university sector over the longer term. The DES has indicated that income from student fees will increase relative to the block grant, the intention being to encourage universities to take on extra students at a cost substantially below the average cost of tuition per graduate. The government is eager to expand the number of graduates by encouraging an increase in the participation rate in higher education and by inducing universities to provide more places for mature students. This extra throughput, however, has to be achieved at lower unit costs.

The UFC has taken a similar line to the DES by requiring universities to bid competitively for funded students. The guide price established by the UFC for each subject area sets an upper limit to the income available per student. The fact that the guide prices are based upon historical cost data indicates that the intention is to reduce unit costs since it is the UFC's expectation that some universities will bid at below the guide prices in subjects in which they have spare capacity.

Thus, although the higher education sector is being encouraged to expand its output of graduates in the 1990s (and beyond), this expansion will have to be achieved at lower unit costs than in the past. The upward trend in student numbers is therefore expected to be accompanied by a continuation of the downward trend in unit costs. The cry is for an expansion of higher education – but at lower cost per student.

Appendix to Chapter 3

A chronology of some of the main events in the history of public funding to the universities: 1889 to 1990

1889	Grant of £15,000 made by the Treasury to the universities. *Ad hoc* committee set up to distribute the money.
1906	*Ad hoc* committee for distributing money to the universities made into a continuing body.
1910	Committee transferred to the jurisdiction of the Board of Education.
1918	High inflation rates and low numbers caused by shortage of money in the universities.
1919	UGC created.
1925	Quinquennial funding began.
1936	Chairmanship of the UGC made full-time post.
1939	Exchequer grants to the universities were still only one-third of the universities' income.
1944	Education Act – ensured an increase in the number of students qualified for university.
1945	The CVCP and UGC developed a plan for the universities requiring vast sums of public money.
1946/47	Exchequer grants were one-half of the universities' income.
1947/52	UGC used earmarked grants in allocating money to individual universities.
1952	Earmarked grants ended, but UGC guidelines on spending became more detailed.
1957–67	Student numbers more than doubled. The number of institutions on the grants list doubled with the addition of ex-CATs and new universities.
1960	Anderson Report – recommended a maintenance grant for every student qualified for and able to get a place at university.
1963	Robbins Report – recommended a place at university for every student qualified and wanting one.
1964	UGC moved under the jurisdiction of the DES.
1965	Crosland's announcement of the binary policy.
1967	UGC began the practice of written as opposed to oral guidelines.

1968	Comptroller and Auditor-General given access to UGC and university records.
1972	The White Paper (DES) indicated that grants to universities per student would fall.
1973	World economic crisis.
1974/75	No supplementation of the grant despite an inflation rate of 20 per cent. The size of the grants for the final two years of the quinquennium were not made known until six months before receipt.
1977	The end of the quinquennial system of funding and the start of the rolling triennium.
1979	Election of the Thatcher government. The UGC told the DES that reductions in university funding in excess of 2.5 per cent in real resources would cause chaos.
1979/80	Overseas entrants no longer subsidized. Level funding announced for home students.
1981/84	Planned cuts in the real recurrent grant of 8.5 per cent. The CVCP estimated that overall cuts would amount to 15 per cent.
1982	Merrison Report (ABRC/UGC) – recommended more funds to go to research, and the direction of resources to respond to research strengths.
1984	*A Strategy for Higher Education into the 1990s* was published by the UGC. It confirmed that new methods of selective funding were planned.
1985	Jarratt Report (CVCP). *Higher Education into the 1990s* (DES Green Paper).
1985/86	A new model of resource allocation introduced by the UGC for the distribution of the 1986/87 grant. UGC research selectivity exercise.
1987	Croham Report (DES) *Higher Education: Meeting the Challenge* (DES White Paper). *A Strategy for the Science Base* (ABRC). The Education Reform Bill (DES).
1989	Consultation paper on shifting the balance of public funding from block grants to fees. Replacement of UGC by UFC. DES proposal to shift the balance of public funding from block grants to student fees. UFC research selectivity exercise. UFC proposal to change method of funding: universities to bid for funded students and research component of block grant to be influenced by research selectivity exercise.
1990	Guide prices published by UFC as basis of bidding for funded students (1991/92 – 1994/95 planning period).

4

Inputs, Processes and Outputs in the University Sector: The University Production Function

Introduction

The purpose of evaluation is to discover whether there is a better way of doing things. As far as the university sector is concerned, evaluation involves investigating whether universities could achieve their objectives more efficiently and more effectively. One approach to this task of evaluating universities is to compare their performance across a range of indicators. But if this comparative approach is to be adopted, it is essential to compare like with like. This means that any observed differences in performance must take account of any corresponding differences in the particular circumstances of each institution. It is entirely pointless to compare degree results between universities, for example, unless account is taken of differences in the ability of student entrants. Lancaster cannot expect as high a proportion of first class honours graduates as Cambridge since its student entrants are generally of lower academic ability than those at Cambridge.

A potentially useful framework for undertaking a comparative study of the performance of universities is provided by production theory, the purpose of which is to investigate the way in which inputs are transformed into outputs. Production theory provides a useful starting-point since it requires a clear statement of the outputs universities aim to produce and the inputs they need to produce these outputs. This chapter therefore draws upon production theory in order to investigate the relationship between inputs and outputs in the university sector.

If universities are to be evaluated, it is therefore necessary to acquire information about

1. the outputs which universities aim to produce
2. the inputs which universities need to produce these outputs
3. quantitative measurements of each university's inputs and outputs
4. the technical relationship between inputs and outputs.

This chapter focuses entirely on specifying the inputs and outputs of the university production process. Attempts to measure the quantitative relationship between specific inputs and specific outputs are made in later chapters.

The purpose of attempting to measure the technical relationship between inputs and outputs in the university sector is to provide a bench-mark against which each university can be compared. This is the crux of the methodological approach used in the next five chapters of this book. Since the production function provides quantitative estimates of the link between inputs and outputs, it is possible (at least in principle) to estimate what each university *could* have produced with the inputs available to it. The production function also provides information about the likely effect on output of changing the amount and combination of inputs used by individual institutions.

Once a university production function has been estimated from data on inputs for all UK universities, it is consequently possible to obtain an estimate of the extent to which each institution's *actual* output matches up to its *expected* output. This methodological approach forms the basis of the remaining chapters of this book. The present chapter simply provides some background information about the links between inputs and outputs in the university production system as a whole.

The production function

In a simplified theoretical world, a production unit (such as a firm or a plant within a firm) is assumed to produce a single homogeneous commodity and this can be achieved in various ways depending upon the chosen production technique. Writing the production function in general form, we have

$$y = f(l,k,t,c,r)$$

where

y = output (e.g. teaching and research)
l = labour inputs (e.g. academic and non-academic staff)
k = capital inputs (e.g. buildings and equipment)
t = technical knowledge (e.g. knowledge of academic staff)
c = consumables (e.g. heating and telephones)
r = raw material (e.g. students).

A problem which arises in attempting to apply production theory to the university sector is that universities produce more than one output. Moreover, these outputs are quite different and there is no obvious way of adding them together. In the case of private sector firms, output can be measured in monetary units (e.g. total sales or value added). This is not possible in the university sector. Since universities are multi-product organizations, it is necessary to specify the individual outputs which are produced and to show the extent to which these individual outputs are dependent upon the wide variety of inputs required.

A further problem with attempting to estimate a production function for the university sector (or parts of this sector) is that inputs are often used to produce more than one output and there is no obvious way of attributing specific inputs to specific outputs. Time spent on reading articles and books for research purposes, for example, often provides useful input into teaching; and teaching (particularly at the postgraduate level) may also have feedback effects on research. Since research output and teaching output cannot be added together in any meaningful way, this makes it difficult to estimate input and output relationships for specific outputs.

There is also a simultaneity problem since universities (or departments within universities) which gain a high reputation for their research output are often able to attract students of higher academic ability than universities with a poorer research record. Some support for this hypothesis is offered by the highly significant positive correlation between A level score and the UFC's research rating across universities ($r = 0.66$). Research output may therefore affect teaching output indirectly by affecting the inputs which determine teaching output. Ideally such interrelationships should be taken into account explicitly when attempting to estimate input–output relationships.

Finally, there is the absolutely critical problem of identifying and measuring the inputs and outputs of the higher education sector at the institutional level. The next two sections deal specifically with this issue.

University outputs

To discover what the university sector produces, it is useful to begin by investigating what it is that universities aim to achieve. We need to know their objectives. In the private sector, firms produce goods and services in order to provide income for their owners. Their primary aim is usually taken to be profit maximization over the long term. Higher education is driven by a more complex set of objectives. Blaug (1968), for example, suggests that the purpose of higher education is

1. to select the most able for leadership in industry and government
2. to cultivate talent for the sake of self-enrichment
3. to promote scholarship and research
4. to preserve and disseminate cultural values.

Other objectives can be added to Blaug's list:

5. to provide skills which will be valuable both to the person acquiring those skills and to society more generally (Robbins 1963; Jarratt 1985)
6. to promote the notion of public service (Robbins 1963; Jarratt 1985)
7. to provide greater equality of opportunity (Brandl 1970)
8. to provide an independent source of social and political comment (i.e.

independent of the government, political parties and other institutions) (Layard and Verry 1975)
9. to undertake applied research of relevance to increasing the productive efficiency of the economy and to improving the well-being of
humankind.

Since universities are constrained in their efforts to achieve these objectives
by the availability of public funding, they have attempted to push back this
financial constraint by adding a further objective:

10. to reduce their dependency on public funds by undertaking income-
generating activities (such as putting on short courses, attracting
students from overseas, and undertaking consultancy and research
work for government and industry).

The most recent attempt to articulate the aims of the university sector is
contained in a circular from the UFC. The general aim as stated by the
UFC, is

> The maintenance and development of universities as high-quality and
> cost-effective institutions, providing for the advancement of knowl-
> edge, the pursuit of scholarship and the education of students, thereby
> playing their parts in meeting national needs.
>
> (UFC 1989a: Annex B)

In addition to this *general* objective, the UFC has set out several *specific* aims.
Universities will be expected

1. to provide an expanding range of services to cater for the growing needs
of society
2. to provide more opportunities for people to participate in university
education, thereby raising the participation rate of under-represented
groups
3. to maintain and enhance scholarship and research of high quality and to
make this more accessible to the public at large
4. to participate more fully in local and regional activities as centres of
expertise
5. to obtain a greater proportion of their income from non-government
sources
6. to develop more efficient management systems
7. to become more outward-looking by expanding their activities at local,
regional and international levels.

Finally, universities will be encouraged 'to exercise their autonomy to the
maximum degree consistent with full accountability for their use of [public]
funds' (UFC 1989a: Annex B).

These various attempts to specify the objectives of universities suggest
that they aim to produce four main categories of output:

1. output derived from teaching activities

2. output derived from research activities
3. output derived from consultancy and related activities
4. cultural and social outputs.

Although there is little dispute about exactly what the higher education sector produces when the outputs are stated in broad and very general terms, serious problems arise when *quantifiable* measurements of these outputs are required. Examples are not difficult to find. How can the extent to which universities 'cultivate talent for the sake of self-enrichment' or 'preserve and disseminate cultural values' be quantified? Similar questions can be asked about the wider benefits accruing to society as a result of training and education at a high academic level. Is it possible to assess in any convincing way the importance of higher educational institutions as sources of social and political comment, or as sources of ideas and inventions which help to shape the future of humankind? Indeed, it may be asked whether there is any point in attempting to measure the extent to which the higher education sector is achieving objectives which are themselves not subject to quantifiable measurement.

Take research output as an example. How should research output be measured? A monetary measure of the *value* of research output does not exist since the results of virtually all academic research become a public good through the publication of articles in learned journals and books. This suggests that the *amount* of research produced by a university could be measured by the quantity of publications. But this ignores the *quality* of the research being produced. The recent research selectivity exercise by the UFC (1989c) attempted to combine *qualitative* assessment of the research output of individual departments in each university with the quantitative information supplied to the UFC. Having obtained quantitative data of every university's research output over the period 1984–88, the UFC's subject committees then appraised the quality of this research (though how carefully this was done is another matter) in order to produce an overall assessment on a five-point scale. The UFC's research selectivity exercise therefore provides us with a quantitative measure of each university's research output (by cost centre) which is intended to take quality into account as well as quantity. The problems of measuring research output will be considered further in Chapter 9.

A similar argument holds for the teaching function of universities. Detailed information exists on the number of graduates, the classification of their degrees and their degree subject. Something is also known about the first destination of graduates after their graduation and about the salaries of graduates with different types of degrees (though this is available only at the national level and not for individual institutions). Exactly how this information should be assembled to produce a measure of the teaching output of individual institutions is not, however, entirely obvious.

Measuring the output of universities is therefore an extremely complex problem. This does not mean, however, that the higher education sector

Table 4.1 Various output measures by university, 1987/88

University	% of under-graduates not completing their degree course[1]	% of graduates with a first or upper second[2]	% of graduates proceeding to further education or training[3]	% of graduates proceeding to permanent employment[3]	% of graduates unemployed or in a short-term job
Aston	16.8	58.7	8.0	86.6	5.4
Bath	14.1	59.8	12.6	81.6	5.8
Birmingham	10.5	39.5	25.2	68.2	6.6
Bradford	16.0	45.6	11.9	75.8	12.3
Bristol	7.3	53.2	22.8	68.7	8.5
Brunel	21.8	45.6	16.0	80.6	3.4
Cambridge	3.4	69.3	36.8	54.6	8.6
City	19.3	48.1	8.7	86.1	5.2
Durham	5.2	49.0	31.4	62.4	6.2
East Anglia	9.6	48.8	27.8	58.3	13.9
Essex	14.6	48.2	32.6	58.6	8.8
Exeter	8.8	47.4	24.2	64.7	11.1
Hull	12.3	44.4	27.4	65.1	7.5
Keele	16.3	46.4	31.6	51.2	17.2
Kent	13.3	51.1	26.3	66.6	7.1
Lancaster	8.7	53.6	24.6	67.7	7.7
Leeds	10.9	41.6	23.6	66.0	10.4
Leicester	9.7	45.4	33.3	57.3	9.4
Liverpool	14.3	37.4	23.8	63.3	12.9
London	16.5	43.3	23.2	66.1	10.7
Loughborough	10.3	51.1	12.9	75.8	11.3
Manchester	12.8	45.8	20.9	67.5	11.6
UMIST	14.8	43.0	14.9	73.5	11.6
Newcastle	16.9	40.2	19.2	72.4	8.4
Nottingham	9.2	52.5	19.4	70.6	10.0
Oxford	7.0	58.8	36.8	55.0	8.2
Reading	12.0	52.6	24.1	68.5	7.4
Salford	19.5	50.5	12.5	81.1	6.4
Sheffield	9.9	46.4	23.4	62.7	13.9
Southampton	9.1	45.4	24.1	68.0	7.9
Surrey	14.7	47.4	18.9	72.5	8.6
Sussex	12.2	44.8	29.5	56.9	13.6
Warwick	11.5	48.9	21.2	67.6	11.2
York	8.7	58.5	24.6	61.2	14.2
Aberdeen	23.6	35.8	32.4	61.1	6.5
Dundee	22.4	30.7	30.0	62.8	7.2
Edinburgh	14.0	42.2	26.2	62.9	10.9
Glasgow	20.8	28.8	32.0	60.5	7.5
Heriot-Watt	21.5	35.6	18.2	75.2	6.6
St Andrews	11.8	50.0	32.3	55.3	12.4
Stirling	14.9	37.9	18.7	70.4	10.9
Strathclyde	21.6	41.4	20.6	71.0	8.4
Queen's	11.5	36.3	33.2	59.1	7.7
Ulster	15.9	36.4	16.6	67.3	16.1
Wales	15.7	41.8	31.2	56.8	12.0
All universities	13.3	45.9	25.0	65.1	9.9

Notes:
1. Percentage of 1980 entrants not completing by 1986
2. 1988 graduates
3. Status of 1988 graduates (who are available for employment and of known destination) at 31 December 1988

Source: Universities' Statistical Record, Cheltenham.

Table 4.2 Income from research grants and contracts and other services rendered per full-time academic by university 1987/88 (£ thousands)

University	Research grants and contracts						Other services rendered			
	Total	Research councils	UK government	Charitable bodies	Industry	Other	Total	Short courses	Government and hospitals	Other
Aston	8.8	2.6	2.3	1.3	1.5	1.1	4.3	2.8	1.1	0.4
Bath	9.7	3.5	2.6	0.6	1.9	1.2	1.9	0.7	0.1	1.1
Birmingham	9.9	3.8	1.8	2.2	1.3	0.9	8.2	4.0	1.5	2.7
Bradford	6.8	1.8	1.2	0.9	2.0	0.9	3.7	2.9	0.0	0.8
Bristol	10.7	4.5	2.3	2.5	0.7	0.7	3.2	0.9	1.2	1.0
Brunel	13.2	3.7	4.0	1.6	2.4	1.6	2.8	1.7	0.3	0.7
Cambridge	12.8	6.9	1.0	2.6	1.4	0.9	1.6	0.8	0.5	0.3
City	6.9	2.2	1.5	0.5	1.7	1.0	9.8	8.6	0.0	1.2
Durham	8.0	3.7	1.5	0.4	1.5	0.9	4.2	3.1	0.3	0.8
East Anglia	6.4	2.0	1.7	0.7	1.1	0.9	0.7	0.5	0.0	0.2
Essex	8.7	3.4	1.3	0.6	2.6	0.8	1.9	1.4	0.0	0.5
Exeter	5.6	2.1	1.4	0.7	0.5	0.9	2.7	0.9	1.0	0.9
Hull	4.6	2.3	0.7	0.2	0.9	0.4	2.0	1.0	0.3	0.8
Keele	7.0	2.3	2.1	1.7	0.7	0.2	2.0	1.8	0.0	0.1
Kent	9.6	3.3	3.8	0.3	1.1	1.0	0.7	0.2	0.0	0.5
Lancaster	6.2	3.9	1.0	0.2	0.5	0.6	3.2	0.5	0.0	2.7
Leeds	7.9	2.9	1.3	1.6	1.3	0.8	5.5	1.2	1.9	2.4
Leicester	9.4	3.9	1.2	1.6	1.9	0.8	3.6	0.5	2.8	0.3
Liverpool	10.0	3.0	1.5	3.0	1.4	1.1	3.0	0.3	1.7	1.1
London	16.9	4.5	2.3	5.2	2.1	2.8	4.6	0.5	3.3	0.8

Loughborough	12.6	5.0	2.9	0.2	3.2	1.3	3.1	2.5	0.0	0.6
Manchester	8.5	3.6	1.9	1.8	0.7	0.4	3.6	1.3	0.9	1.4
UMIST	14.7	5.0	1.9	0.2	5.1	2.5	2.5	0.6	0.0	1.8
Newcastle	9.8	3.1	1.8	2.2	1.4	1.4	2.5	0.7	0.7	1.1
Nottingham	9.9	3.3	1.3	2.4	2.1	0.8	2.3	0.4	0.3	1.6
Oxford	16.8	7.7	2.0	3.8	1.1	2.1	2.0	0.6	0.6	0.9
Reading	10.0	3.5	2.0	1.3	1.5	1.7	3.0	2.5	0.4	0.1
Salford	8.5	4.5	1.4	0.4	1.5	0.7	20.4	1.1	6.6	12.7
Sheffield	9.3	4.0	1.5	1.6	1.4	0.8	2.1	0.6	0.6	0.9
Southampton	13.4	4.0	3.3	2.0	2.1	2.0	3.7	1.0	0.7	1.9
Surrey	13.9	4.5	3.5	1.9	2.5	1.6	7.7	2.6	0.1	5.1
Sussex	10.4	5.0	1.3	1.2	1.5	1.3	1.4	1.0	0.0	0.4
Warwick	12.5	6.0	1.9	0.5	2.6	1.5	8.2	5.9	0.0	2.3
York	10.6	4.6	2.6	2.1	0.5	1.0	2.1	0.7	0.0	1.3
Aberdeen	7.3	2.0	1.9	1.6	1.2	0.7	5.2	0.3	4.7	0.2
Dundee	12.6	2.8	2.7	3.0	2.7	1.4	2.3	0.8	0.9	0.6
Edinburgh	12.2	5.3	2.8	2.2	1.2	0.7	4.1	0.3	2.1	1.7
Glasgow	12.0	5.1	1.4	2.8	1.3	1.4	4.2	0.7	1.1	2.4
Heriot-Watt	16.2	5.2	2.4	0.1	7.3	1.3	4.7	0.7	0.0	4.0
St Andrews	6.5	2.9	1.0	1.7	0.4	0.4	1.7	0.3	0.1	1.2
Stirling	7.0	2.0	2.1	0.5	1.1	1.3	5.3	4.7	0.0	0.5
Strathclyde	10.1	3.0	2.7	0.7	1.9	1.8	1.8	1.0	0.1	0.8
Queen's	6.4	1.8	1.7	1.2	0.9	0.8	4.6	0.0	4.3	0.3
Ulster	3.2	0.7	0.9	0.2	0.1	1.3	1.3	0.5	0.0	0.9
Wales	9.0	2.0	2.4	1.5	1.7	1.5	2.8	0.9	1.0	0.9
All universities	11.4	4.0	2.0	2.3	1.7	1.5	3.9	1.2	1.4	1.3

Source: University Statistics: Finance, 1987/88, Tables 3 and 9.

should not *attempt* to measure its output since there can be little hope of progress towards developing appropriate methods of evaluation unless satisfactory measures of output can be constructed. In fact, the higher education sector has no alternative but to develop such measures. The funding agencies – and indeed the government itself – are committed to imposing more rigorous methods of evaluation on the higher education sector.

In view of the requirement imposed on the higher education sector to construct and use performance indicators, it is important to examine what kinds of output measure actually exist. Several variables can be constructed which measure various aspects of each university's activities. The variables given in Table 4.1, for example, provide information which relates to the annual output of graduates. Non-completion rates, degree results and the first destination of graduates after leaving university all relate in some way to the success or otherwise of each university's graduates. Since universities aim to produce as many 'successful' students as possible from any given entry cohort, these various measures can consequently be used as indicators of each university's output.

Attempts to measure other types of outputs which are produced by the university sector are equally problematic. The difficulty of measuring research output has already been mentioned. A similar problem arises in attempting to measure the services rendered to government departments and to the private sector. Since universities sell their services to government and industry, however, it is possible to estimate the output arising from their services by the payments made for them. Table 4.2 provides this information for several services (including research). It shows the amount of income received (per full-time academic) from various income-providing organizations. The research grant data reveal substantial disparities in the extent to which individual institutions are able to attract different types of income. This is likely to be strongly influenced by the subject mix of institutions.

University inputs

The inputs used by the university sector can be broadly classified into four main groups: labour services, capital services, consumables and students. Technical knowledge is omitted since it is assumed that this is embodied in labour and capital services. The linkages between these inputs and the outputs of the university sector are shown in broad terms in Figure 4.1.

One of the most critical inputs of universities is the students whom they are able to attract. Universities have to operate in a competitive environment as far as acquiring students is concerned. In general they attempt to attract students of the highest academic calibre, a characteristic which can be expected to have an effect on several university outputs. The academic ability of students, for example, may be expected to affect their exam

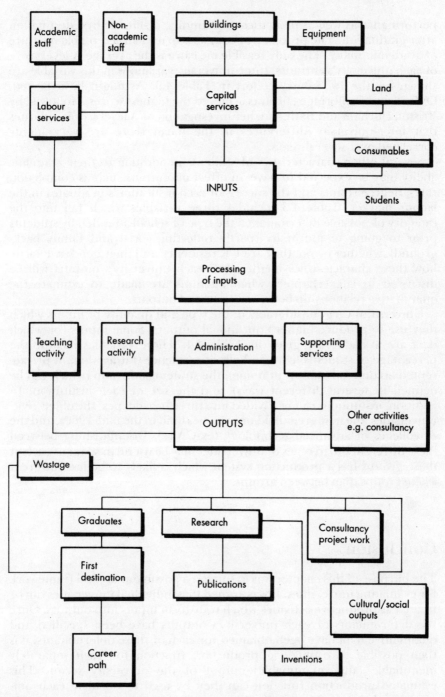

Figure 4.1 Inputs and outputs in the university sector

performance as well as their success in finding a suitable first destination after graduation. The problem, of course, is to find an acceptable measure of academic ability. The only feasible measure is the average A level score of each university's entrants. Inter-university variations in this variable are shown for the 1985 entry cohort in Table 4.3. As might be expected, Oxford and Cambridge entrants achieved the highest scores – followed by Bristol, Durham and Bath. Further investigation of A level scores indicates that inter-university differences in the mean score are very highly correlated over several years.

Several other characteristics of students in addition to their academic ability may be expected to have an effect on outputs such as completion rates, degree results and the success of each institution's graduates in the labour market. Table 4.3 includes three variables which fall into the category of possible determinants: the type of school attended by students prior to going to university (partly reflecting social and family background), whether or not they are UK residents, and their gender. Exactly how these characteristics might affect each university's outputs will be discussed in later chapters when attempts are made to estimate the quantitative relationship between inputs and outputs.

Universities vary considerably in the type and quantity of inputs which they use to produce higher educational outputs. Some inputs for which data are available are given in Table 4.4. These variables include the percentage of students living in halls of residence (rather than in private rented accommodation or at home), the student/staff ratio (which can be defined in several different ways), and the size of each institution. In addition, institutions can be divided into three broad types: the older 'civic' universities, the new greenfield universities built in the mid-1960s, and the ex-colleges of advanced technology (ex-CATs). Distinguishing between these different broad types of universities may be useful in so far as each of these groups has a production system which is likely to be less different *within* groups than between groups.

Conclusion

The purpose of this chapter was to suggest a possible analytical framework for evaluating universities. It was argued that individual universities can be treated as productive activities which transform inputs into outputs. Once the determinants of each university's outputs have been specified and quantitative data have been obtained for each of these determinants, it is then possible to estimate a production function for each separately identifiable (and quantifiable) output of the university sector. This estimated production function can then be used to calculate each university's *relative* efficiency in producing each of its outputs.

Table 4.3   Some major characteristics of each university's students

University	Average A level[1] score of 1985 entrants	% of graduates[2] who attended a grammar or independent school	% of graduates[2] who attended a comprehensive school	% of graduates[3] from overseas	% of graduates[4] who were females
Aston	11.4	31.0	56.1	1.7	39.8
Bath	12.4	34.7	46.4	7.9	34.7
Birmingham	11.4	42.1	43.9	5.9	43.7
Bradford	10.0	24.3	56.2	4.2	41.7
Bristol	12.7	56.5	30.6	5.8	42.8
Brunel	10.6	25.6	56.7	2.7	29.5
Cambridge	14.1	62.7	23.1	6.3	37.7
City	10.0	34.6	47.1	12.7	31.8
Durham	12.5	51.3	35.7	1.7	42.4
East Anglia	10.0	33.9	47.4	8.9	48.3
Essex	8.8	22.7	54.5	15.3	42.1
Exeter	11.1	52.0	35.0	1.9	47.5
Hull	10.0	28.5	53.3	5.6	47.6
Keele	9.1	28.3	52.8	15.7	47.3
Kent	10.2	29.3	52.8	15.9	45.3
Lancaster	10.0	25.5	54.0	4.9	46.1
Leeds	10.7	33.3	50.0	5.4	42.6
Leicester	10.4	30.7	53.5	3.4	46.9
Liverpool	10.7	31.1	50.7	3.4	41.4
London	10.9	43.9	34.9	14.9	45.1
Loughborough	11.3	27.8	50.6	8.5	30.3
Manchester	11.6	36.0	44.7	5.5	42.6
UMIST	10.7	29.2	49.6	16.4	34.4
Newcastle	10.2	30.6	46.2	7.8	40.1
Nottingham	11.6	39.5	46.5	9.8	43.7
Oxford	13.5	62.4	24.9	6.7	40.8
Reading	10.1	42.0	44.4	7.3	47.2
Salford	10.1	17.6	49.0	15.4	32.2
Sheffield	11.4	28.1	50.6	3.1	43.1
Southampton	12.0	44.6	42.6	5.1	40.7
Surrey	10.8	30.5	48.5	11.0	40.9
Sussex	10.2	28.3	53.1	5.6	47.0
Warwick	11.0	31.8	51.4	8.1	46.8
York	11.7	33.5	48.2	2.5	41.4
Aberdeen	10.1	15.0	7.1	10.9	47.3
Dundee	9.4	21.1	19.0	3.9	42.5
Edinburgh	12.3	29.2	8.8	2.4	47.3
Glasgow	10.9	5.9	2.7	7.6	50.4
Heriot-Watt	10.0	11.4	7.3	17.3	34.9
St Andrews	11.6	46.0	16.0	6.6	52.0
Stirling	9.5	18.2	17.4	5.4	51.7
Strathclyde	9.7	3.6	1.8	10.9	39.3
Queen's	9.8	88.5	0.6	4.3	45.7
Ulster	7.4	28.3	4.6	7.9	50.3
Wales	9.3	24.4	58.2	7.4	47.4
All universities	11.0	36.9	37.1	7.9	43.6

Notes:
1. The average is based on only those entrants to the university with two or more A levels:
    A = 5, B = 4, C = 3, D = 2, E = 1
2. 1988 first degree graduates with UK domicile
3. All first degree graduates, 1987–88
4. First degree UK domiciled graduates of known destination, 1987–88

Sources: Universities' Statistical Record, Cheltenham; *University Statistics*, vol. 2.

Table 4.4 Some university-related characteristics

University	% of students living at home	% of students living in halls of residence[1]	Student/staff ratio (full-time academic staff)[2]	Student/staff ratio (excluding research only staff)[3]	Full-time equivalent students[4]	Full-time academic staff[5]	Type of university New	Ex-CAT	Other
Aston	16.8	42.7	9.9	13.2	3549	359	0	1	0
Bath	5.2	33.5	7.5	10.5	3950	524	0	1	0
Birmingham	12.0	40.6	6.3	9.0	9360	1492	0	0	1
Bradford	5.5	29.6	8.6	10.7	4439	518	0	1	0
Bristol	4.9	41.7	6.1	9.5	7398	1219	0	0	1
Brunel	19.0	56.1	9.1	13.0	3427	376	0	1	0
Cambridge	1.6	78.4	6.9	11.5	13085	1901	0	0	1
City	27.5	33.0	9.0	10.9	3355	372	0	1	0
Durham	4.2	78.2	8.2	11.2	5101	622	0	0	1
East Anglia	5.0	54.3	9.0	11.0	4506	502	1	0	0
Essex	8.1	71.0	8.6	8.7	3257	379	1	0	0
Exeter	5.4	57.3	9.0	10.9	5147	571	0	0	1
Hull	5.7	57.8	10.3	12.2	5033	490	0	0	1
Keele	5.9	88.0	8.9	10.3	2959	331	0	0	1
Kent	4.9	34.7	9.0	11.7	4339	483	1	0	0
Lancaster	6.1	55.1	8.1	10.6	4837	594	1	0	0
Leeds	7.2	39.2	7.1	9.4	10163	1441	0	0	1
Leicester	7.6	67.5	6.6	9.4	4946	746	0	0	1
Liverpool	21.7	40.1	6.7	9.0	8268	1233	0	0	1
London	23.0	31.0	5.2	8.2	45758	8751	0	0	1
Loughborough	10.1	71.1	7.3	10.4	5424	746	0	1	0
Manchester	13.6	41.5	6.5	8.7	11761	1821	0	0	1
UMIST	10.2	41.4	6.3	10.0	4303	685	0	1	0

Newcastle	11.7	44.6	6.5	9.2	7974	1234	0	1
Nottingham	6.5	57.5	7.0	10.3	7719	1103	0	1
Oxford	1.1	67.4	6.9	10.6	13583	1977	0	1
Reading	5.2	61.9	7.5	10.3	5809	778	0	1
Salford	17.6	48.0	10.3	12.3	4383	426	1	0
Sheffield	8.3	39.5	7.8	10.5	8432	1082	0	1
Southampton	1.7	45.3	5.8	9.6	6756	1156	0	1
Surrey	7.6	53.4	6.1	10.6	3678	607	1	0
Sussex	6.0	42.8	7.2	10.6	4384	605	0	1
Warwick	8.6	66.1	8.1	11.4	6532	808	0	1
York	4.1	74.3	8.1	12.2	3854	478	1	0
Aberdeen	20.1	45.3	7.6	10.4	5919	776	0	1
Dundee	22.6	53.3	6.6	9.7	3466	522	0	1
Edinburgh	21.7	34.0	6.1	8.6	10512	1735	0	1
Glasgow	63.2	12.3	7.6	10.6	11314	1479	0	1
Heriot-Watt	28.6	25.6	7.9	11.2	3307	416	0	1
St Andrews	1.9	72.2	9.0	11.3	3702	413	0	1
Stirling	12.2	61.6	8.9	11.6	3240	365	1	0
Strathclyde	65.7	13.8	7.9	11.6	7925	1009	0	1
Queen's	45.9	22.1	8.6	11.4	7908	922	0	1
Ulster	24.5	21.3	11.4	12.7	9956	874	1	0
Wales	9.3	46.6	7.9	10.6	20944	2635	0	1
All universities	15.1	45.7	7.1	10.1	336348	47674	—	—

Notes:

1. The most recently available published data are for 1979
2. Full-time equivalent students to full-time academic staff in 1987/88
3. Full-time equivalent students to full-time teaching and research staff (excluding research only staff) in 1987/88
4. Full-time equivalent students, 1987/88
5. All full-time academic staff including 'research only' staff, 1987/88

Sources: Statistics of Education: Universities, 1979; University Statistics, vols 1 and 3, 1987/88.

In effect, the evaluation process compares the *actual value* of a particular university's output with the *value that would have been expected* given the inputs available to that university. The outputs to which this method has been applied in Chapters 6 to 9 are

1. the degree results of each university's graduates
2. the non-completion rate of each university's student entrants
3. the success of each university's annual crop of graduates in obtaining a satisfactory first destination after graduation
4. research output as indicated by the research rating exercise undertaken by the UFC for the period 1984–88.

We turn first, however, to an investigation of inter-university differences in unit costs. In particular, the next chapter examines costs per student and attempts to identify and measure the influence of those factors which determine the level of unit costs in each institution.

5

Unit Costs: Differences between Universities

Introduction

The steady growth in the public funding of the UK university sector which began at the end of the Second World War came to a sudden halt in the mid-1970s. After a short spell of growth during 1979–81 public funding again fell in real terms during the 1980s. This reversal in the public funding of universities was accompanied by demands from the government for higher standards and increased efficiency. The government has been particularly concerned that procedures should be developed for assessing the performance of universities, the aim being to obtain a more efficient use of scarce public funds:

> The essential purposes of performance measurement in education are to introduce into considerations of policy and the management of the education system at national and institutional level some concrete information on the extent to which the benefits expected from education expenditure are actually secured, and to facilitate comparisons in terms of effectiveness and efficiency as between various parts of the system and as between different points in time.
>
> (DES 1985: 49)

This chapter investigates the possibility of constructing a performance indicator based upon cost per student at the institutional level. The intention is to establish the extent to which inter-university differences in cost per student are explained by corresponding variations in the type of inputs used by each institution. It is important to discover the determinants of inter-university differences in cost per student if this variable is to be of any value as a performance indicator. If we know why cost per student varies between institutions, this should provide some clues as to how individual universities might be able to reduce their unit costs, thereby increasing their economic efficiency.

A further reason for evaluating cost per student as a potential performance indicator is that this variable appears regularly in lists of suggested indicators (Jarratt 1985; DES 1985, 1987b; CVCP 1987; Sizer 1988). The

CVCP, for example, has already produced a set of management statistics and so-called performance indicators in which cost per student has a prominent role. The popularity of cost per student as a performance indicator is hardly surprising since not only are the data readily available for entire institutions, and for individual departments within institutions, but also the government itself has focused attention on unit costs across the entire public sector. Reducing unit costs in all publicly funded organizations has become a primary economic objective of policy-makers during the 1980s.

The remainder of this chapter is in five sections. The first section defines unit costs and describes the data used to measure cost per student at the institutional level. The second section examines inter-university differences in cost per student for the period 1981–88 and the third section discusses some possible explanations of these differences. The relative importance of these factors in explaining (statistically) the inter-university differences in cost per student are investigated in the fourth section with the aid of multiple regression analysis. The fifth section investigates the possibility of constructing a performance indicator based upon cost per student.

Measuring unit costs

Unit costs are defined in this chapter in terms of cost *per student*. It could be argued that cost *per student* is inappropriate since unit costs are supposed to be a measure of cost per unit of output and the output of universities is graduates not students. Indeed, students are inputs into the university production process, which means that cost per student measures cost per unit of input. Cost per graduate and cost per student will be identical, of course, if all students become graduates, which would require the non-completion rate to be zero. For UK universities as a whole, the non-completion rate is about 13 per cent (see Chapter 6). Since this varies substantially between universities, however, this suggests that cost per graduate is a more appropriate measure than cost per student.

One problem with using cost per graduate (rather than cost per student) is the implicit assumption that those students who do not complete their degree course (through failure, illness, transfer to another institution or other reasons) obtain zero value from attending university. Since this is unlikely to be the case, the number of students registered for courses during any one year is used in this chapter as a proxy for output. A similar approach to measuring output is suggested by Nevin (1985), who uses a weighted combination of staff, postgraduates and undergraduates as an index of output in his attempt to calculate cost per unit of output for UK universities. His argument is that staff produce research output and so should be included in the calculation of unit costs. A major problem with this approach is that the weights that have to be attached to staff and students are entirely arbitrary.

Problems also arise in deciding which elements of *expenditure* to include in calculating cost per student. Total university expenditure is split into two components: recurrent expenditure and capital expenditure. Since capital expenditure can vary considerably from year to year, this element is excluded from the measure of university costs. Moreover, within the recurrent component of expenditure, many of the items cover expenditure which does not relate directly to the output of graduates (such as expenditure on research activities, short courses and project work undertaken for outside agencies). Hence in order to focus specifically on the teaching aspects of a university's activities, total general expenditure *on academic departments* is used as the measure of costs. This comprised 41 per cent of the total recurrent expenditure of all UK universities in 1987/88, varying from 36 per cent at Heriot-Watt to 55 per cent at Ulster. Other recurrent cost items which are obviously important in the teaching function of universities (such as administration, central services, academic services and maintenance costs) were not included in the measure of costs since these activities are also important for other university functions in addition to those directed specifically at the tuition of students. To include these further cost items in the measure of cost per student, it would be necessary to find ways of allocating these costs between the various outputs produced by universities. This has recently been done for each cost centre in the university sector as a whole but not yet for individual institutions (UFC 1989a). Unit cost (*UC*) is therefore defined as follows:

$$UC = \frac{\text{General expenditure on academic departments}}{\text{Full-time equivalent students}}$$

Full-time equivalent students include undergraduates, taught postgraduates and research postgraduates. The same definition is used by the CVCP in its *University Management Statistics and Performance Indicators, UK* (CVCP 1989).

Although cost per student is defined in this chapter in terms of expenditure on academic departments, it is useful to note that there is a high correlation (across universities) between various measures of unit costs. Three such measures are given in Table 5.1.

Inter-university differences in cost per student and the influence of subject mix

There is a tremendous variation in cost per student between UK universities (see Table 5.2). In 1987/88, for example, cost per student was below £2,600 at Essex, Kent, Stirling and Ulster compared to over £3,600 at

Table 5.1   Cost per student in UK universities, 1987/88

University	Total recurrent expenditure per FTE student	General academic and related expenditure per FTE student[1]	General academic expenditure per FTE student
Aston	7520	5709	2807
Bath	7471	5738	3242
Birmingham	9252	6379	3549
Bradford	6723	5395	3150
Bristol	8742	6353	4001
Brunel	7545	5659	3286
Cambridge	7647	5411	3419
City	8385	6180	3489
Durham	6649	5113	2832
East Anglia	6352	5048	2959
Essex	6252	4777	2511
Exeter	5640	4665	2855
Hull	5799	4614	2692
Keele	6413	5202	2780
Kent	5829	4619	2512
Lancaster	5914	4756	2982
Leeds	8272	6266	3809
Leicester	7705	5644	3336
Liverpool	9223	7028	3892
London	12569	8229	4525
Loughborough	7434	5429	3276
Manchester	8601	6721	3785
UMIST	9398	6537	4233
Newcastle	8347	6312	3723
Nottingham	7919	6033	3448
Oxford	8566	5691	3233
Reading	7202	5496	3446
Salford	8033	5217	3068
Sheffield	7724	5834	3431
Southampton	9010	6142	3783
Surrey	9212	5993	3516
Sussex	7467	5572	3132
Warwick	7600	5132	2817
York	6641	4814	2745
Aberdeen	8012	5835	3375
Dundee	9257	6573	3692
Edinburgh	9995	6929	3885
Glasgow	8565	6087	3635
Heriot-Watt	8948	5980	3226
St Andrews	6531	5368	2770
Stirling	6395	4772	2554
Strathclyde	6989	5290	3033
Queen's	6659	5101	2929
Ulster	4329	3924	2386
Wales	7009	5175	3060
All universities	8377	6026	3465

Note:
1. This includes general academic expenditure on departments and academic services, general educational expenditure, administration and central services, maintenance and running costs, and expenditure on staff and student facilities

Source: University Statistics: Finance, vol. 3, 1987/88, Tables 1 and 6.

Table 5.2   Actual unit costs by university: 1980/81 to 1987/88

University	Actual unit costs (£)[1]							
	1980/81	*1981/82*	*1982/83*	*1983/84*	*1984/85*	*1985/86*	*1986/87*	*1987/88*
Aston	2130	2163	2230	2355	2405	2636	2617	2807
Bath	2050	2131	2338	2450	2651	2869	3002	3242
Birmingham	2678	2750	2849	3045	3090	3305	3335	3549
Bradford	2065	2201	2279	2386	2530	2681	2789	3150
Bristol	2585	2689	2755	2968	3284	3544	3797	4001
Brunel	2376	2479	2561	2839	2856	2885	2926	3286
Cambridge	2217	2354	2464	2616	2848	3036	3201	3419
City	2854	2893	2866	3298	3045	3150	3466	3489
Durham	1971	2049	2138	2352	2407	2529	2641	2832
East Anglia	1850	2025	2262	2522	2666	2787	2853	2959
Essex	1663	1634	1739	1872	2198	2305	2372	2511
Exeter	1809	1908	2106	2230	2328	2534	2661	2855
Hull	1736	1788	1846	2099	2375	2507	2598	2692
Keele	1961	1978	2035	2185	2265	2487	2580	2780
Kent	1637	1589	1675	1782	1959	2148	2310	2512
Lancaster	1968	2059	2180	2350	2674	2776	2927	2982
Leeds	2392	2454	2589	2815	3128	3381	3613	3809
Leicester	2112	2198	2371	2580	2815	3045	3132	3336
Liverpool	2539	2710	2841	2997	3102	3342	3596	3892
London	2998	3072	3196	3450	3634	3979	4293	4525
Loughborough	1815	1938	2055	2312	2664	2819	3139	3276
Manchester	2528	2646	2762	2823	3118	3310	3519	3785
UMIST	2909	2805	2760	3112	3549	4006	3963	4233
Newcastle	2406	2524	2632	2862	3028	3274	3430	3723
Nottingham	2203	2309	2373	2719	2843	3036	3183	3448
Oxford	2168	2272	2383	2566	2705	2910	3083	3233
Reading	2279	2390	2475	2628	2859	3048	3172	3446
Salford	2381	2382	2510	2563	2649	2786	2972	3068
Sheffield	2412	2508	2604	2819	2978	3248	3162	3431
Southampton	2550	2575	2670	2763	3034	3206	3436	3783
Surrey	2571	2678	2772	2974	3282	3325	3454	3516
Sussex	2110	2173	2198	2320	2529	2652	2827	3132
Warwick	1809	1807	2009	2166	2358	2573	2749	2817
York	1676	1709	1865	2143	2195	2387	2566	2745
Aberdeen	2688	2681	2582	2816	2952	3202	3235	3375
Dundee	2885	2910	2980	2806	3251	3443	3585	3692
Edinburgh	2494	2529	2651	2824	3006	3389	3695	3885
Glasgow	2640	2606	2686	2813	3040	3235	3512	3635
Heriot-Watt	1968	2102	2228	2514	2727	2895	3154	3226
St Andrews	1921	1972	2023	2122	2265	2413	2590	2770
Stirling	1667	1801	1911	2218	2246	2438	2420	2554
Strathclyde	2237	2338	2419	2636	2543	2637	2795	3033
Queen's	2480	2630	2725	2883	2900	2954	3044	2929
Ulster	2213	2208	2220	2150	1584	2039	2176	2386
Wales	2118	2260	2452	2731	2807	2972	2904	3060

Note:

1. See p. 67 for the definition of unit costs

Source: University Statistics: Finance, 1980/81 to 1987/88 inclusive.

Bristol, Leeds, Liverpool, London, Manchester, UMIST, Newcastle, Southampton, Dundee, Edinburgh and Glasgow. These differences *between* universities contrast strongly with the stability of cost per student *within* universities over time (allowing, of course, for inflation).

This stability in inter-university differences in cost per student over time suggests the existence of at least one fundamental causal factor, namely the subject mix. This factor has a predominating role to play in explaining inter-university variations in cost per student. In 1987/88, for example, cost per student varied between under £2,000 in law and accountancy to over £5,000 in the physical sciences (see Table 5.3). Given these vast differences in cost per student between subjects and the differences in subject mix between universities, inter-university differences in cost per student can be *expected* to be substantial. Inter-university comparisons in cost per student therefore need to take into account inter-university differences in subject mix if cost comparisons are to be useful. This can be done by calculating the costs per student which each university could be *expected* to have on the basis of its subject mix. The formula used to calculate the *expected* cost per student for any given university is given in the appendix to this chapter (pp. 79–80).

When the *expected* cost per student given for each university in Table 5.4 and in Figure 5.1 is compared with the *actual* cost per student, it is found that around 70 per cent of the variation in *actual* cost per student is accounted for by *expected* cost per student (i.e. taking subject mix into account). Table 5.5 shows that the inter-university variation in cost per student accounted for by subject mix during 1984/85–86/87 varied between 66 per cent and 72 per cent. This leaves about 30 per cent of the variation in cost per student to be explained by other factors. Exactly what these factors might be is discussed in the next section. Before that, however, it is useful to note that there is a considerable degree of stability in actual minus expected cost per student (see Table 5.4) from one year to the next. This is reflected by the very high correlation between *actual* minus *expected* costs per student for 1984/85, 1985/86 and 1986/87.

Some explanations of inter-university differences in cost per student

It was shown in the previous section that inter-university variations in cost per student can be accounted for to a substantial extent by corresponding variations in subject mix. About 30 per cent of the variation remains unexplained, however, even when subject mix is taken into account. What factors might be expected to explain this remaining variation?

First, the mix of students may have an effect on cost per student (Bowen 1980). In calculating cost per student for each institution, no account was taken of inter-university differences in student mix even though this varies considerably between universities. In 1987/88, for example, around 90 per

Table 5.3   Unit costs by cost centre, 1984/85 to 1987/88 (all UK universities)

Cost centre[1]	Unit costs[2]			
	1984/85[3]	*1985/86*[3]	*1986/87*[3]	*1987/88*[3]
Law	1283	1390	1444	1555
Accountancy	1448	1543	1592	1711
Nursing	1498	1874	1845	2325
Business and management studies	1857	1977	2088	2232
Humanities	1890	1996	2072	2200
Mathematics	1899	2096	2238	2411
Other social studies	1902	1999	2088	2209
Language-based studies	1987	2149	2281	2371
Computer science	1995	2460	2817	3075
Education	2254	2359	2462	2711
Psychology	2351	2494	2487	2568
Geography	2390	2622	2734	2948
Creative arts	2425	2631	2709	2780
Architecture	2425	2499	2728	3032
Other studies allied to medicine	2807	3258	3354	3613
Electrical and electronic engineering	3134	3364	3500	3695
Planning	3229	3435	3316	3381
Civil engineering	3266	3461	3727	4101
Other technologies	3327	3661	4043	4033
Agriculture and forestry	3361	3647	3704	3935
General engineering	3385	3620	3657	3949
Pharmacy	3400	3605	3733	4007
Mechanical and production engineering	3672	4003	4203	4445
Biochemistry	3835	4009	4245	4426
Chemical engineering	3849	4056	4542	4587
Anatomy and physiology	3882	4108	4340	4589
Pharmacology	3929	4365	4635	4956
Other physical sciences	3957	4318	4570	4989
Mineral engineering	4025	4406	4491	4962
Pre-clinical studies	4211	4299	4556	4735
Chemistry	4277	4592	4814	5063
Other biological sciences	4279	4557	4732	4926
Physics	4468	4833	5235	5642
Metallurgy and materials	4960	5128	5211	5706
Clinical dentistry	5853	6262	7054	7508
Clinical medicine	6022	6597	7193	7626
Veterinary science	7873	8163	8450	8980

Notes:
1. The cost centres are arranged in ascending order according to the 1984/85 value of unit costs
2. Unit costs are defined to be the ratio of total general expenditure on academic departments in cost centre *j* to full-time equivalent students in cost centre *j* (the data were not published by cost centre prior to 1984/85)
3. The four columns are highly correlated ($r > 0.9$ for all pairs of years)

Source: University Statistics: Finance, various issues.

Table 5.4   Expected unit costs, 1984/85 to 1986/87

University	Expected cost per student[1]			Actual − expected cost per student		
	1984/85	*1985/86*	*1986/87*	*1984/85*	*1985/86*	*1986/87*
Aston	2811	2946	3048	−406	−310	−431
Bath	2890	3110	3300	−239	−242	−298
Birmingham	3023	3293	3424	67	66	−89
Bradford	2780	2932	3076	−249	−251	−287
Bristol	3133	3356	3576	151	187	220
Brunel	2948	3107	3239	−92	−222	−312
Cambridge	2787	2970	3137	61	65	63
City	2537	2771	2911	508	380	556
Durham	2547	2688	2804	−139	−159	−163
East Anglia	2410	2584	2733	256	203	120
Essex	2352	2495	2614	−153	−190	−242
Exeter	2404	2554	2699	−76	−20	−38
Hull	2288	2465	2590	87	42	8
Keele	2334	2522	2655	−69	−35	−75
Kent	2189	2375	2525	−231	−227	−216
Lancaster	2345	2498	2605	330	277	321
Leeds	3090	3307	3511	38	73	102
Leicester	2787	3007	3178	28	38	−47
Liverpool	3339	3561	3759	−236	−219	−163
London	3389	3646	3864	245	333	429
Loughborough	2847	3086	3245	−183	−267	−106
Manchester	3011	3229	3397	108	82	122
UMIST	2950	3205	3425	598	802	538
Newcastle	3186	3407	3622	−158	−133	−191
Nottingham	3054	3255	3420	−212	−219	−237
Oxford	2668	2854	3008	38	57	75
Reading	2758	2958	3107	101	90	65
Salford	2911	3088	3269	−262	−302	−297
Sheffield	3012	3265	3399	−34	−18	−237
Southampton	2956	3164	3344	78	42	92
Surrey	3032	3202	3390	250	123	64
Sussex	2543	2740	2883	−14	−87	−57
Warwick	2334	2497	2635	24	76	114
York	2540	2787	2876	−345	−401	−310
Aberdeen	2932	3156	3297	20	47	−61
Dundee	3223	3466	3734	28	−23	−149
Edinburgh	3007	3217	3418	−1	172	277
Glasgow	3198	3440	3673	157	−205	−162
Heriot-Watt	2926	3161	3302	−199	−266	−148
St Andrews	2630	2790	3057	−365	−377	−467
Stirling	2316	2478	2563	−70	−39	−143
Strathclyde	2735	2911	3054	−192	−274	−259
Queen's	2838	3060	3258	62	−106	−214
Ulster	2385	2582	2711	−800	−543	−535
Wales	2749	2941	3094	58	−81	−189

Note:
1. See pp. 79–80 for the definition of expected unit costs

Source: University Statistics: Finance, various issues and own calculations.

Table 5.5 The percentage of inter-university differences in cost per student accounted for by subject mix

	1984/85	*1985/86*	*1986/87*
Inter-university variations in cost per student accounted for by subject mix (%)	66	70	72
Inter-university variations in cost per student to be explained by other factors (%)	34	30	28
Total (%)	100	100	100

cent of the students at St Andrews were undergraduates compared to only 72 per cent at City. Since costs per student are likely to be higher for postgraduates than for undergraduates (since postgraduates often require more personal supervision), it follows that the ratio of undergraduates to postgraduates will be negatively related to cost per student. The percentage of each university's students who are undergraduates is therefore used as an explanatory variable in the statistical analysis of inter-university variations in cost per student on pp. 74–5.

Second, there are differences in the *type* of degree course taken by undergraduates and postgraduates and these may affect cost per student. Undergraduates, for example, may undertake honours degrees or ordinary degrees. The percentage of graduates obtaining honours (compared with ordinary) degrees varies substantially between universities. In 1987, for example, 53 per cent of graduates at Glasgow obtained honours degrees compared with virtually 100 per cent at Bath. For postgraduates, there is an obvious distinction between taught courses and degrees based entirely upon research. The effect of degree mix (measured by the percentage of graduates obtaining honours degrees and by the percentage of postgraduates on taught courses) on cost per student is uncertain *a priori*.

Third, two factors related to staff inputs are likely to affect cost per student. Older staff will in general have higher salaries, thus raising cost per student in those universities in which the average age of staff is relatively high. The same argument holds for the percentage of university staff who are professors. In addition, universities with a high student/staff ratio can be expected to have a lower cost per student than universities in which the student/staff ratio is low. This follows directly from the fact that the cost of academic staff is a substantial proportion of total recurrent costs (29 per cent in 1987/88).

Fourth, universities are involved in research as well as teaching and the level of research activity could raise costs. Expenditure on academic departments, for example, may be higher in those universities which have a

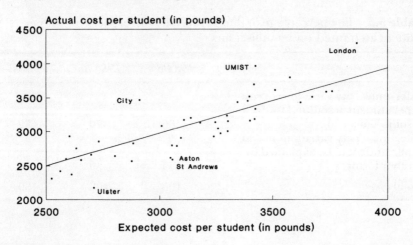

Figure 5.1   Actual cost per student v. expected cost per student by university, 1986/87

Note: Cost = general expenditure on academic departments; students = full-time equivalent students.

high research commitment. The UFC's rating of each university's research output (for 1984 to 1988 inclusive) is therefore expected to be positively related to cost per student.

Fifth, economic theory suggests that *unit* costs of production will tend to fall as producing units increase in size since they will benefit from scale economies. The fact that diseconomies of scale may occur when producing units become very large suggests a non-linear relationship between cost per student and the size of institutions (falling at first and then rising as size increases).

Statistical analysis of inter-university variations in cost per student

Multiple regression analysis has been used to investigate inter-university variations in cost per student. Attention is concentrated here only on inter-university differences in cost per student which cannot be explained by corresponding inter-university differences in subject mix. The dependent variable is therefore *actual* minus *expected* cost per student (as given in Table 5.4 for the years 1984/85 to 1986/87 inclusive). All the variables identified (in the previous section) as possible determinants were included in the regression analysis. Only those results which turned out to be statistically significant, however, are discussed here. Details of the regression analysis are given in the appendix to this chapter (pp. 70–80).

Three main findings emerge from the estimated regression equations. First, the student/staff ratio is highly significant in explaining inter-university differences in *actual* minus *expected* costs per student. The regression equations given in the appendix to this chapter indicate that an increase in the student/staff ratio by one unit is associated with a reduction in the cost per student of around £80 (or about 2.5 per cent of the cost per student for UK universities as a whole).

Second, the student mix of universities (reflected by the percentage of undergraduate students in universities) is highly significant in explaining inter-university differences in *actual* minus *expected* costs *only* when all forty-five universities are included in the analysis. When three universities (namely City, UMIST and Ulster) are excluded, the variable is no longer an important determinant. The effect of student mix in explaining inter-university variations in unit costs must therefore be regarded as being uncertain.

The third main finding of the regression analysis is that inter-university variations in *actual* minus *expected* cost per student were found to be unrelated to corresponding variations in the following variables: the staff mix of universities; type of degree undertaken by each university's students; the UFC's rating of each university's research (1984–88); the average age of staff and the size of each university. The absence of a significant relationship between a university's size and cost per student is especially interesting since it suggests that scale economies are unimportant in higher education (at least in the size range of UK universities).

These findings indicate that around 80 per cent of the inter-university variation in cost per student is accounted for by only two explanatory variables:

1. the subject mix
2. the student/staff ratio

Construction of a performance indicator based upon cost per student

It has already been shown that a large proportion of the variation between universities in cost per student can be accounted for by subject mix. In addition, the student/staff ratio is significantly negatively related to cost per student. These two results suggest that if inter-university comparisons in cost per student are to serve any useful purpose, *it is necessary to allow for inter-university differences in both the subject mix and the student/staff ratio*. If these two factors are not taken into account, inter-university comparisons in cost per student would be of little value since they would mainly reflect inter-university differences in subject mix and the student/staff ratio.

The importance of subject mix in determining each university's cost per student has already been clearly demonstrated on pp. 67–70, where each university's *actual* cost per student was compared with its *expected* cost per student. The latter was calculated from information about each university's subject mix and the cost per student for each subject in the UK as a whole. It was shown that inter-university variations in subject mix accounted for around 70 per cent of inter-university variations in cost per student. This approach can be extended to take inter-university variations in the student/staff ratio into account *in addition to* inter-university variations in subject mix. This can be done by utilizing the results of the regression analysis discussed in the previous section.

The method is as follows:

1. The influence of subject mix on cost per student is estimated by subtracting the *expected* cost per student from the *actual* cost per student:

$$C = UC - UC^e$$

where:

C = indicator of cost per student after controlling for subject mix
UC = actual cost per student
UC^e = expected cost per student given each university's subject mix
      and cost per student in each subject for the UK as a whole.

For example, Cambridge's *actual* cost per student (UC) in 1985/86 was £3,036 and its *expected* cost per student (UC^e) was £2,970. The difference (C) is therefore £66. Cost per student at Cambridge in 1985/86 was therefore £66 *above* what would have been expected given its subject mix.

2. The influence of the student/staff ratio on cost per student is now estimated by regressing C (cost per student after controlling for subject mix) on the student/staff ratio across all universities. The estimated equation for 1985/86, for example, was as follows:

$$C = 625 - (89.8 \times \text{STUDSTAFF})$$

where

STUDSTAFF = ratio of full-time equivalent students to full-time
               academic staff.

3. This equation can now be used to estimate each university's *expected* unit costs given its student/staff ratio. This is done by substituting the actual value of STUDSTAFF for each university into the above equation. Thus, for Cambridge, with its student/staff ratio of 7.17 we find that

$$C^* = 625 - (89.8 \times 7.17) = -18.8$$

This is now compared with the actual value of C for Cambridge to provide an indicator of this university's performance as far as unit costs are concerned:

Performance indicator based on unit costs $= C - C^*$

For Cambridge, $C - C^* = 84.8$ (since $C = 66$ and $C^* = -18.8$). This means that cost per student at Cambridge in 1985/86 was £84.8 higher than it could have been expected to be *given* its subject mix *and* its student/staff ratio.

A performance indicator (calculated in this way) based upon cost per student is given in Table 5.6 for 1984/85, 1985/86 and 1986/87. Two points are particularly noteworthy. The first is the very weak relationship between the performance indicator (i.e. $C - C^*$) in any one year and the actual cost per student (i.e. UC) in the same year. The second and most striking result is the remarkable stability in this indicator over the three years for which it has been calculated ($r > 0.9$ for any pair of consecutive years). One interpretation of this result is that some universities have been consistently more costly (per student) than others, even after allowing for inter-university differences in subject mix and the student/staff ratio. The obvious implication of this is that further investigation is necessary to explain why some universities are consistently more costly than others, even after allowing for these two factors.

The danger with this interpretation of the performance indicators displayed in Table 5.6 is that they are essentially the unexplained residuals of regression models and *there are potentially serious problems with using these variables as indicators of performance*. The high positive correlation of the residuals for consecutive years suggests that there could be *at least one* important explanatory variable omitted from the regression model. The use of the residuals to indicate performance is based on the assumption that the missing variable is a measure of efficiency. This assumption could, however, be incorrect and there might be other factors, unrelated to efficiency, which have been omitted.

There is a far more serious objection to the use of regression residuals to indicate performance. One of the basic assumptions underlying the method of ordinary least squares regression is that the unexplained residual is a random variable. In cases (such as this) where the residual is found *not* to be a random variable, the estimated coefficients in the associated regression equation could be biased. Thus if at least one important explanatory variable has been omitted from the regression equations reported in this chapter (causing the observed correlation of the residuals in Table 5.6), and even if that missing variable could safely be assumed to be university efficiency, the assessment of universities based on the residuals could be inaccurate, owing to the misspecification of the regression model.

Of course, had the regression residuals displayed in Table 5.6 been random variables, the resulting rankings of universities would also have been random, and therefore useless in performance assessment.

Table 5.6   A performance indicator based upon cost per student ($C - C^*$), 1984/85 to 1986/87

University	$C - C^*$		
	1984/85	*1985/86*	*1986/87*
Aston	−256.7	−29.5	−117.7
Bath	−161.1	−132.8	−218.9
Birmingham	−14.3	−16.7	−151.6
Bradford	−84.6	−66.0	−82.4
Bristol	81.3	111.8	147.4
Brunel	12.7	−80.0	−124.0
Cambridge	72.3	84.8	74.1
City	674.8	579.9	715.7
Durham	−44.0	−18.3	21.8
East Anglia	349.3	334.9	299.0
Essex	−45.6	−86.7	−87.1
Exeter	120.5	186.2	195.9
Hull	274.3	271.5	295.4
Keele	97.5	160.5	227.1
Kent	−39.0	−24.9	14.2
Lancaster	370.0	341.9	396.7
Leeds	42.9	84.4	118.1
Leicester	35.1	34.7	−34.3
Liverpool	−208.2	−176.8	−121.6
London	129.7	198.2	281.5
Loughborough	−175.3	−230.7	−81.2
Manchester	71.8	64.3	103.2
UMIST	524.9	727.0	451.9
Newcastle	−210.1	−172.9	−215.3
Nottingham	−208.3	−235.0	−224.8
Oxford	−15.3	21.6	49.5
Reading	136.0	141.1	119.9
Salford	39.9	−63.5	−78.9
Sheffield	23.9	34.2	−123.4
Southampton	−7.8	−39.1	44.7
Surrey	166.6	32.7	16.4
Sussex	−20.9	−70.3	−9.1
Warwick	119.2	146.6	200.5
York	−288.1	−326.2	−217.3
Aberdeen	33.6	90.9	−6.2
Dundee	−7.4	−41.2	−178.7
Edinburgh	−28.3	126.5	202.5
Glasgow	−95.2	−122.1	−78.0
Heriot-Watt	−149.4	−138.7	76.3
St Andrews	−223.4	−217.3	−285.7
Stirling	62.5	73.9	40.7
Strathclyde	−105.8	−180.4	−151.7
Queen's	83.1	−42.8	−100.9
Ulster	−355.0	−100.8	−75.9
Wales	68.5	−26.4	−79.6

Note:
The regression equation used to calculate C^* in each year was estimated with City, UMIST and Ulster excluded from the model. The values of $C - C^*$ for these three universities should therefore be treated with even more caution than those of other universities. See pp. 76–7 for definitions of C and C^*.

Conclusion

Cost per student varies substantially between universities. By far the most important factor responsible for these differences in cost per student between universities is the subject mix, which explains about 70 per cent of the inter-university variation in this variable. Moreover, a further 10 per cent of the variation can be explained by one other factor: the student/staff ratio. This variable has a significant negative effect on cost per student. The student mix of universities measured by the percentage of undergraduate students was significant only when three universities (City, UMIST and Ulster) were included in the analysis. The effect of this variable on cost per student must therefore be regarded as uncertain. Other factors which were expected to have an effect on cost per student (such as the size of a university, and the age and seniority of its staff) were found to be unrelated. There was no evidence, for example, that universities are subject to either economies or diseconomies of scale, at least within the size range of UK universities.

The critical question to which we sought an answer at the beginning of this chapter was whether a useful performance indicator based upon cost per student could be constructed. If inter-university comparisons are to have any meaning, it is necessary *at least* to take into account inter-university differences in subject mix. It is also possible to allow for differences between universities in the student/staff ratio. *It is far from certain, however, whether such an indicator would be useful for evaluating the performance of universities.* An individual university, for example, could reduce its unit costs by raising its student/staff ratio. But the consequence of this action may well be a decline in research output or a decline in the quality of teaching. Reducing cost per student may therefore result in a worse *overall* performance.

This is not to argue that individual universities should not take a cold, hard look at their unit costs compared to other universities, but exactly how they respond to an apparently inferior cost position is something which must be very carefully considered. The potential consequences of any action to reduce cost per student will need to be assessed with great care.

Appendix to Chapter 5

Calculation of expected cost per student

$$UC^*_i = \sum_j \left(\frac{FTE_{ij}}{FTE_i}\right) \left(\frac{TC_j}{FTE_j}\right)$$

i = universities $1, \ldots 45$
j = cost centres $1, \ldots 37$
UC^*_i = expected cost per student of university i

FTE_{ij} = full-time equivalent students at university i in cost centre j
FTE_i = full-time equivalent students in university i
TC_{ij} = total general expenditure on academic departments in cost centre j in all UK universities
FTE_j = full-time equivalent students in cost centre j in all UK universities.

Estimated regression equations: dependent variable = $UC - UC^*$

Explanatory variables	Estimated coefficients					
	1984/85		1985/86		1986/87	
	(1)	*(2)*	*(3)*	*(4)*	*(5)*	*(6)*
CONSTANT	2094	579	1939	625	2129	649
	(4.46)	(3.53)	(3.95)	(3.70)	(4.17)	(3.73)
%UNDERGRAD	−18.1		−16.4		−19.3	
	(−3.03)		(−2.62)		(−2.90)	
STUDSTAFF	−83.0	−80.4	−85.8	−89.8	−82.8	−94.4
	(−3.92)	(−3.87)	(−3.69)	(−4.12)	(−3.65)	(−4.26)
$\bar{R}^2$	0.42	0.26	0.36	0.28	0.40	0.30
n	45	42	45	42	45	42

Notes:
1. ( ) = t-ratios
2. All estimated coefficients are significant at the 1 per cent level or less
3. Definition of variables:
   UC = cost per student (as defined on p. 67)
   UC^* = expected cost per student (as defined on p. 70 and above)
   %UNDERGRAD = undergraduates as a percentage of total students
   STUDSTAFF = ratio of full-time equivalent students to full-time academic staff
4. City, UMIST and Ulster are included only in equations *(1)*, *(3)* and *(5)*

Source: J. Johnes 1990b.

6
Non-Completion Rates:
Differences between Universities

Introduction

This chapter is concerned with the non-completion rate of undergraduate
entrants into UK universities. Earlier research into non-completion rates in
the UK has focused primarily upon the reasons why *individual* students
have not completed their courses (see, for example, Miller 1970; C.L. Jones
et al. 1973; Entwistle and Wilson 1977; J. Johnes 1990a). This chapter
concentrates on non-completion at the institutional level. It is important to
examine institutional differences in non-completion since the disparity
between universities is immense. This was recognized as long ago as 1968,
when the University Grants Committee published its *Enquiry into Student
Progress*. The non-completion rate of the 1980 entrants into UK universities varied between less than 10 per cent at twelve universities to over 20 per
cent at six other universities. It is the purpose of this chapter to examine the
reasons for the wide disparity between institutions in their non-completion
rates.

An investigation into inter-university differences in the non-completion
rate is required for two reasons. First, the non-completion rate may be used
as a performance indicator by those administering the funding of higher
education. It is therefore important to know why the non-completion rate
varies so much between institutions. Second, the universities themselves
should be interested in discovering why their non-completion rate differs
from those of other universities. Those universities with a consistently high
non-completion rate should be particularly interested in such an investigation.

This chapter is in four sections. The first section defines the non-
completion rate and provides estimates for all UK universities over a
seven-year period; this allows longer-term trends to be detected. The
second identifies a range of factors which may be expected *a priori* to
determine the non-completion rate. This is followed in the third section by
a discussion of statistical tests of the contribution of each of these factors to
explaining inter-university differences in the non-completion rate. The
fourth section proposes a method of constructing a performance indicator
for individual institutions which is based upon the non-completion rate.

Non-completion rates in UK universities

The entry cohort method of measuring non-completion

The non-completion rate is defined here as the proportion of any given entry cohort of undergraduates who had not completed their degree course (at the university at which they originally registered) within six years of their registration. Thus for the 1980 entry cohort, the non-completion rate is calculated as follows:

$$\text{Non-completion rate for 1980 entry cohort} = \frac{\begin{pmatrix}\text{Number of under-}\\\text{graduate entrants in}\\1980\end{pmatrix} - \begin{pmatrix}\text{Number of under-}\\\text{graduate entrants in}\\1980\text{ who had gradu-}\\\text{ated by }1986\end{pmatrix}}{\text{Number of undergraduate entrants in }1980} \times 100$$

The use of a six-year cut-off point means that any students who eventually obtained their degree after six years are assumed not to have completed their degree course. The number completing after six years is likely to be very small.

The term 'non-completion' is preferred to 'wastage' since non-completion occurs for reasons other than students failing to meet required academic standards. Many students who 'drop out' of one higher education institution, for example, subsequently 'drop into' another one. Some students discover that their initial choice of degree course is in some way inappropriate and consequently switch to another course. Switching courses within institutions at the end of the first year of higher education is the usual method by which students are able to match their preferences to the courses that are available, but transferring to another institution is sometimes a necessary method of adjustment. Some attrition is therefore inevitable (and indeed desirable) as students realize that their goals and aspirations are more likely to be met by switching courses and institutions (Tinto 1982). According to data supplied by the Universities Statistical Record, Cheltenham, 7.1 per cent of all non-completers in the 1979 entry cohort and 8.3 per cent in the 1980 entry cohort transferred to another institution.

The non-completion rate of UK universities

Non-completion rates are given in Table 6.1 for all UK universities using the 1975 to 1981 entry cohorts. The two main features of these non-completion rates are first, the remarkable differences in the non-completion rate between universities during any given year, and second, the remarkable stability of the non-completion rates within each university over time. This stability of the non-completion rate within institutions over

Table 6.1 Estimated non-completion rates in UK universities for each undergraduate entry cohort during 1975–81

University	Entry cohort (year)						
	1975	1976	1977	1978	1979	1980	1981
Aston	20.4	17.3	20.8	19.9	17.1	16.8	16.4
Bath	15.6	19.3	17.2	15.0	11.4	14.1	14.3
Birmingham	12.6	12.4	10.7	11.7	11.5	10.5	9.8
Bradford	13.6	13.0	16.7	15.4	15.2	16.0	15.9
Bristol	10.3	12.3	10.4	8.8	8.3	7.3	9.7
Brunel	27.3	26.3	27.6	22.7	22.5	21.8	18.6
Cambridge	4.3	3.7	4.2	3.3	3.6	3.4	9.2
City	20.9	25.2	24.0	23.9	19.1	19.3	18.5
Durham	5.4	6.3	6.0	7.8	5.9	5.2	6.1
East Anglia	13.7	12.6	9.6	12.0	12.8	9.6	9.9
Essex	18.3	18.2	19.6	15.8	14.4	14.6	16.0
Exeter	12.6	9.7	11.7	9.4	10.3	8.8	8.9
Hull	12.5	14.7	13.4	13.2	12.8	12.3	12.4
Keele	22.0	18.5	17.9	16.4	16.6	16.3	18.6
Kent	17.1	15.1	15.7	13.2	11.9	13.3	13.8
Lancaster	13.8	14.4	13.5	12.5	11.4	8.7	10.4
Leeds	21.3	17.5	16.4	9.4	11.7	10.9	11.5
Leicester	11.8	11.5	11.8	11.4	12.2	9.7	11.1
Liverpool	12.6	13.9	13.6	15.4	14.7	14.3	13.4
London	18.8	19.5	18.6	17.3	15.7	16.5	20.0
Loughborough	14.0	13.7	9.7	12.7	11.8	10.3	8.1
Manchester	14.5	13.6	14.8	14.2	13.9	12.8	16.1
UMIST	22.5	18.9	16.1	17.4	18.6	14.8	16.5
Newcastle	18.1	16.1	18.8	19.5	18.2	16.9	18.5
Nottingham	10.9	11.0	11.0	9.7	9.4	9.2	9.3
Oxford	7.4	7.8	7.3	7.0	6.3	7.0	7.9
Reading	17.3	12.4	16.3	14.5	13.3	12.0	11.1
Salford	27.6	24.0	22.2	20.6	20.8	19.5	18.9
Sheffield	14.4	12.9	13.5	10.1	11.2	9.9	12.8
Southampton	11.6	11.0	8.9	11.5	10.9	9.1	10.5
Surrey	15.0	16.6	19.5	19.6	14.7	14.7	15.5
Sussex	11.0	12.1	12.0	10.8	12.7	12.2	12.7
Warwick	15.8	15.0	13.9	13.5	10.2	11.5	10.8
York	9.0	10.3	11.5	9.7	9.0	8.7	8.6
Aberdeen	21.3	20.3	22.0	23.3	22.4	23.6	20.0
Dundee	24.2	20.9	20.8	22.7	19.7	22.4	25.7
Edinburgh	18.1	19.3	19.6	21.5	16.9	14.0	17.2
Glasgow	20.1	20.8	21.4	20.3	21.0	20.8	21.4
Heriot-Watt	27.2	24.9	26.1	24.0	22.8	21.5	21.7
St Andrews	12.9	14.1	13.9	12.2	16.1	11.8	19.9
Stirling	14.0	14.9	14.8	12.9	14.6	14.9	9.6
Strathclyde	24.5	23.0	21.2	25.9	20.9	21.6	19.0
Queen's	15.8	13.9	13.8	14.4	12.3	11.5	11.7
Ulster	15.2	18.6	13.6	18.6	16.4	15.9	19.2
Wales	18.8	17.3	18.6	16.7	16.9	15.7	16.0
All universities	15.8	15.4	15.3	14.7	13.8	13.3	14.4

Note:
It should be noted that these non-completion rates were calculated from data supplied by university registrars to the Universities Statistical Record and that there may be inaccuracies in this database.

Source: Universities' Statistical Record, Cheltenham.

time is reflected by the very high correlation between the adjacent columns of Table 6.1. Thus universities which have a high non-completion rate for any one entry cohort tend to have high non-completion rates for the entry cohorts in other years. In other words, many universities have a persistently high non-completion rate while others have a persistently low non-completion rate. Those universities with a persistently low non-completion rate (e.g. under 10 per cent over several years) include Bristol, Cambridge, Durham, Oxford and York. By contrast, several universities had non-completion rates which exceeded 20 per cent over several years. These include Brunel, City, Salford, Aberdeen, Dundee, Heriot-Watt and Strathclyde.

The substantial disparities in the non-completion rate between universities coupled with the general stability in these inter-university disparities over time suggests the existence of some fundamental cause or causes. Some of the possible causes are investigated on pp. 89–96.

The time-profile of non-completion

The entry cohort method of measuring the non-completion rate has one potentially serious drawback: it does not take the time profile of non-completion into account. The time profile of non-completion, for example, may be entirely different for two universities which have exactly the same non-completion rate. Thus university *A*'s non-completers may all leave in their first year while university *B*'s non-completers may all fail at the end of their course. The time profile of each university's non-completers for the 1979 cohort is given in Table 6.2. This shows the proportion of non-completers who left at the end of each calendar year following their entry. For the university sector as a whole, Table 6.2 indicates that 53 per cent of all non-completers left within fifteen months of starting their degree. The proportion then declines exponentially and approaches zero in the sixth year. It tails off gradually in this way since many non-completers may take a year (or more) out of university before deciding to withdraw.

The surprising feature of the time profile of non-completers given in Table 6.2 is the vast difference between institutions. This is illustrated in Figure 6.1 using the 1979 entry cohort of two universities. Three-quarters of the non-completers at Warwick left within fifteen months of starting their course whereas only 20 per cent did so at Edinburgh. Indeed, the peak in the time-profile of non-completion at Edinburgh did not occur until the third year after the 1979 cohort began their courses. It should be noted, however, that there is some concern about the accuracy of the data describing the time profile of non-completers. A recent report on non-completion rates in Scotland suggests that the data supplied by registrars may contain inconsistencies, with the result that the time profile for individual institutions may not be accurate (Universities of Scotland 1989).

Table 6.2 The percentage of non-graduates leaving in each year after entry from the 1979 entry cohort

University	% leaving in each year						
	1979[1]	1980	1981	1982	1983	1984	1985
Aston	9.3	42.4	25.7	14.9	3.0	3.7	1.1
Bath	13.5	55.0	19.8	4.5	5.4	1.8	0.0
Birmingham	16.1	42.9	21.5	9.1	1.9	8.5	0.0
Bradford	11.7	40.4	24.6	15.2	3.5	4.1	0.6
Bristol	12.0	52.7	25.7	4.8	3.0	0.0	1.8
Brunel	7.9	40.0	26.1	14.5	9.7	1.2	0.6
Cambridge	3.3	59.3	19.8	11.0	5.5	0.0	1.1
City	7.5	38.4	39.7	8.2	6.2	0.0	0.0
Durham	10.9	52.5	24.8	5.9	5.0	1.0	0.0
East Anglia	8.0	65.6	9.8	12.9	2.5	1.2	0.0
Essex	11.9	51.5	22.4	9.0	4.5	0.7	0.0
Exeter	12.5	54.3	17.4	10.3	4.3	1.1	0.0
Hull	5.1	50.9	23.1	17.6	3.2	0.0	0.0
Keele	5.5	56.3	21.9	11.7	3.1	1.6	0.0
Kent	12.0	42.7	28.2	11.1	3.4	2.6	0.0
Lancaster	11.7	46.2	20.0	15.9	4.8	1.4	0.0
Leeds	14.7	32.0	22.9	25.8	2.6	1.3	0.8
Leicester	13.5	47.2	19.7	10.7	6.2	2.8	0.0
Liverpool	11.7	49.8	16.4	14.6	6.0	0.7	0.7
London[2]	9.2	44.7	12.4	13.3	4.5	5.9	10.0
Loughborough	8.2	47.9	22.7	12.4	7.2	0.5	1.0
Manchester	9.5	57.5	18.1	13.3	0.7	0.5	0.5
UMIST	8.8	53.7	28.8	7.8	0.5	0.5	0.0
Newcastle	2.9	61.5	21.1	8.6	3.4	1.7	0.7
Nottingham	13.2	53.7	16.8	9.5	6.3	0.5	0.0
Oxford	0.5	40.1	12.0	37.5	8.9	1.0	0.0
Reading	16.0	60.8	16.5	3.8	2.5	0.4	0.0
Salford	12.3	47.2	26.2	9.1	5.2	0.0	0.0
Sheffield	16.7	48.6	19.0	14.3	1.4	0.0	0.0
Southampton	8.3	40.9	29.5	17.4	3.8	0.0	0.0
Surrey	11.5	31.7	30.9	17.3	2.9	4.3	1.4
Sussex	0.7	50.0	24.3	14.0	2.9	8.1	0.0
Warwick	10.2	64.6	9.2	11.2	2.9	1.5	0.5
York	9.7	54.8	16.1	10.8	7.5	0.0	1.1
Aberdeen	8.2	45.7	24.7	16.5	4.8	0.0	0.0
Dundee	5.1	47.1	20.3	18.1	8.0	0.7	0.7
Edinburgh	3.8	16.7	18.9	46.7	4.3	8.6	1.0
Glasgow	3.8	8.6	42.0	20.0	14.4	8.3	2.9
Heriot-Watt	6.9	33.0	32.5	16.3	7.4	2.5	1.5
St Andrews	0.0	50.8	18.3	11.9	7.1	7.9	4.0
Stirling	10.1	52.9	20.2	5.9	8.4	1.7	0.8
Strathclyde	5.6	36.3	36.5	14.1	6.6	0.7	0.2
Queen's	6.4	40.6	24.3	16.3	9.9	2.5	0.0
Ulster	8.0	60.0	18.7	8.0	4.0	1.3	0.0
Wales	8.0	43.7	33.6	9.4	3.2	1.6	0.4
All universities	8.8	44.5	23.4	14.5	4.8	2.6	1.5

Notes:
1. Percentage of 1979 non-graduates leaving from October to December
2. The figures given for London are affected by the movement of medical students between Schools. There may be similar problems in other universities but we have no further information on this potentially important factor

Source: Universities' Statistical Record, Cheltenham.

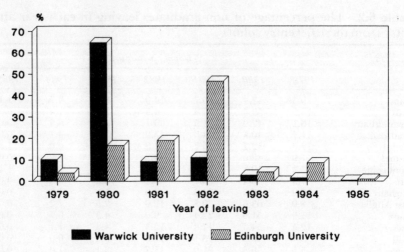

Figure 6.1 Percentage of non-completers leaving in each year after entry: 1979 entry cohort

An alternative measure of non-completion: the percentage of the leaving cohort who did not complete their course

Since 1988 the CVCP has included a measure of the success rate of each university's students (by cost centre) in its annual publication *University Management Statistics and Performance Indicators*. This success rate is defined as follows:

$$\text{Success rate of leavers} = \frac{\text{Number of leavers who successfully obtained a qualification in year } t}{\text{Total number of leavers in year } t} \times 100$$

The non-completion rate of a given leaving cohort is therefore obtained by subtracting the success rate from 100 per cent. In practice, the CVCP has produced a success rate based on leavers over a three-year period in order to reduce the influence of temporary fluctuations in this variable. The non-completion rate based upon three leaving cohorts (1986–88) is given for each UK university in Table 6.3. The non-completion rate based upon three entry cohorts (1979–81) is included for comparative purposes.

Since the non-completion rate can be calculated for either any given entry cohort or for any given leaving cohort of students, it is useful to investigate the differences between these two measures. The primary difference between these two approaches is that the entry cohort approach measures the non-completion rate of students entering university at a

Table 6.3   Two estimates of the non-completion rate in
UK universities

University	Non-completion rates based upon:	
	Leaving cohorts 1986–88[1]	*Entry cohorts 1979–81*
Aston	15.2	16.8
Bath	13.0	13.2
Birmingham	11.4	10.6
Bradford	12.5	15.7
Bristol	9.0	8.4
Brunel	20.3	21.1
Cambridge	3.1	5.4
City	18.6	19.0
Durham	6.5	5.7
East Anglia	11.2	10.8
Essex	14.4	15.1
Exeter	9.9	9.4
Hull	9.1	12.5
Keele	13.3	17.2
Kent	13.2	13.0
Lancaster	10.0	10.1
Leeds	10.9	11.4
Leicester	11.5	11.0
Liverpool	13.6	14.2
London	19.1	17.4
Loughborough	9.5	10.1
Manchester	12.0	14.3
UMIST	15.4	16.5
Newcastle	15.4	17.9
Nottingham	8.3	9.3
Oxford	5.4	7.1
Reading	12.6	12.1
Salford	14.6	19.8
Sheffield	11.1	11.3
Southampton	9.7	10.2
Surrey	15.3	15.0
Sussex	11.5	12.5
Warwick	11.4	10.8
York	7.7	8.8
Aberdeen	12.6	22.0
Dundee	22.4	22.8
Edinburgh	11.2	16.0
Glasgow	20.3	21.1
Heriot-Watt	23.0	22.0
St Andrews	12.3	16.0
Stirling	13.0	13.3
Strathclyde	14.3	20.5
Queen's	14.4	11.8
Ulster	18.7	17.4
Wales	13.5	16.2
All universities	12.9	13.9

Note:
1. Calculated from data given in CVCP 1989.

specific point in time whereas the leaving cohort approach measures the non-completion rate of students who entered university over several years. This means that the entry cohort approach produces a measure of the probability of non-completion for a specific group of *entrants* whereas the leaving cohort approach produces a measure of the probability of non-completion for a specific group of *leavers*. The advantage of the leaving cohort approach is that it provides an up-to-date measure of non-completion whereas the entry cohort approach is inevitably out of date (because it must allow at least six years for students to pass through the system). The advantage of the entry cohort approach is that it is easier to investigate the statistical relationship between this variable and its potential determinants since the available database provides information about student entrants in specific years (e.g. the mean A level score of students by university is available for entry cohorts and not leaving cohorts).

In spite of these differences between the two methods of calculating a non-completion rate for UK universities, it is nevertheless interesting to compare the estimates obtained by using each of these methods. This is done in Figure 6.2, which shows the relationship between the non-completion rate based upon three entry cohorts (1979–81) and the non-completion rate based upon three leaving cohorts (1986–88). The correlation between these two estimates is extremely high ($r = 0.87$) even though they cover different groups of students. (Moreover, the correlation increases to 0.93 when three outliers, namely Salford, Dundee and Strathclyde, are excluded.) This suggests not only that the two approaches

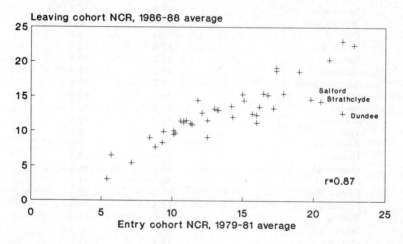

Figure 6.2   Comparison between two alternative non-completion rates for all UK universities

Notes:
1. NCR = non-completion rate (%)
2. Leaving cohort NCR excludes medics
3. See text for definitions.

produce similar estimates of the non-completion rate but that the non-completion rate in individual universities (with the possible exceptions of Salford, Dundee and Strathclyde) has remained very stable during the 1980s. The reasons for the stability in the non-completion rate within universities over time are investigated in the next two sections.

Some explanations of inter-university differences in non-completion rates

Students leave university before the completion of their course for many reasons. Among the most common of these are unsatisfactory academic progress, examination failure, dissatisfaction with the course, dissatisfaction with social life at university, poor health, financial difficulties and family problems. Not all those who leave university prematurely necessarily quit higher education since some transfer to another institution (which may be a polytechnic or a college).

If inter-university differences in non-completion rates are to be explained, it is first necessary to identify those explanatory variables for which adequate quantitative measures can be obtained. This requirement eliminates the possibility of including variables such as those which directly measure the quality of supervision and the quality of life at each institution. The influence of such variables can be measured indirectly only by including proxy variables such as the student/staff ratio and measures of the types of accommodation used by students at each institution. This pragmatic approach is necessary if an attempt is to be made to explain (statistically) inter-university differences in the non-completion rate.

It is useful to divide the factors which can be expected to influence each institution's non-completion rate into two broad categories: those which relate to the students themselves and those which relate to the individual institution.

Student-related factors

Earlier work indicates that several factors influence the probability that any *individual* student will leave university prematurely (J. Johnes 1990a). These are gender, academic ability (as reflected by A level score), type of school attended immediately before university, and father's occupation. The influence of gender on the non-completion rate is evident from Table 6.4, which shows that the non-completion rate for university undergraduates as a whole has been significantly higher for men than for women during the entire study period. On average, the male non-completion rate has been 44 per cent higher than that for females. Although the underlying reasons for this are unknown, it is nevertheless important to take the gender-mix of universities into account if inter-university differences in

Table 6.4   Non-completion rates in the UK university sector: men, women and total (1975–81 undergraduate entry cohorts)

Entry cohort (year)	Non-completion rates		
	Men	Women	Total
1975	17.4	12.8	15.8
1976	17.1	12.3	15.4
1977	17.2	11.9	15.3
1978	16.6	11.4	14.7
1979	15.7	10.9	13.8
1980	15.3	10.2	13.3
1981	16.6	11.1	14.4

Source: Universities' Statistical Record, Cheltenham.

the non-completion rate are to be explained. Universities with a high proportion of men, for example, are likely to have a higher non-completion rate than universities with a low proportion. It is therefore more useful to investigate inter-university variations in the non-completion rate for men and women separately.

Academic ability is known to have a negative effect on the probability of an individual student not completing (Marsh 1966; Panos and Astin 1968; Krishnan and Clelland 1973; Astin 1975; Astin *et al.* 1987; J. Johnes 1990a). Students with a high level of academic ability are less likely to fail examinations than those with low academic ability. The average A level score of each university's intake of students is therefore used as an indicator of the academic ability of each institution's students. We expect the non-completion rate to be higher in universities with a low average A level score.

The way in which the socio-economic background of students affects the non-completion rate is less obvious than the effect of academic ability. It seems reasonable to assume, however, that students whose parents are themselves well educated (e.g. those in professional occupations) will be more able to draw upon family support than students whose parents have not had similar experience. The socio-economic background of students is measured by using the percentage of each university's intake of students who attended either an independent school or a grammar school. The non-completion rate is expected to be lower in those universities which have a high proportion of students coming from independent or grammar schools. This variable may be measuring not only social class, however, but also the type of training that students receive before entering university. Independent and grammar schools may provide more appropriate training in the types of study skills required at university than is provided by comprehensive and secondary modern schools. This is obviously a gross over-generalization but is nevertheless worthy of investigation.

University-related factors

Previous research has indicated that the non-completion rate is higher in some subjects than in others (Robbins 1963; Wankowski 1972; Powell 1973; De Rome and Lewin 1984; J. Johnes 1990a). This is confirmed by data obtained from the Universities Statistical Record. Table 6.5 shows that the non-completion rate is higher in the sciences, for example, than in business studies and language courses. Since the differences in the non-completion rate between the main subject groups remain very stable over a number of years, this suggests that there is some underlying cause. One possibility is that it is easier to fail some subjects than others. Whatever the underlying cause may be, it is important to allow for differences in the subject mix of institutions when seeking explanations of inter-institutional variations in the non-completion rate.

The influence of subject mix on the non-completion rate is confirmed by Figure 6.3, which shows the relationship between the *actual* and the *expected* non-completion rate for all UK universities. The expected non-completion rate is the rate that each university would be expected to have given:

1. each university's subject mix
2. the non-completion rate for each subject group in the UK as a whole as shown in Table 6.6. (The CVCP's publication *University Management Statistics and Performance Indicators* (1989) provides this information for twenty main subject groups. Medicine and dentistry are omitted.)

Table 6.5 Non-completion rates in the UK university sector by main subject group (1975–79 undergraduate entry cohorts)

Main subject group	Entry cohort (year)				
	1975	1976	1977	1978	1979
Education	0.3	3.4	3.7	5.1	3.9
Agriculture and related studies	9.1	8.0	7.2	8.5	8.0
Business and related studies	9.1	9.1	7.2	7.1	7.6
Languages	10.4	8.4	8.2	6.4	7.3
Architecture, planning	19.1	16.2	24.6	23.7	19.7
Engineering, technology	19.5	19.6	19.2	18.6	17.2
Medicine, dentistry	19.7	18.4	18.1	17.9	17.1
Sciences	20.5	19.5	21.0	20.0	19.2
Other arts	21.2	22.1	23.3	22.2	18.4
All subjects	15.8	15.4	15.3	14.7	13.8

Note:
Non-completion rates cannot be calculated for individual subjects for the 1980 or 1981 entry cohorts since the classification of subjects was changed in 1985/86

Source: Universities' Statistical Record, Cheltenham.

Table 6.6   Non-completion rates in the UK university sector by main academic subject group (excluding medicine and dentistry), 1986–88 leaving cohorts

Academic subject group	%
Humanities	9
Agriculture and related topics	9
Social studies	10
Topics allied to medicine	10
Education	10
Business and administration	10
Languages and related topics	10
Biological sciences	11
Creative arts	12
Physical sciences	13
Mass communications, etc.	13
Combined science and social studies/arts	13
Combined social studies and arts	14
Mathematical sciences	15
Arts combinations	15
Social studies combinations	17
Engineering and technology	17
Science combinations	22
Architecture, planning, etc.	23
General and broad combinations	28

Source: CVCP 1989.

The method of calculating the expected non-completion rate is explained in the appendix to this chapter (pp. 100–1). It is clear from Figure 6.3 that inter-university variations in the actual non-completion rate are not explained by subject mix alone. The correlation between the actual and expected non-completion rate is statistically significant but still rather low ($r = 0.53$).

Several other university-related factors may be expected to have an effect on the non-completion rate. These are the student/staff ratio, the length of course and the type of accommodation used by students. A higher student/staff ratio can be expected to raise the non-completion rate since this would indicate that less personal supervision was available to students. Similarly universities with a greater proportion of students on four-year (or longer) degree courses can be expected to have higher non-completion rates since the probability of a problem arising is likely to increase as the duration of a course increases. With regard to the type of accommodation used by students, it has been shown that living at home during term time increases the chances of an individual student not completing (Chickering and Kuper 1971). This may be because such students have a lower degree of involvement in the academic and social activities at university (either

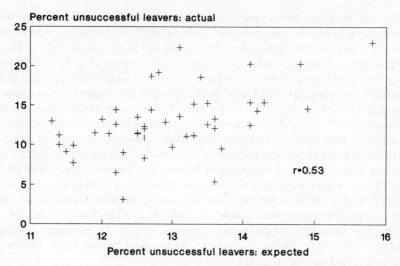

Figure 6.3   Per cent unsuccessful leavers: actual v. expected, 1986–88
Source: CVCP 1989.

through choice or of necessity) and this, it is argued, has a detrimental effect on their chances of completion (Astin 1975). On the other hand, students who live in university accommodation may be more independently minded and will have greater access to the activities and facilities offered by the university, including counselling services. Universities with a greater proportion of their students living in halls of residence may therefore be expected to have lower non-completion rates.

Not all university-related factors which may affect an institution's non-completion rate are easily measurable. It is therefore useful to allow for differences in the characteristics of universities by grouping universities into separate (broad) categories. Four different types of universities are identified in the following statistical analysis. First, ex-colleges of advanced technology tend to be more vocationally oriented and to have closer links with industry than other types of universities. The non-completion rates of these institutions are likely to be lower since they may be expected to attract students with a strong vocational motivation, a characteristic which has an established negative effect on the likelihood of non-completion (Summerskill 1962).

Second, the new greenfield universities established in the mid-1960s are all campus universities and this characteristic may have an effect on the quality of life of students at those institutions. Whether this will have a positive or a negative effect on the non-completion rate is impossible to say.

Third, there are distinct differences between the Scottish university system and that which operates in the rest of the UK and this may have an effect on Scottish non-completion rates. One of the most important differences between Scottish and non-Scottish universities which may adversely affect the non-completion rate in Scotland is that a larger proportion of Scottish students undertake a four-year degree course than is the case in the rest of the UK, where three-year degree courses are more common. Another special factor in Scotland is the higher proportion of entrants who are under 18. Data for the 1987 leaving cohort, for example, indicate that 67 per cent of all Scottish entrants were 18 or under compared to only 38 per cent in England and Wales. Moreover, 16 per cent of entrants to Scottish universities were 17 or under compared to under 1 per cent for universities in England and Wales. The higher proportion of 17- and 18-year-olds entering Scottish universities compared to universities in the rest of the UK may be expected to have a detrimental effect on their non-completion rates since younger students are less likely to be able to handle the pressures of pursuing a degree course. In addition, younger students are more likely to change their mind about their choice of institution and course than are older students.

Finally, it has been suggested that the Scottish non-completion rate is higher because Scotland has a higher proportion of its relevant age group proceeding to university than is the case in England and Wales (Universities of Scotland 1989: 6). In 1986, for example, 8.5 per cent of the relevant age group proceeded to university in Scotland compared to only 6.8 per cent in England and Wales. The strength of this argument rests on the relationship between the age participation rate and academic ability. If academic ability declines sharply as the age participation rate increases, this can be expected to lead to an increase in the non-completion rate, as argued previously. This hypothesis of a negative effect of age participation rate and academic ability receives some support from the fact that 33 per cent of Scottish entrants (in 1985/86) had fewer than three A levels or fewer than five Scottish highers compared to only 22 per cent of entrants to universities in England and Wales (CVCP 1988).

Statistical analysis of inter-university differences in the non-completion rate

Extensive empirical tests were undertaken in order to measure the influence of the variables discussed in the previous section on inter-university variations in the non-completion rate. Multiple regression analysis was used to estimate the relationship between several explanatory variables and the non-completion rate (calculated using the entry cohort method). Separate equations were estimated for male and female non-completion rates in view of the much higher non-completion rates experienced by male undergraduates. A sample of the estimated equations is provided in the appendix to this chapter (pp. 100–1). The analysis was undertaken on the entry cohorts for 1979 and 1980.

The firmest result to emerge from our statistical analysis is that A level score plays a crucial role in explaining inter-university differences in the non-completion rate. The higher the A level score, the lower the non-completion rate was found to be. This is consistent with the view that students with lower ability are likely to find it more difficult to complete a degree course and are consequently more likely to drop out. For example, in the case of male undergraduates, a one-point increase in the A level score was found to be associated with a two percentage point decrease in the non-completion rate. This means that a four-point difference in A level score between institutions (e.g. an eight-point average compared to a twelve-point average) is associated with an eight percentage point difference in the non-completion rate. The effect of A level score on the female non-completion rate was considerably weaker, though still statistically significant: a three-point increase in an institution's A level score is associated with a two percentage point reduction in the female non-completion rate. The highly significant relationship between A level score and the non-completion rate obtained in all our statistical tests offers strong support for the view that academic ability is an important factor in determining a university's non-completion rate.

The second very firm result is that the non-completion rate in Scottish universities is significantly higher than in non-Scottish universities (McPherson and Paterson 1990; J. Johnes and Taylor 1990). On average, the non-completion rate is four percentage points higher in Scottish universities than in the rest of the UK even when several other factors have already been taken into account. This difference was greater for men, however, than for women. The higher non-completion rates in Scottish universities are possibly a result of three factors: the lower age on entry of the majority of Scottish undergraduates; the higher proportion of Scottish undergraduates who embark on a four-year degree course and the higher age participation rate in Scottish universities. All these factors could lead to a higher non-completion rate. An additional possible explanation of the significantly higher non-completion rate in Scotland is that the academic ability of entrants into Scottish universities has been overestimated in the statistical analysis. Academic ability has been proxied using the mean A level score of *A level qualified entrants*, yet the majority of entrants to Scottish universities have Scottish highers and not A levels. In 1988, for example, 20 per cent of entrants to Scottish universities had three or more A levels compared to 47 per cent who had five or more Scottish highers. Nevertheless, there is a highly significant positive correlation between the mean A level score and the mean Scottish highers score (by subject) in Scottish universities ($r = 0.69$ using 1985 data). This suggests that mean A level score may well be an adequate proxy for the academic ability of entrants to Scottish universities.

Several further results are of interest. First, universities with a large proportion of their students in halls of residence tend to have lower non-completion rates. This supports the view that residence in university premises tends to reduce non-completion. Second, the non-completion rate was found to be lower in universities with a high proportion of students reading business studies (for men) and languages (for women). This confirms our expectations based upon the much lower non-completion rates found in these two subject groups for the UK as a whole.

Third, the effect of the student/staff ratio on non-completion rate proved inconclusive, this variable having a significant negative coefficient in the regression equations for 1980 only. This result indicates that, for the 1980 entry cohort, a higher student/staff ratio is associated with a reduction in the non-completion rate. The reason for this is probably related to the subject mix of universities, which determines the student/staff ratio (see Chapter 2). It is possible that the effect of the subject mix on the non-completion rate is not being adequately measured in our statistical analysis by the two subject mix variables.

Finally, it is worth noting that the statistical results obtained for the two entry cohorts (1979 and 1980) are very similar. Not only are the estimated coefficients very similar for these two years (with the exception of the coefficient on the student/staff ratio), the explanatory power is very similar as well. For men and women combined, over 80 per cent of the variation in non-completion rates is explained (statistically) by only four explanatory variables.

Construction of a performance indicator based upon the non-completion rate

It was shown in the previous section that differences in the non-completion rate between universities can be explained by factors such as differences in the academic ability of each university's student entrants. This means that comparisons of the actual non-completion rate between universities are unlikely to be very helpful unless such factors are taken into account. It is therefore necessary to compute a *standardized* non-completion rate for each university which takes into account inter-university differences in factors such as the academic ability of each university's student entrants (as reflected by A level score) and the subject mix of each university. Once a *standardized* non-completion rate has been calculated, this can then be used as the bench-mark against which each university's *actual* non-completion rate should be compared. This can be expressed either as a ratio (actual/standardized) or as a difference (actual − standardized). In the case of the difference between the actual to the standardized non-completion rate, a difference exceeding zero indicates that a university has a higher than *expected* non-completion rate.

But how should a standardized non-completion rate be calculated? One possibility is to utilize the estimated regression equations discussed in the previous section (see appendix, pp. 100–1, for details). Since the regression equations provide information about the extent to which inter-university variations in the non-completion rate are explained by factors such as the A level score of each university's student entrants, it is possible to estimate each university's *expected* non-completion rate given the actual value of these factors for each university. In the case of A level score, for example, the actual value of this variable is substituted into the regression equation to provide an estimated non-completion rate for each university. Thus to compute a standardized non-completion rate for each university which allows for inter-university differences in ALEVEL, BUS+LANG, HALL and SCOTTISH (see appendix, pp. 100–1, for details), the actual value of each of these variables *for each university separately* is substituted into the estimated regression equation. For 1980 entrants, for example, the estimated non-completion rate for each university (NCR^*) is calculated as follows:

$$NCR^* = 36.46 - (1.59 \times \text{ALEVEL}) - (0.14 \times \text{BUS} + \text{LANG}) - (0.063 \times \text{HALL}) + (4.05 \times \text{SCOTTISH})$$

The non-completion rate performance indicator is then given by

$$NCR - NCR^*$$

for each university.

To illustrate the importance of taking inter-university differences in inputs into account when computing performance indicators, the values of $NCR - NCR^*$ are given for each university in Table 6.7 for the 1979 and 1980 entry cohorts. The two outstanding features of these results are, first, the low correlation between the actual non-completion rate (NCR) and $NCR - NCR^*$ ($r = 0.42$ for 1980). This confirms the view that the actual non-completion rate should not be used as a performance indicator *per se*. Whether $NCR - NCR^*$ should be used as a performance indicator, however, is also in doubt. It should first be noted that NCR^* has been calculated by including *all* explanatory variables in the estimating equation. This may be a misleading indicator of performance, however, since it effectively raises NCR^* for Scottish universities by about five percentage points (since this is the value of the estimated coefficient on SCOTTISH in the relevant equation). Since the higher non-completion rate in Scottish universities may be due to a higher proportion of young entrants than in the rest of the UK, or because of longer courses and a higher age participation ratio, it could be argued that NCR^* for Scottish universities should reflect these fundamental differences. The value of SCOTTISH (which is unity for all Scottish universities and zero otherwise) would not in this case be substituted into the estimated regression equation. Scottish universities would then perform less well on this particular indicator than those universities in the rest of the UK.

A further problem with this method of calculating NCR^* is that it is based upon an estimated regression equation which may be incomplete (see the discussion on pp. 75–7). *Only those variables for which data could be readily*

Table 6.7   A performance indicator based upon non-completion rates (*NCR − NCR**), 1979 and 1980 entry cohorts

University	NCR − NCR*	
	1979	*1980*
Aston	−1.5	−1.4
Bath	−1.8	−1.5
Birmingham	−1.2	−1.6
Bradford	−3.0	−1.8
Bristol	−1.4	−1.4
Brunel	5.2	4.7
Cambridge	−1.3	−1.0
City	2.2	2.0
Durham	−1.6	−1.7
East Anglia	−0.5	−2.2
Essex	−2.4	−0.8
Exeter	−0.2	−0.7
Hull	1.2	1.7
Keele	5.8	6.1
Kent	−1.0	0.9
Lancaster	−0.4	−2.3
Leeds	−1.8	−2.2
Leicester	−0.5	−2.1
Liverpool	1.0	0.8
London	0.9	2.1
Loughborough	−1.6	−2.3
Manchester	1.2	0.5
UMIST	2.3	−1.7
Newcastle	1.6	0.9
Nottingham	−2.2	−2.1
Oxford	1.3	2.6
Reading	1.2	0.4
Salford	1.8	0.8
Sheffield	−1.7	−1.9
Southampton	−0.4	−1.2
Surrey	−3.1	−2.9
Sussex	−0.1	−0.0
Warwick	−2.0	0.7
York	0.3	0.5
Aberdeen	−1.0	1.2
Dundee	1.4	3.8
Edinburgh	1.2	0.8
Glasgow	1.3	0.8
Heriot-Watt	0.8	−0.6
St Andrews	1.9	−0.7
Stirling	−4.9	−2.7
Strathclyde	−2.5	−1.4
Queen's	−3.0	−3.7
Ulster	−0.9	−2.4
Wales	1.3	0.1

Note:
See p. 82 for the definition of *NCR* and p. 97 for the definition of *NCR**.

obtained are included in the regression analysis. There may therefore be 'missing variables' and this could lead to inappropriate estimates of NCR^*. Despite these various problems, using $NCR - NCR^*$ as a performance indicator is, in our view, more appropriate than using NCR *per se*.

Conclusion

There has been increasing interest in undergraduate non-completion rates in the UK in recent years, especially as a result of the government's call for the development of performance indicators. The fact that over 13 per cent of those who start a university course do not complete it is now regarded as a cause for concern. Since the non-completion rate varies considerably between universities, this chapter has examined some of the possible reasons underlying these disparities. Detailed statistical analysis of differences in non-completion rates between institutions is particularly important in view of the proposed use of this variable as a performance indicator.

The statistical analysis of the 1979 and 1980 entry cohorts indicates that inter-university variations in the non-completion rate are explained by three main factors: the average A level score of each university's new entrants, the proportion of each university's students taking business studies or language courses, and the proportion of each university's students accommodated in a hall of residence. In addition, Scottish universities generally had substantially higher non-completion rates than universities elsewhere in the UK. This is probably related to the fact that Scottish students tend to enter university a year younger than their non-Scottish counterparts. In addition, a larger proportion of Scottish entrants are on four-year degree courses than in the rest of the UK and the age participation rate is higher in Scottish universities. All three factors could help to explain the higher non-completion rates in Scotland.

As far as using the non-completion rate as a performance indicator is concerned, the main conclusion to be drawn is that inter-university comparisons are of little value *per se*. For such comparisons to be of some value (either to the universities themselves or to policy-makers interested in measuring the efficiency of each institution), each university's non-completion rate would first need to be 'corrected' for at least some of the factors responsible for causing inter-university disparities in this variable. It is particularly important to allow for differences between universities in the quality of their student entrants since students with high A level scores are more likely to complete their degree course than those with low scores. When differences between universities in the A level score of their student entrants are taken into account (along with other explanatory variables), this has a dramatic effect on the measured performance of many universities with respect to their non-completion rate. Thus the actual non-completion rate is unlikely to provide useful information about a university's performance.

Appendix to Chapter 6

Calculation of the expected non-completion rate

$$\text{Expected non-completion rate in university } i = 100 \sum_j \left(\frac{N_{ij}}{N_i}\right)\left(\frac{SR_j}{N_j}\right)$$

where

N_{ij} = total number of leavers in university i in subject j
N_i = total number of leavers in university i
SR_j = leavers who successfully completed their course in subject j in UK universities as a whole
N_j = total number of leavers in UK universities as a whole.

Estimated weighted regression equations: dependent variable = non-completion rate

Explanatory variables	Estimated coefficients							
	1979				1980			
	Equation number							
	(1)	*(2)*	*(3)*	*(4)*	*(5)*	*(6)*	*(7)*	*(8)*
CONSTANT	35.76	38.65	37.11	35.76	36.46	42.19	36.12	38.33
	(19.10)	(10.24)	(18.81)	(14.50)	(18.27)	(12.38)	(16.20)	(15.48)
ALEVEL	−1.55	−1.66	−1.71	−1.54	−1.59	−1.79	−1.59	−1.74
	(−9.27)	(−7.82)	(−9.55)	(−7.14)	(−9.00)	(−9.13)	(−7.91)	(−8.05)
BUS + LANG	−0.12	−0.12	−0.12	−0.13	−0.14	−0.14	−0.13	−0.15
	(−4.67)	(−4.31)	(−4.33)	(−4.82)	(−5.06)	(−4.96)	(−3.90)	(−5.47)
HALL	−0.065	−0.057	−0.059	−0.061	−0.063	−0.049	−0.067	−0.066
	(−3.50)	(−2.81)	(−2.83)	(−3.00)	(−3.12)	(−2.40)	(−2.84)	(−3.12)
SCOTTISH	4.44	4.62		4.44	4.05	4.44		4.04
	(5.24)	(5.29)		(5.23)	(4.65)	(5.16)		(4.78)
STUDSTAFF		−0.31				−0.63		
		(−0.88)				(−2.04)		
$\bar{R}^2$	0.84	0.84	0.81	0.77	0.83	0.84	0.77	0.79
n	45	45	37	43	45	45	37	43

Notes:

1. ( ) = t-ratios
2. A t-ratio $\geqslant 1.96$ indicates significance at the 5% level or less; a t-ratio $\geqslant 2.58$ indicates significance at the 1% level or less (using a two-tailed test)
3. Definition of variables

ALEVEL　　　= average A level score of undergraduate entrants (only students with two or more A levels are included)
BUS + LANG = percentage of undergraduate entrants undertaking business, social science or language courses
HALL　　　　= percentage of full-time students living in halls of residence
SCOTTISH　 = 1 if a university is located in Scotland and 0 otherwise
STUDSTAFF = ratio of full-time equivalent students to full-time academic staff

4. The non-completion rate has been calculated using the entry cohort method.

Source: J. Johnes and Taylor 1989a.

Estimated weighted regression equations: dependent variable = non-completion rate (men only)

Explanatory variables	Estimated coefficients							
	1979				1980			
	Equation number							
	(1)	(2)	(3)	(4)	(5)	(6)	(7)	(8)
CONSTANT	41.58	45.52	43.48	40.93	43.96	49.86	44.39	45.08
	(18.90)	(10.46)	(20.15)	(14.11)	(17.16)	(11.69)	(16.78)	(14.20)
ALEVEL	−2.03	−2.18	−2.26	−1.91	−2.24	−2.45	−2.30	−2.34
	(−10.48)	(−8.95)	(−11.52)	(−7.58)	(−10.17)	(−9.92)	(−9.82)	(−8.49)
BUSINESS	−0.15	−0.14	−0.17	−0.15	−0.20	−0.20	−0.20	−0.21
	(−3.59)	(−3.37)	(−4.07)	(−3.61)	(−4.13)	(−4.14)	(−3.77)	(−4.19)
HALL	−0.073	−0.062	−0.056	−0.064	−0.060	−0.046	−0.060	−0.062
	(−3.50)	(−2.71)	(−2.53)	(−2.77)	(−2.59)	(−1.87)	(−2.32)	(−2.41)
SCOTTISH	5.34	5.53		5.36	6.13	6.43		6.15
	(5.46)	(5.57)		(5.40)	(5.89)	(6.23)		(5.85)
STUDSTAFF		−0.41				−0.63		
		(−1.05)				(−1.71)		
$\bar{R}^2$	0.84	0.84	0.84	0.74	0.84	0.84	0.81	0.77
n	45	45	37	43	45	45	37	43

Notes:
1. See notes to previous table
2. BUSINESS = percentage of undergraduate entrants undertaking business or social science courses.

Source: J. Johnes and Taylor 1989a.

Estimated weighted regression equations: dependent variable = non-completion rate (women only)

Explanatory variables	Estimated coefficients							
	1979				1980			
	Equation number							
	(1)	(2)	(3)	(4)	(5)	(6)	(7)	(8)
CONSTANT	22.32	29.64	24.49	21.79	21.49	30.85	22.02	21.76
	(10.55)	(6.79)	(11.06)	(7.69)	(9.89)	(8.12)	(8.98)	(7.70)
ALEVEL	−0.74	−1.03	−0.88	−0.69	−0.59	−0.91	−0.68	−0.61
	(−3.61)	(−4.11)	(−4.07)	(−2.67)	(−2.78)	(−4.05)	(−2.81)	(−2.31)
LANGUAGES	−0.064	−0.045	−0.084	−0.069	−0.081	−0.070	−0.059	−0.092
	(−1.69)	(−1.17)	(−1.97)	(−1.78)	(−2.01)	(−1.87)	(−1.18)	(−2.26)
HALL	−0.075	−0.056	−0.082	−0.071	−0.088	−0.066	−0.093	−0.086
	(−3.50)	(−2.44)	(−3.59)	(−2.99)	(−3.85)	(−2.94)	(−3.49)	(−3.46)
SCOTTISH	4.20	4.80		4.18	2.28	3.05		2.22
	(4.11)	(4.62)		(4.06)	(2.20)	(3.08)		(2.16)
STUDSTAFF		−0.77				−1.02		
		(−1.90)				(−2.89)		
$\bar{R}^2$	0.65	0.68	0.56	0.57	0.59	0.66	0.45	0.52
n	45	45	37	43	45	45	37	43

Notes:
1. See notes to previous table
2. LANGUAGES = percentage of undergraduate entrants undertaking language courses.

Source: J. Johnes and Taylor 1989a.

7

Degree Results: Differences between Universities

Introduction

One of the primary outputs of the university sector is graduates. Resources such as teaching staff are employed for the specific purpose of disseminating knowledge to every institution's student entrants and a high proportion of these will ultimately obtain a degree or diploma. The *quantity* of graduates, however, is only one aspect of each university's contribution to the creation of human capital since the *quality* of education may vary between institutions. But if the quality of education at different institutions is to be measured, this raises the critical question of how to measure the quality of graduates. The most obvious (but by no means the only) approach is to construct a measure of output based upon the degree results obtained by each university's annual output of graduates. Degree results are an attractive variable for measuring the quality of education since a degree is the most obvious outcome of teaching activity.

This points in the direction of using the degree results achieved by graduates in each institution as a performance indicator. It will be shown in this chapter that the proportion of graduates gaining a first or an upper second varies considerably between UK universities and it therefore seems appropriate to investigate the extent to which this variation in degree results reflects the quality of tuition. Are universities which award a high proportion of firsts and upper seconds more efficient than universities which produce a low proportion? Do they provide better tuition? Or is it simply that differences in the quality of the raw material (i.e. the innate academic ability of students) explain these inter-university disparities in degree results? Answers to these questions are of interest not only to the universities themselves but also to those who fund them (i.e. taxpayers) and to potential students. Universities will be interested in comparing the performance of their own students in final degree examinations with those of other institutions while potential students will be interested in discovering how their chance of obtaining a 'good' degree varies between universities.

The purpose of this chapter is to investigate why degree results vary between universities. Attention is concentrated specifically on first degrees since this represents the bulk of each institution's teaching output. It is particularly important to undertake such an investigation in view of the fact that degree results have been proposed as a performance indicator. This is made clear in the 1987 White Paper:

> Academic standards and the quality of teaching in higher education need to be judged by reference mainly to student's achievements. The numbers and class distribution of degrees awarded provide some measure as, conversely, do non-completion rates.
>
> (DES 1987b: 28)

But if degree results are to be used as a performance indicator it is important to know why they differ between institutions. If they differ because of factors such as differences in the innate ability of student entrants, any comparisons in degree results between institutions will be worthless unless such factors are taken into account. Ideally this means that any performance indicator based on degree results will have to be 'corrected' to allow for inter-university differences in degree results which are due to factors unrelated to the teaching process – since it is the effectiveness of the teaching process which degree results are supposedly measuring.

This chapter is in four sections. The first section discusses two alternative methods of measuring degree results at the institutional level and provides these for every UK university for the period 1976–88. The second suggests why degree results might vary between universities, distinguishing between student-related and university-related factors. This is followed in the third section by a statistical analysis of inter-university variations in degree results. Multiple regression analysis is used to estimate the effect of various factors on degree results. The fourth section proposes a method of constructing a performance indicator for each university based upon degree results.

Two measures of degree results

Two alternative measures of degree performance are used in the present chapter. They are as follows:

$$\text{DEGREE RESULT} = \frac{I + II.1}{G - II} \times 100$$

$$\text{DEGREE SCORE} = \frac{(75 \times \text{I}) + (65 \times \text{II.1}) + (60 \times \text{II}) + (55 \times \text{II.2}) + (45 \times \text{III}) + (40 \times \text{PASS/ORD})}{G}$$

where

I	= number of graduates with a first class honours degree
II.1	= number of graduates with an upper second class honours degree
II	= number of graduates with an undivided second class honours degree
II.2	= number of graduates with a lower second class honours degree
III	= number of graduates with a third class honours degree
PASS/ORD	= number of graduates with a pass or ordinary degree
G	= total number of graduates

DEGREE RESULT and DEGREE SCORE turn out to be closely correlated in practice. This can be seen from Figure 7.1, which shows DEGREE RESULT and DEGREE SCORE for the UK university sector as a whole for the period 1976–88. The correlation between DEGREE RESULT and DEGREE SCORE is 0.99. The correlation between these two measures of degree results is also very high across universities ($r = 0.92$ for 1988).

A major problem arises in any comparisons of degree results which involve Scottish universities. The latter offer two quite separate degree

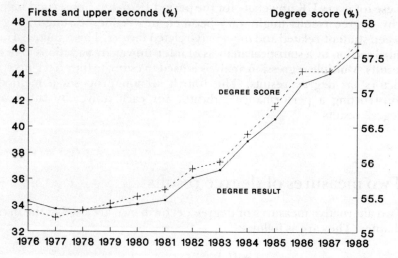

Figure 7.1 DEGREE RESULT and DEGREE SCORE: all UK universities, 1976–88

Source: Universities' Statistical Record, Cheltenham (unpublished data).

schemes: a three-year non-honours degree and a four-year honours degree. It is important to note that the non-honours scheme is valued in its own right and is recorded as an ordinary degree. Scottish universities point out that the ordinary degree is different from a pass degree on an honours degree scheme. In 1988, for example, pass or ordinary degrees constituted 34 per cent of total degrees awarded by Scottish universities (ranging from 16 per cent at St Andrews to 48 per cent at Glasgow) compared with only 9 per cent in the rest of the UK. This raises the question of whether ordinary degrees should be equated with pass degrees in measuring degree results. In practice, any decision about how to treat ordinary degrees is ultimately arbitrary and there seems little alternative but to group ordinary degrees with pass degrees. (They are in fact grouped together in the data supplied by the Universities Statistical Record, Cheltenham.)

Information on degree results for all UK universities is provided in Table 7.1 for the period 1976–88. (Oxford is included only from 1986 onwards since second class honours degrees were undivided until 1986.) From Table 7.1, it can be seen that the proportion of graduates gaining firsts or upper seconds varies considerably between universities. The proportion of firsts and upper seconds at Bath, Bristol, Cambridge, Nottingham, Sussex and York, for example, has been consistently higher than in most other universities. At the opposite end of the scale are Hull, Leeds, Liverpool, Newcastle, Salford and Ulster.

Further scrutiny of Table 7.1 indicates that the variation in degree results *between* universities during any single year is far greater than the variation *within* universities over time. This is the case despite the fact that there has been a significant – and in some cases very substantial – increase in the percentage gaining a first or upper second over time. At Lough-borough, for example, the percentage increased from an average of 32.2 per cent during 1976–81 to 46.1 per cent during 1982–88. Increases at other universities were less dramatic but have still been considerable, particularly since 1981. Another significant feature of the percentage gaining a first or upper second is the remarkably stable pattern across universities over a long period of time. This is reflected by the very high correlation in the percentage gaining a first or upper second (within each university) in adjacent years. Indeed, there is a high correlation in the percentage of firsts and upper seconds awarded by universities over the entire study period (J. Johnes and Taylor 1987).

The stability of the percentage of graduates gaining a first or upper second (within universities) over time strongly suggests the existence of some underlying causal factors which determine the inter-university pattern of degree results. One reason for this stability may be that the percentage of firsts and upper seconds in any one year is predetermined by 'an institution's preconception of the appropriate percentage' (Bee and Dolton 1985). In other words, the past determines the present. An alternative view is that the variation in degree results between universities is a result of fundamental differences in factors such as the ability of students,

Table 7.1 Percentage of graduates with a first or upper second class honours degree in UK universities, 1976 to 1988

University	DEGREE RESULT												
	1976	1977	1978	1979	1980	1981	1982	1983	1984	1985	1986	1987	1988
Aston	31.4	33.1	29.7	28.4	29.5	31.4	34.7	36.3	38.1	43.8	48.1	55.4	58.7
Bath	39.6	38.4	42.0	41.6	40.7	45.6	44.8	45.6	49.1	56.7	57.7	60.3	59.8
Birmingham	34.8	30.3	30.7	31.4	30.8	29.7	33.0	35.6	36.7	36.7	43.3	41.6	39.5
Bradford	37.6	42.0	37.9	37.2	36.8	37.9	37.0	41.2	42.1	39.6	41.9	46.1	45.6
Bristol	39.2	40.3	43.2	44.3	44.2	44.6	43.3	47.1	49.1	47.6	52.1	51.9	53.2
Brunel	35.1	32.5	41.8	41.8	38.4	42.0	41.3	42.1	44.1	45.7	45.9	47.3	45.6
Cambridge	61.6	63.6	61.9	64.4	63.6	63.1	65.7	66.5	67.4	66.0	66.2	68.6	69.3
City	32.0	35.0	35.0	32.5	34.3	32.2	34.8	34.5	37.6	41.5	45.3	42.8	48.1
Durham	37.0	38.4	36.8	35.6	32.9	34.8	40.0	43.9	43.3	47.9	47.8	45.9	49.0
East Anglia	36.8	36.2	36.2	35.0	32.3	29.3	29.0	32.8	39.8	42.0	42.9	51.1	48.8
Essex	41.9	39.0	35.3	37.4	35.3	34.2	38.6	41.2	38.5	44.5	43.5	48.9	48.2
Exeter	38.8	39.9	37.9	36.7	37.6	36.6	40.0	41.0	42.8	45.3	45.1	43.7	47.4
Hull	31.5	32.3	29.8	29.6	28.5	29.9	34.4	29.9	30.6	37.4	41.9	44.5	44.4
Keele	37.3	33.9	36.2	37.1	39.8	32.8	36.0	37.4	38.9	38.3	42.5	45.2	46.4
Kent	32.2	32.2	27.7	29.8	28.1	30.3	35.5	38.3	36.1	36.7	43.6	47.3	51.1
Lancaster	38.7	34.5	36.0	31.0	32.0	33.1	36.4	36.6	41.3	41.0	43.5	49.0	53.6
Leeds	37.5	29.8	29.7	28.9	32.0	34.1	34.1	32.1	35.3	36.3	37.8	37.0	41.6
Leicester	38.9	35.7	39.4	41.5	36.1	36.6	34.3	35.5	40.3	39.1	42.4	41.9	45.4
Liverpool	32.3	30.7	30.6	30.1	29.2	30.3	31.3	32.9	33.8	33.6	35.0	37.4	37.4
London	33.5	33.5	32.7	33.8	34.7	34.2	35.8	35.7	39.2	40.7	43.2	42.2	43.3
Loughborough	32.1	30.7	32.1	29.7	33.6	35.2	39.5	42.3	45.2	47.2	47.2	50.4	51.1
Manchester	33.4	35.6	33.5	33.9	36.8	35.5	38.2	38.0	39.2	42.9	40.7	43.9	45.8

University												
UMIST	36.5	38.7	34.6	33.0	36.9	34.3	37.7	37.0	34.7	40.0	42.3	41.2	43.0
Newcastle	25.5	29.3	28.2	28.9	26.9	29.3	29.4	29.6	31.9	35.9	35.2	37.8	40.2
Nottingham	41.8	40.0	41.9	43.1	44.1	42.8	44.5	44.8	47.6	47.1	47.3	51.8	52.5
Oxford											56.8	58.6	58.8
Reading	38.7	40.6	37.1	38.7	37.0	40.0	42.8	41.2	42.7	42.5	51.1	48.3	52.6
Salford	28.3	28.6	29.2	26.5	27.4	28.7	28.2	31.0	32.4	37.9	43.9	42.4	50.5
Sheffield	36.4	36.8	34.6	36.2	35.8	34.4	35.6	39.0	36.9	41.2	41.4	44.5	46.4
Southampton	37.6	37.1	38.9	40.2	38.6	40.1	41.1	41.9	45.6	44.1	43.4	43.7	45.4
Surrey	38.2	36.0	37.6	37.1	36.0	38.0	36.5	42.3	44.9	45.1	43.6	44.2	47.4
Sussex	44.1	40.8	41.9	43.8	42.4	42.8	42.1	45.3	41.4	42.8	44.1	44.9	44.8
Warwick	37.1	35.7	33.2	34.3	30.9	33.2	32.8	34.8	38.2	41.3	47.7	47.1	48.9
York	45.2	48.3	45.1	49.1	48.9	43.7	48.7	51.0	51.2	52.9	54.0	56.4	58.5
Aberdeen	22.2	22.6	23.8	24.1	26.1	25.2	27.7	26.0	27.5	33.1	33.3	31.1	35.8
Dundee	22.3	17.0	20.9	18.9	20.0	21.7	26.0	25.8	27.1	25.4	31.8	29.7	30.7
Edinburgh						30.9	33.6	31.0	36.3	38.0	37.7	37.6	42.2
Glasgow	16.6	15.9	17.5						23.5	27.1	29.8	27.0	28.8
Heriot-Watt	18.8	22.8	23.3	21.5	19.7	22.2	25.7	25.0	29.8	26.6	28.2	33.1	35.6
St Andrews	35.0	30.7	30.3	36.2	33.6	38.8	38.8	38.2	38.2	44.8	47.8	44.0	50.0
Stirling	18.8	18.9	17.6	21.7	17.9	20.6	24.3	21.0	26.7	30.3	32.5	33.7	37.9
Strathclyde	20.3	18.5	20.8	21.3	22.7	24.6	21.6	24.1	27.1	33.6	39.1	39.3	41.4
Queen's	25.2	22.3	21.7	24.5	29.0	26.2	27.2	29.7	32.2	31.9	33.4	34.9	36.3
Ulster	35.3	35.1	32.0	32.0	37.3	34.2	33.7	30.8	29.4	28.2	33.3	32.7	36.4
Wales	33.8	32.5	32.5	32.6	32.4	31.5	33.8	33.7	35.3	37.8	39.1	38.6	41.8

Note:
The precise definition of DEGREE RESULT is given on pp. 103–4. Several universities were awarded undivided seconds during 1976–88.
DEGREE RESULT has not been calculated in cases where the percentage of graduates awarded undivided seconds exceeds 20 per cent.

Source: Universities' Statistical Record, Cheltenham.

standards of teaching and the facilities available to both students and staff at each institution. It is this second view which we investigate in the remainder of this chapter.

Some explanations of inter-university differences in degree results

This section investigates the view that variations in degree results between universities can be explained by factors which relate either to each university's students or to the universities themselves. Students are the essential raw material inputs which universities convert into graduates through teaching and related processes. It is therefore appropriate to search for measurable variables which can be used to describe those aspects of student-related inputs and university-related processes which are likely to have an effect on each university's degree results. *Only those variables for which data can be readily obtained are considered here.* It is useful to distinguish between those factors which relate to the raw material input (the students) and those which relate to the inputs provided by each institution in support of the teaching process.

Student-related factors

Several student-related factors may be expected to affect their degree results. First, degree results are likely to be better for those with high academic ability. There is plenty of evidence to demonstrate that the academic ability of *individual* students (measured by school qualifications) has a positive effect on their degree result, although the relationship is often only weak (Freeman 1970; Kapur 1972; Entwistle and Wilson 1977; Tarsh 1982; Crum and Parikh 1983; Sear 1983). The only available measure of the academic ability of each university's annual intake of new students is their average A level score, which is expected to be positively related to the average degree result obtained by each university's graduates. A level score is by no means a perfect indicator of academic ability since it will depend on quality of schooling, support from parents and the personality traits of each individual student. On average across all student entrants in an institution, however, it seems likely that average A level score will be an adequate proxy of the academic ability of each university's annual intake of students.

The use of A level score as an explanatory variable in a model to explain degree results is supported by the high positive correlation between these two variables at national level. Allowing for a three-year lag of the percentage obtaining a first or upper second (DEGREE RESULT) behind

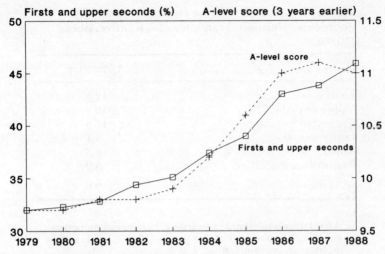

Figure 7.2 Degree results v. A level score: UK universities, 1979–88

Source: Universities' Statistical Record, Cheltenham (unpublished data).

A level score, the correlation between these two variables was 0.98 for the period 1979–88 (see Figure 7.2). Similarly a correlation of 0.98 was obtained between DEGREE SCORE and A level score. Moreover, the regression of DEGREE RESULT on A level score indicates that a one-point increase in A level score has been associated with a 7.5 percentage point increase in the percentage of graduates obtaining a first or upper second (at national level). Further support for using A level score as an explanatory variable is provided by data obtained from the National Survey of Graduates and Diplomates. Table 7.2 indicates a clear positive relationship between degree class and A level score.

One of the problems with using A level score as an indicator of academic ability is that the majority of entrants into Scottish universities take Scottish highers and not A levels. Since any method of converting Scottish highers into A level equivalents would be arbitrary, the A level score of A level qualified entrants is used as a measure of academic ability of all entrants to Scottish universities in spite of obvious problems with this approach. The existence of a highly significant positive correlation, however, between A level scores and Scottish highers across Scottish universities (using data obtained from the CVCP's *University Management Statistics and Performance Indicators*) offers some support for the use of A level score as a proxy variable. It may be noted at this point, however, that the statistical analysis of degree results reported in the next section is undertaken both with and without Scottish universities.

Second, degree results may be affected by whether or not a student lives at home during term time. Students who live at home may have less opportunity to obtain the full benefit of university facilities (such as the

Table 7.2   Mean A level (or equivalent) score by degree classification: graduates of UK universities (1980)

Degree class	A level score
First	12.8
Upper second	10.8
Undivided second	11.8
Lower second	9.1
Third	8.3
Pass, ordinary or other	3.9
All classes	9.6

Note:
1. A level score is calculated by awarding the following numerical marks to each grade: A = 5, B = 4, C = 3, D = 2, E = 1; and for Scottish highers: A = 3, B = 2, C = 1.
2. Sample size = 4864.

Source: National Survey of 1980 Graduates and Diplomates (1987).

library, computers or the laboratories) because a greater proportion of their time may be spent travelling between home and university or they may become more involved in domestic (non-academic) activities. This may consequently result in work of lower standard compared to those students who live away from home during term time. A further possibility is that students who live at home during their degree course are less adventurous and less independently minded than students who live away from home. They may also be less financially independent.

Third, students whose first language is not English may be at a disadvantage in taking a degree in the UK and may therefore achieve a poorer degree as a consequence. Working in the opposite direction is the possibility that students from abroad may have more initiative, ambition and self-reliance than students who study in their home country. The way in which the percentage of each university's graduates who come from overseas will affect its degree results is therefore uncertain.

Fourth, since a higher proportion of female graduates obtain a first or an upper second on average than male graduates for the UK as a whole (see Figure 7.3), it is worth testing whether the ratio of male to female graduates plays any part in explaining inter-university differences in degree results.

University-related factors

A university-related factor which may be expected to have considerable impact on degree results is the quality of each institution's teaching. Since

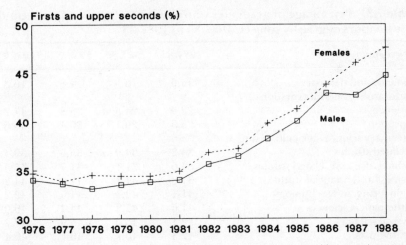

Figure 7.3 Percentage of graduates obtaining a first or upper second: males and females, 1976–88

Source: Universities' Statistical Record, Cheltenham (unpublished data).

no direct measure of teaching *quality* is available at the institutional level, it is necessary to fall back upon *quantitative* measures such as the student/staff ratio. Students at universities with a high student/staff ratio may receive less personal tuition than students at universities in which the student/staff ratio is low. The student/staff ratio can therefore be expected to be negatively related to degree results.

A second factor which may influence a university's degree result is its subject mix (Nevin 1972). Table 7.3 indicates very wide variations between subjects at national level in the percentage of firsts and upper seconds. Moreover, these intersubject differences are highly correlated over time. It follows that the subject mix of an institution can be expected to affect its degree results. Universities with a high proportion of subjects in which a high proportion of firsts and upper seconds are awarded can be expected to have a higher than average proportion of firsts and upper seconds.

Third, degree results may vary between different types of universities. The new greenfield universities and the ex-colleges of advanced technology (ex-CATS) established in the 1960s, for example, have developed along different lines from the older 'civic' universities and this may have an effect on degree results. Both the ex-CATs and the new greenfield universities have been keen, for example, to introduce a substantial coursework element into their assessment procedures. Whether these procedures differ substantially from those used in the older civic universities, however, is unknown since many universities have shifted towards the incorporation of coursework assessment into the determination of their degree results in recent years. In addition, Scottish universities require

Table 7.3 Percentage of graduates who obtained a first or upper second class honours degree by subject, 1984/85 to 1987/88

Subject group	1984/85	1985/86	1986/87	1987/88
Medicine and dentistry	14.6	16.5	14.8	16.3
Librarianship and information science	22.9	24.8	35.8	47.2
Education	25.3	29.1	30.4	36.6
Veterinary science, agriculture and related studies	34.2	34.9	35.5	39.4
Architecture and related studies	34.6	31.1	31.7	35.3
Business and financial studies	37.8	41.1	41.0	44.2
Engineering and technology	41.1	42.3	41.5	42.2
Mathematical sciences	41.6	43.2	44.4	46.0
Physical sciences	42.1	46.0	45.9	47.2
Creative arts	42.3	46.1	46.1	46.4
Social sciences	43.3	46.1	47.6	48.2
Studies allied to medicine	47.9	50.6	55.1	58.3
Languages and related studies	49.1	52.0	55.6	56.6
Biological sciences	49.2	53.2	53.5	55.2
Humanities	50.1	52.5	53.3	55.3

Note:
The formula for calculating the percentage of graduates with a first or upper second class honours degree is given on pp. 103–4.

Source: Unpublished data, Universities' Statistical Record, Cheltenham.

separate treatment since they award a far larger proportion of ordinary degrees than other UK universities.

Finally, several other university-related factors which may have an effect on degree results are included in the statistical analysis in the next section. These additional variables are the age of a university, its size, library expenditure as a percentage of total expenditure, and the UFC research rating of universities for 1984–88. Thus students at universities which spend a high proportion of their income on their libraries may provide better access to relevant books and articles and they may be expected to improve their prospects of gaining a good degree. The effect of a university's commitment to research on its teaching is uncertain. On the one hand universities in which the staff are highly committed to research may have less time for undergraduates and this could result in less intensive tuition and consequently poorer degree results. On the other hand, good quality research might actually improve teaching effectiveness and hence the quality of degrees obtained (Voeks 1962; Hammond *et al.* 1969; Hayes 1971; Harry and Goldner 1972; Aleamoni and Yimer 1973; Linsky and Straus 1975; Dent and Lewis 1976). Any attempt to suggest how the age or the size of a university might affect degree results would be purely speculative.

Statistical analysis of inter-university differences in degree results

Multiple regression methods were used to estimate the extent to which differences in degree results between universities could be explained (statistically) by the student-related and university-related factors identified in the previous section. Two variables have been used to measure the average degree result in each university. These are the mean degree score (DEGREE SCORE) and the percentage of firsts and upper seconds (DEGREE RESULT) as defined on pp. 103–4.

The regression analysis was undertaken for four separate years 1983–86 inclusive. Both DEGREE SCORE and DEGREE RESULT were used as dependent variables. A selection of estimated regression equations is given in the appendix to this chapter (pp. 119–20). The main results obtained from the statistical analysis are as follows. First, over 80 per cent of the variation in DEGREE SCORE and DEGREE RESULTS is explained by six explanatory variables. These are

1. the mean A level score of entrants
2. the percentage of students who live at home
3. library expenditure as a percentage of total expenditure
4. whether or not a university is an ex-college of advanced technology
5. whether or not a university is one of the new greenfield universities established in 1964/65
6. whether or not a university is located in Scotland.

The second main result obtained from the regression analysis is that each of the explanatory variables has a similar effect on degree results in all four years. This means that the results appear to be robust. Third, several explanatory variables were found to be *unrelated* to both DEGREE SCORE and DEGREE RESULT. These are the percentage of students from overseas, the ratio of male to female graduates, the student/staff ratio, the subject mix, the age and size of each university and the UFC rating of each university's research over the period 1984–88.

One of the most interesting results obtained from the regression analysis is the highly significant positive relationship between A level score and degree results. This indicates that the academic ability of each university's student entrants has a substantial impact upon their subsequent degree results. The equations using DEGREE RESULT as the dependent variable imply that a one-point increase in A level score is associated with an increase of between three and four percentage points in the proportion of graduates with a first or an upper second. This result is very firm and is not disturbed when either Scottish universities or Oxford and Cambridge (where A level scores are very high) are excluded from the analysis.

The importance of A level score as an explanatory variable conflicts with previous research which indicates at best only a weak positive relationship between A level score and degree result for individual students (e.g. Sear

1983). The most likely explanation for these conflicting results is that many of the factors which affect an *individual's* degree results (such as motivation and commitment to study) will cancel out when the relationship is being tested at the *institutional* level (as in the present study). The absence of a strong statistical relationship between A level score and degree results in the cross-sectional analysis of *individual* graduates may therefore be consistent with the highly significant relationship found in the present highly aggregated analysis of degree results for *entire institutions*.

Third, very little evidence could be found to indicate that inter-university variations in degree results were associated with corresponding variations in subject mix. This is a surprising result in view of the substantial differences in degree results across subjects. The only finding of interest as far as subject mix is concerned is that universities with a high proportion of arts graduates tend to have poorer degree results. But this relationship is statistically rather weak.

Fourth, there is considerable evidence that degree results vary significantly between different broad types of universities. The regression results indicate that the percentage of firsts and upper seconds is about six to seven percentage points lower in Scottish universities (on average), six percentage points higher in the ex-CATs, and about four percentage points higher in the new greenfield universities than in the older civics. The lower percentage of firsts and upper seconds in Scottish universities is a direct consequence of the long tradition of awarding ordinary degrees for three-year courses in Scotland (as explained earlier). Exactly why the ex-CATs and the new greenfield universities should award a higher proportion of firsts and upper seconds is uncertain, but it is possible that it has something to do with different methods of assessing students in these institutions compared to the civics.

Finally, two other variables were found to be significantly related to DEGREE RESULT and DEGREE SCORE: the percentage of students who live at home is negatively related to degree results; and library expenditure as a proportion of total spending is positively related to degree results. Degree results therefore tend to be better in those universities which give library expenditure a relatively high priority (or perhaps can afford to do so) and which have a high proportion of their students who do not live at home during term time. It should also be noted that none of the statistical results is disturbed when Scottish universities are excluded from the regression analysis.

Construction of a performance indicator based upon degree results

It was shown in the previous section that differences in degree results between universities are strongly influenced by both student-related and university-related factors. As far as can be ascertained, however, none of these is specifically related to the quality of teaching at each institution. The student/staff ratio, for example, was found to be unrelated to inter-university variations in degree results. This was not the case, however, for A level scores: the highly significant coefficient on the A level score variable clearly indicates that a university's degree results are likely to be strongly affected by the A level scores achieved by its student entrants. It would therefore be entirely inappropriate *not* to take differences in A level scores into account when comparing degree results between universities since individual universities have only limited control over the mean A level score of their students. This is because universities *generally* aim to attract students with as high an A level score as they can (in spite of the fact that many academics and university administrators believe that there is very little correlation between A level scores and the degree results ultimately obtained by students).

The substantial influence of a university's average A level score on its degree results suggests that each university's degree results should be compared not with the average for all universities (when assessing its performance) but with a *standardized* value of degree results for each university based upon the variables which explain inter-university variations in degree results. The difference between the *actual* and the *standardized* degree result for each university can then be used to indicate the extent to which differences in degree results between universities have *not* been explained by the variables included in the model. Thus for the percentage of firsts and upper seconds, the performance indicator would be given by:

DEGREE RESULT − DEGREE RESULT*

where DEGREE RESULT* (the standardized degree result) is computed for each university by substituting actual values of each explanatory variable into the appropriate regression equation. For example, the standardized degree result for each university's 1986 graduates would be calculated as follows:

DEGREE RESULT* = −3.26 + (3.26 × ALEVEL) −
(0.05 × LIVEHOME) + (7.05 × EXCAT) + (2.88 × NEW) −
(6.85 × SCOTTISH) + (2.94 × LIBRARY)

The explanatory variables are as defined in the appendix (pp. 119–20).

This performance indicator for degree results is given for UK universities for 1983–86 in Table 7.4. The most interesting result is the low correlation between

DEGREE RESULT
and DEGREE RESULT − DEGREE RESULT*.

The correlation coefficient does not exceed 0.42 in any year. Inter-university comparisons in *actual* degree results are therefore unlikely to be helpful in evaluating the performance of individual institutions. Whether

Table 7.4   A performance indicator based upon the percentage of graduates with a first or upper second

University	DEGREE RESULT − DEGREE RESULT*			
	1983	*1984*	*1985*	*1986*
Aston	2.4	0.4	3.7	2.4
Bath	−6.5	−4.1	0.8	1.8
Birmingham	−1.3	−2.4	−2.4	0.5
Bradford	3.6	2.5	−2.9	−3.2
Bristol	0.6	1.9	0.5	4.8
Brunel	3.5	2.1	2.7	1.3
Cambridge	8.4	7.4	1.7	4.2
City	−3.1	−0.7	−1.4	−0.6
Durham	−4.0	−7.2	−4.0	−3.6
East Anglia	−5.4	0.8	0.1	−0.8
Essex	7.2	4.7	7.0	1.8
Exeter	−1.6	−1.3	−1.1	−3.7
Hull	−3.6	−5.7	−3.5	0.1
Keele	3.2	2.9	1.4	−0.2
Kent	−0.2	−4.2	−5.4	−2.5
Lancaster	−2.4	0.2	−0.3	−0.7
Leeds	−3.2	−1.0	−2.0	−1.3
Leicester	−1.6	0.8	−2.8	−0.4
Liverpool	0.2	−0.9	−2.4	−2.8
London	0.3	3.1	2.6	2.2
Loughborough	−2.7	−1.4	−0.6	−2.7
Manchester	0.8	0.6	2.9	−0.9
UMIST	−1.3	−4.1	−2.0	−1.5
Newcastle	−4.3	−3.6	−1.9	−4.5
Nottingham	5.1	5.4	4.9	3.4
Oxford	—	—	—	−5.0
Reading	2.6	2.9	2.6	8.8
Salford	1.0	−1.5	0.3	1.3
Sheffield	0.2	−3.1	0.2	−2.3
Southampton	−0.6	2.0	−0.0	−1.2
Surrey	2.3	1.0	−2.0	−1.5
Sussex	1.8	−2.4	−2.0	−2.5
Warwick	−7.6	−3.0	−3.4	2.7
York	4.4	3.2	6.4	4.8
Aberdeen	0.3	1.4	1.9	0.7
Dundee	2.5	−0.0	−2.3	−0.8
Edinburgh	−1.2	1.0	0.8	0.6
Glasgow	—	−4.6	−2.4	−3.9
Heriot-Watt	−1.5	3.4	−2.7	−3.8
St Andrews	0.9	−1.0	2.9	5.0
Stirling	−3.2	−2.6	−2.1	−4.3
Strathclyde	2.3	2.5	4.0	6.6
Queen's	−1.6	1.2	−1.9	−2.3
Ulster	−0.3	0.3	0.7	2.5
Wales	3.7	3.1	3.6	1.7

Note:
See pp. 103–4 for definition of DEGREE RESULT and p. 115 for definition of DEGREE RESULT*. Values of DEGREE RESULT − DEGREE RESULT* are missing in cases where the percentage of undivided seconds awarded exceeds 20 per cent.

inter-university comparisons in DEGREE RESULT – DEGREE RESULT* are useful for this purpose, however, is also questionable. It is by no means clear that inter-university variations in this indicator can be attributed entirely to corresponding variations in teaching quality. Indeed, this would be a rash assumption. It should be remembered that a very high proportion of the variation in degree results between universities is accounted for by factors which do *not* include a measure of teaching quality. The fact that the variation in DEGREE RESULT – DEGREE RESULT* is far smaller than in DEGREE RESULT alone suggests that there is relatively little scope for using degree results as a performance indicator once inter-university variations in the various explanatory variables (such as mean A level score) have been taken into account.

A further interesting result to emerge from inter-university comparisons in DEGREE RESULT – DEGREE RESULT* is that this variable is highly correlated with itself for the four years for which it has been calculated. Thus the stability over time in DEGREE RESULT – DEGREE RESULT* suggests that at least one other important explanatory variable which has had a consistent effect on degree results has been omitted from the regression model. Whether this missing variable is teaching quality is unknown. The general problems with using a regression residual as a performance indicator (see pp. 75–7) are also applicable here.

Conclusion

The performance of graduates in final degree examinations varies considerably between UK universities. Some universities consistently award a high proportion of firsts and upper seconds, for example, while others consistently award a much lower proportion. In other words, there is a high degree of stability in the university 'league table' of degree results over many years.

Since the government has indicated that variations in degree results between universities should be used as a performance indicator (presumably to reflect inter-university differences in the quality of teaching), it is important that these variations in degree results should be carefully and thoroughly investigated. It would be entirely wrong to use degree results as a performance indicator in the absence of a detailed statistical inquiry into why degree results vary between institutions. The purpose of this chapter was therefore to investigate the causes of inter-university variations in degree results since this is a necessary first step towards constructing a performance indicator based upon this variable. Using regression analysis, it was found that over 80 per cent of the variation between universities in degree results can be explained (statistically) by a set of plausible explanatory variables, the main one being the mean A level score of each university's student entrants.

Although the importance of A level score as an explanatory variable is hardly surprising, it is nevertheless an important result for those intent on using degree results as a performance indicator. In particular, it would clearly be wrong to compare degree results between universities without taking into account differences in the mean A level score of each university's student entrants. Other variables also played an important part in explaining inter-university differences in degree results. These include the percentage of students living at home during term time and type of university (i.e. ex-CATs, new greenfield universities, civics and Scottish universities).

Since a substantial proportion of the inter-university variation in degree results can be explained by a set of explanatory variables which do not include a direct measure of teaching inputs, it is tempting to assume that the remaining unexplained variation must be due to inter-university variations in the quality of teaching. But this would be an entirely speculative conclusion since the unexplained variation may be a result of other factors in addition to variations in teaching quality. Thus although a performance indicator can be constructed based upon the variation in degree results *not* accounted for by explanatory variables such as A level score, it is by no means certain that such an indicator would be useful for measuring performance.

Finally, a further problem of using degree results as a performance indicator needs to be underlined. Degree results are under the direct control of each university's examining body, and although these are advised by independent external examiners there may nevertheless be a strong temptation for universities to award more 'good' degrees if those with unfavourable degree results are seen to be penalized in the allocation of funds. This would inevitably result in a general upward trend in degree results and a narrowing of differences between universities. It may therefore be inappropriate to use degree results as a target variable since this variable is itself determined by those who are affected by it.

Appendix to Chapter 7

Estimated regression equations: dependent variable = DEGREE SCORE

Explanatory variables	1982/83		1983/84		1984/85		1985/86	
	(1)	*(2)*	*(1)*	*(2)*	*(1)*	*(2)*	*(1)*	*(2)*
CONSTANT	47.71	48.82	47.87	47.60	47.49	49.35	50.25	51.31
	(37.49)	(37.56)	(38.66)	(37.68)	(29.45)	(34.02)	(28.60)	(29.09)
ALEVEL	0.65	0.57	0.64	0.67	0.66	0.59	0.50	0.48
	(6.28)	(5.49)	(6.49)	(6.89)	(5.15)	(5.28)	(3.38)	(3.28)
LIVEHOME	−0.071	−0.081	−0.061	−0.060	−0.048	−0.070	−0.051	−0.075
	(−6.14)	(−4.93)	(−5.84)	(−4.02)	(−3.55)	(−4.16)	(−3.38)	(−3.60)
EXCAT	2.61	2.34	2.33	2.09	2.20	2.03	2.08	1.82
	(6.90)	(6.41)	(6.97)	(6.63)	(5.62)	(6.14)	(4.90)	(4.64)
NEW	0.91	1.09	0.91	1.15	0.70	1.03	0.60	0.90
	(2.20)	(2.55)	(2.52)	(3.14)	(1.58)	(2.62)	(1.25)	(1.88)
SCOTTISH	−4.02		−3.66		−3.46		−3.24	
	(−10.26)		(−10.34)		(−7.96)		(−6.56)	
LIBRARY	0.79	0.73	0.76	0.76	0.82	0.57	0.66	0.51
	(5.21)	(4.75)	(5.42)	(5.69)	(4.17)	(3.40)	(3.53)	(2.84)
$\bar{R}^2$	0.91	0.80	0.91	0.82	0.87	0.79	0.82	0.70

Notes:
1. ( ) = *t*-ratios
2. Oxford is excluded from the regression analyses for 1982/83, 1983/84 and 1984/85 since a large proportion of seconds were undivided until 1985/86
3. Scottish universities are excluded from equation (2) in all three years
4. For further results see J. Johnes and Taylor (1987)
5. Definition of variables

DEGREE SCORE	= as defined on pp. 103–4
ALEVEL	= average A level score of A level qualified undergraduate entrants three years previously: A = 5, B = 4, C = 3, D = 2, E = 1
LIVEHOME	= percentage of each university's students living at home
EXCAT	= binary variable for ex-colleges of advanced technology; EXCAT = 1 for ex-CATS and 0 otherwise
NEW	= binary variable for new greenfield universities; NEW = 1 for new university and 0 otherwise
SCOTTISH	= binary variable for Scottish universities; SCOTTISH = 1 for universities located in Scotland and 0 otherwise
LIBRARY	= recurrent library expenditure (excluding wages and salaries) as a percentage of total recurrent expenditure

Source: J. Johnes and Taylor 1987.

Estimated regression equations: dependent variable = DEGREE RESULT

Explanatory variables	1982/83		1983/84		1984/85		1985/86	
	(1)	*(2)*	*(1)*	*(2)*	*(1)*	*(2)*	*(1)*	*(2)*
CONSTANT	−7.34	−5.32	−7.84	−10.95	−11.15	−9.50	−3.26	−3.18
	(−1.28)	(−0.81)	(−1.45)	(−1.72)	(−2.08)	(−1.54)	(−0.57)	(−0.52)
ALEVEL	3.85	3.73	3.89	4.13	3.76	3.78	3.26	3.45
	(8.22)	(7.05)	(9.30)	(8.48)	(8.83)	(7.92)	(6.84)	(6.79)
LIVEHOME	−0.10	−0.15	−0.14	−0.11	−0.06	−0.08	−0.05	−0.06
	(−1.76)	(−1.80)	(−3.07)	(−1.45)	(−1.43)	(−1.07)	(−1.01)	(−0.87)
EXCAT	8.50	8.26	7.87	7.32	8.25	7.95	7.05	6.62
	(5.15)	(4.46)	(5.41)	(4.61)	(6.35)	(5.67)	(5.13)	(4.86)
NEW	4.60	4.40	3.98	4.56	2.42	3.44	2.88	4.17
	(2.54)	(2.04)	(2.52)	(2.46)	(1.64)	(2.05)	(1.86)	(2.50)
SCOTTISH	−8.25		−7.08		−6.41		−6.85	
	(−4.85)		(−4.59)		(−4.44)		(−4.29)	
LIBRARY	2.03	1.96	2.24	2.34	3.37	2.88	2.94	2.38
	(3.10)	(2.53)	(3.69)	(3.46)	(5.18)	(4.06)	(4.86)	(3.85)
$\bar{R}^2$	0.80	0.71	0.83	0.77	0.84	0.80	0.80	0.78

Notes:
1. See notes to previous table
2. A t-ratio $\geqslant 1.96$ indicates significance at the 5% level or less; a t-ratio $\geqslant 2.58$ indicates significance at the 1% level or less (using a two-tailed test)
3. Definition of variables
   DEGREE RESULT = percentage of graduates with a first or upper second (see pp. 103–4 for precise definition)

Source: J. Johnes and Taylor 1987.

8

The First Destination of New Graduates: Differences between Universities

Introduction

Every year, the Careers Advisory Service at each UK university collects information describing the first destinations of their new graduates. These data are collected in order to provide universities with information about the success or otherwise of their graduates in either obtaining a job or proceeding to further study or training. The extent to which a university's graduates have been successful in obtaining a satisfactory first destination is of interest since it allows each university to compare its performance with that of all other universities. Not surprisingly, this has led to the construction of league tables which aim to show which universities have done well and which universities have done badly in producing employable graduates. Publication of these league tables has been defended on the grounds that they provide useful information both to potential university students and to employers of university graduates.

There is, however, a more ominous reason for the recent interest in inter-university differences in the success of graduates in obtaining a satisfactory first destination. The government has made it clear that the success of graduates in the job market is an important indicator of the performance of the university sector. The 1987 White Paper, for example, argued that

> the subsequent employment patterns of students provide some indication of the value of higher education courses to working life.
>
> (DES 1987b: 18)

The use of the first destinations data for constructing performance indicators raises several pertinent questions. Do differences between universities in the success of graduates in obtaining a satisfactory first destination accurately reflect corresponding differences in the value to the economy of each university's graduates? Are universities which have a high proportion of graduates proceeding to permanent employment more efficient and more effective than universities with a low proportion? Indeed, can we rely on the first destinations data for comparing the performance of graduates from different universities in obtaining a satisfactory first destination? All these questions must be answered in the affirmative if the first destinations data are to be used to construct performance indicators.

It is the purpose of this chapter to evaluate the first destinations data as a source of indicators which can be used to assess the performance of individual institutions. Attention is focused on three indicators: the percentage of each university's graduates obtaining a permanent job, the percentage proceeding to further study or training, and the percentage believed to be unemployed six months after graduation. The remainder of this chapter is in five sections. The first section describes the first destinations data and defines three indicators of each university's perform- ance. The second section examines inter-university differences in these three indicators during recent years. The possible reasons for these inter-university disparities in the first destination performance of gradu- ates are then discussed in the third section and these are investigated in a statistical analysis in the fourth section. The fifth section investigates the possibility of constructing performance indicators based upon the first destination of graduates.

The first destination of university graduates

Information is collected annually by the Careers Advisory Service describ- ing the first destination of each university's new crop of graduates. Information is available for 112 separately identifiable subjects (77 subjects before 1986) and for 51 institutions (including the individual Colleges of the University of Wales). Graduates are classified into one of the following six main categories:

1. those entering permanent employment
2. those proceeding to further education or training
3. those believed to be unemployed
4. those currently in a short-term job which is not expected to last for more than three months
5. those not available for employment or further study
6. those whose first destination is unknown.

The purpose of the annual First Destination Survey is to provide each institution with a record of how many of each new crop of graduates in each subject have obtained a satisfactory first destination and how many have failed to do so. This database provides useful feedback information for university careers advisers, who can use the information to help future graduates.

The proportion of graduates in each of the six main first destination categories is given for UK graduates as a whole in Table 8.1 for the years 1976–88. The most striking feature of Table 8.1 is the increasing trend in

Table 8.1 First destination of university graduates 1976–88[1]

| First destination | Year of graduation: % in each category[2] | | | | | | | | | | | | |
	1976	1977	1978	1979	1980	1981	1982	1983	1984	1985	1986	1987	1988
Permanent employment	43.1	46.4	48.7	49.7	50.6	47.6	47.1	49.1	51.8	53.7	54.3	56.0	56.0
Further education or training	34.0	30.5	29.3	26.8	26.7	27.2	25.7	24.7	23.6	22.5	23.5	22.1	21.6
Believed to be unemployed	5.7	5.3	4.4	4.6	8.1	10.2	12.1	10.3	8.6	7.6	6.6	5.6	5.1
Short-term employment	6.2	6.7	6.4	6.6	2.7	2.8	2.6	3.0	3.0	3.0	3.2	3.2	3.4
Unknown destination	9.4	9.3	9.4	9.9	9.4	9.6	10.3	10.8	10.6	10.8	10.4	10.0	9.9
Other[3]	1.7	1.9	1.8	2.3	2.5	2.5	2.3	2.1	2.4	2.5	3.0	3.2	3.9

Notes:
1. These data refer to UK domestically domiciled graduates
2. Errors in summation are due to rounding
3. 'Other' includes those not available for employment or for further education or training

Source: Universities' Statistical Record, Cheltenham.

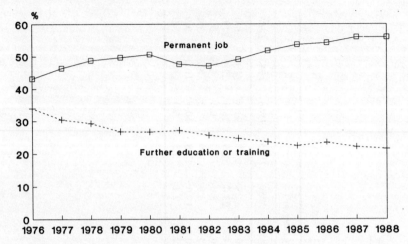

Figure 8.1   Percentage of new graduates proceeding to a permanent job or to further education or training, 1976–88

Source: Universities' Statistical Record, Cheltenham.

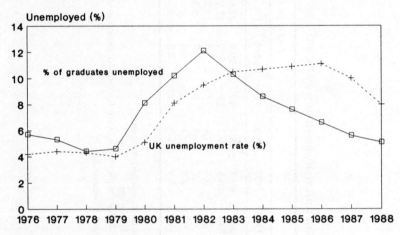

Figure 8.2   Percentage of new graduates believed to be unemployed six months after graduation, 1976–88

Source: Universities' Statistical Record, Cheltenham.

the proportion of graduates entering permanent employment – from 43 per cent in 1976 to 56 per cent in 1988 (see Figure 8.1). The opposite trend has occurred in the proportion of graduates proceeding to further education or training. The other interesting trend is the sharp fall in the proportion of unemployed graduates from the peak of 12 per cent reached in 1982 to under 6 per cent in 1988 (see Figure 8.2).

The success (or otherwise) of each university's graduates in obtaining a satisfactory first destination can be measured in various ways. The three measures constructed and evaluated in this chapter are as follows. First, following G. Johnes *et al.* (1987), a measure of the extent to which graduates have failed to obtain a satisfactory first destination is calculated by expressing the number of graduates who were either still unemployed or in a short-term job as a percentage of total graduates (but excluding those not available for employment and those whose first destination is unknown). This is given by

$$UNEMP = \frac{\text{Graduates believed to be unemployed} + \text{Graduates obtaining a short-term job}}{\substack{\text{Graduates} \\ \text{entering} \\ \text{permanent} \\ \text{employment}} + \substack{\text{Graduates} \\ \text{obtaining a} \\ \text{short-term} \\ \text{job}} + \substack{\text{Graduates} \\ \text{proceeding} \\ \text{to further} \\ \text{education or} \\ \text{training}} + \substack{\text{Graduates} \\ \text{believed to} \\ \text{be} \\ \text{unemployed}}} \times 100$$

Second, two indicators can be constructed, following Taylor (1986a, 1986b), which are based upon the extent to which graduates obtained a satisfactory first destination. One is based upon those graduates obtaining permanent employment (EMPLOY) and the other is based upon those graduates proceeding to further education or training (FURTHER). The same denominator is used as for UNEMP given above:

$$EMPLOY = \frac{\text{Graduates entering permanent employment}}{\substack{\text{Graduates} \\ \text{entering} \\ \text{permanent} \\ \text{employment}} + \substack{\text{Graduates} \\ \text{obtaining a} \\ \text{short-term} \\ \text{job}} + \substack{\text{Graduates} \\ \text{proceeding} \\ \text{to further} \\ \text{education or} \\ \text{training}} + \substack{\text{Graduates} \\ \text{believed to} \\ \text{be} \\ \text{unemployed}}} \times 100$$

$$FURTHER = \frac{\text{Graduates proceeding to further education or training}}{\substack{\text{Graduates} \\ \text{entering} \\ \text{permanent} \\ \text{employment}} + \substack{\text{Graduates} \\ \text{obtaining a} \\ \text{short-term} \\ \text{job}} + \substack{\text{Graduates} \\ \text{proceeding} \\ \text{to further} \\ \text{education or} \\ \text{training}} + \substack{\text{Graduates} \\ \text{believed to} \\ \text{be} \\ \text{unemployed}}} \times 100$$

It should be noted that these three first destination indicators sum to 100 per cent. This means that UNEMP is a composite measure of EMPLOY and FURTHER (since UNEMP = 100 − EMPLOY − FURTHER). The advantage of dividing UNEMP into two component parts is that it provides more information about the relative success of each university's graduates in obtaining a satisfactory first destination. This division proves to be useful later on in this chapter when attempts are made to explain inter-university disparities in the first destinations of each university's graduates.

At first sight, the annual First Destination Survey appears to provide extremely valuable information about inter-university disparities in the success (or otherwise) of their graduates in obtaining a satisfactory first destination. The fact that the three indicators defined above (UNEMP, EMPLOY and FURTHER) can be computed for each university leads inevitably towards making comparisons between universities. Before doing so, however, it is necessary to inject a note of caution concerning the accuracy of the first destinations data itself.

There are three main problems with the first destinations data. First, not all universities stick rigidly to the 31 December deadline laid down by the Universities Statistical Record, Cheltenham, which collates and publishes the data after individual institutions have collected it. This means that those universities which collect data after the deadline are more likely to have a higher proportion of graduates in one of the two successful first destination categories (and a smaller proportion either unemployed or in a short-term job). Second, the data collection methods vary between institutions. Some universities collect data only from the graduates themselves while others acquire the information from wherever they can get it – such as from heads of academic departments and from graduates' parents. Whether these differences in data collection methods result in any bias in the data is unknown. Third, the percentage of graduates in the unknowns category varies substantially between universities (typically from under 5 per cent to over 20 per cent at some universities). If the unknowns tend to be unsuccessful in obtaining a satisfactory first destination, the three first destination measures defined above will favour those universities with a high percentage of unknowns.

Since there is no way of checking the accuracy of the first destinations data, any indicators based upon the first destination of graduates need to be treated with considerable caution. Ideally the data collection methods should be standardized and subject to audit.

Differences between universities in the first destination of graduates

This section provides information for each university about two of the three first destination indicators defined above. Information is provided only for the proportion of graduates obtaining a permanent job (EMPLOY) and for the proportion proceeding to further education or training (FURTHER) since the proportion unemployed (UNEMP) can be obtained from the following identity:

$$UNEMP = 100 - EMPLOY - FURTHER$$

Data describing the proportion of graduates from each university who either entered a permanent job or proceeded to further education or training are given in Table 8.2 for the years 1982/83 to 1987/88. The two

Table 8.2 Percentage of graduates entering permanent employment and proceeding to further education or training, 1982/83 to 1987/88

(a) Percentage of graduates entering permanent employment (EMPLOY)

University	1982/83	1983/84	1984/85	1985/86	1986/87	1987/88
Aston	74.0	77.3	80.5	77.7	84.7	86.6
Bath	70.6	75.9	81.7	76.9	78.7	81.6
Birmingham	59.9	63.8	65.9	65.7	64.8	68.2
Bradford	67.8	72.9	75.6	80.6	78.5	75.8
Bristol	57.5	61.3	61.9	61.6	66.2	68.7
Brunel	73.5	79.6	83.2	78.0	77.2	80.6
Cambridge	53.4	55.2	57.5	53.2	56.0	54.6
City	82.5	86.5	85.0	89.7	88.0	86.1
Durham	55.8	57.9	61.2	60.0	64.8	62.4
East Anglia	47.3	48.0	51.8	52.5	57.5	58.3
Essex	45.3	49.4	55.2	53.5	55.4	58.6
Exeter	59.5	62.3	64.8	62.8	62.5	64.7
Hull	42.3	48.8	56.8	62.3	63.5	65.1
Keele	49.7	49.0	55.2	53.4	59.6	51.2
Kent	51.6	53.1	57.5	62.9	61.7	66.6
Lancaster	51.3	59.6	64.6	66.6	65.3	67.7
Leeds	53.8	57.9	59.9	58.8	64.7	66.0
Leicester	51.4	53.8	58.8	57.0	62.7	57.3
Liverpool	54.7	60.3	58.4	59.5	63.2	63.3
London	60.1	60.3	61.9	64.8	67.3	66.1
Loughborough	74.2	75.3	78.2	79.2	76.0	75.8
Manchester	58.3	60.6	60.5	62.6	65.9	67.5
UMIST	71.0	72.7	76.3	79.4	77.2	73.5
Newcastle	62.6	66.2	69.7	71.5	70.8	72.4
Nottingham	58.8	61.5	62.6	68.2	64.9	70.6
Oxford	52.5	52.0	56.2	55.4	56.4	55.0
Reading	58.2	64.7	67.5	69.4	73.0	68.5
Salford	63.9	72.8	71.9	74.4	73.8	81.1
Sheffield	51.0	58.5	62.3	62.3	63.4	62.7
Southampton	67.2	68.8	69.4	68.3	70.9	68.0
Surrey	66.6	72.9	75.9	76.7	76.1	72.5
Sussex	40.9	49.4	56.2	57.6	59.0	56.9
Warwick	61.8	62.5	63.7	65.0	66.0	67.6
York	53.0	58.2	59.3	56.9	59.3	61.2
Aberdeen	45.5	52.7	54.6	55.8	59.1	61.1
Dundee	54.4	53.8	61.7	57.7	60.8	62.8
Edinburgh	50.4	54.2	58.9	57.2	61.3	62.9
Glasgow	52.1	55.2	59.1	57.1	58.6	60.5
Heriot-Watt	72.4	74.2	76.2	71.5	71.5	75.2
St Andrews	38.5	41.1	47.2	46.9	50.5	55.3
Stirling	56.8	60.1	67.7	62.2	65.7	70.4
Strathclyde	60.9	68.2	70.1	68.7	70.9	71.0
Queen's	50.6	47.7	48.7	51.3	54.6	59.1
Ulster	41.2	47.2	62.8	59.6	64.3	67.3
Wales	45.7	52.0	54.0	56.6	55.9	56.8

Table 8.2   Continued

(b) Percentage of graduates proceeding to further education or training (FURTHER)

University	1982/83	1983/84	1984/85	1985/86	1986/87	1987/88
Aston	15.1	11.6	12.3	12.6	8.7	8.0
Bath	14.9	15.2	13.2	14.5	14.6	12.6
Birmingham	30.1	27.1	23.6	26.1	26.2	25.2
Bradford	16.8	12.8	12.0	10.4	11.1	11.9
Bristol	26.5	27.2	25.1	26.6	23.5	22.8
Brunel	17.2	13.0	11.7	15.6	16.6	16.0
Cambridge	39.1	37.8	34.5	37.6	35.7	36.8
City	8.3	6.9	8.2	5.6	6.7	8.7
Durham	36.9	31.7	32.7	33.5	30.3	31.4
East Anglia	32.6	30.6	28.7	30.4	23.7	27.8
Essex	33.9	29.3	32.5	33.0	32.4	32.6
Exeter	25.1	26.0	25.1	27.1	24.2	24.2
Hull	29.7	29.6	29.6	28.1	27.7	27.4
Keele	36.4	34.0	27.5	32.7	31.0	31.6
Kent	30.2	31.5	25.0	22.3	28.8	26.3
Lancaster	32.9	28.3	22.5	24.0	26.0	24.6
Leeds	27.2	26.3	25.4	26.5	23.5	23.6
Leicester	35.4	31.3	30.3	32.3	28.1	33.3
Liverpool	28.5	25.8	24.2	23.9	21.7	23.8
London	24.3	24.2	23.9	23.4	23.4	23.2
Loughborough	14.2	13.0	11.0	9.8	14.0	12.9
Manchester	25.7	23.4	25.7	25.4	22.8	20.9
UMIST	15.8	14.4	12.3	12.7	13.6	14.9
Newcastle	28.6	24.3	20.9	21.0	21.9	19.2
Nottingham	25.0	26.7	24.4	22.2	25.0	19.4
Oxford	36.3	37.2	35.5	35.1	36.5	36.8
Reading	24.5	22.9	18.3	21.4	19.1	24.1
Salford	20.8	15.9	14.3	15.4	15.6	12.5
Sheffield	27.7	26.7	21.5	24.8	24.1	23.4
Southampton	24.8	23.1	23.0	22.1	23.0	24.1
Surrey	19.7	14.7	13.3	14.1	16.3	18.9
Sussex	33.7	30.7	29.7	26.3	30.1	29.5
Warwick	26.5	23.0	22.3	24.7	20.7	21.2
York	31.8	30.5	26.9	29.6	31.7	24.6
Aberdeen	38.2	32.5	35.5	34.0	32.6	32.4
Dundee	35.6	37.9	31.1	34.2	30.8	30.0
Edinburgh	32.7	33.1	30.3	30.4	28.0	26.2
Glasgow	36.8	34.6	32.2	32.3	32.2	32.0
Heriot-Watt	19.0	20.1	18.8	17.1	20.8	18.2
St Andrews	44.9	48.9	41.6	44.2	42.8	32.3
Stirling	25.0	20.6	19.2	20.9	16.7	18.7
Strathclyde	24.5	19.7	20.0	21.7	21.1	20.6
Queen's	35.5	37.3	34.5	37.1	35.9	33.2
Ulster	18.9	25.0	18.9	20.5	18.0	16.6
Wales	32.0	32.5	31.1	30.8	31.3	31.2

Note: See p. 125 for definition of EMPLOY and FURTHER.

main features of the first destinations data given in Table 8.2 are, first, the existence of vast differences in EMPLOY and FURTHER between universities, and second, the remarkable stability in EMPLOY and FURTHER over time within each university. The proportion obtaining a permanent job, for example, varied between 51.2 per cent at Keele and 86.6 per cent at Aston in 1988, indicating that Aston's graduates have been much more successful in obtaining permanent jobs than those at Keele. On the other hand, 31.6 per cent of Keele's graduates proceeded to further education or training in 1988 compared to only 8 per cent at Aston. Further scrutiny of Table 8.2 indicates that the ex-colleges of advanced technology have a substantially higher proportion of graduates entering permanent jobs than other universities and a much lower proportion proceeding to further education or training.

The remarkable stability over time in both EMPLOY and FURTHER within individual universities suggests the existence of some underlying determining forces. These are discussed in the next section.

Inter-university differences in the first destination of graduates: some possible explanations

A wide range of factors may be expected to have an effect on the first destination of each university's graduates. Since previous empirical work indicates that subject mix is by far the most important explanatory variable, this is treated separately from other possible explanatory variables. The other factors which may be expected to exert some influence on the first destination of each university's graduates are divided into two broad groups: those which are student-related and those which relate to the universities themselves.

Subject mix

The first destination of new graduates varies substantially between degree subjects. This is clear from Table 8.3, which provides information for three first destination categories (EMPLOY, FURTHER and UNEMP) for each subject at national level. Variations between subjects for all three categories are seen to be extremely large. This is especially true for the percentage of graduates proceeding to further education or training which varies from under 1 per cent in medicine and dentistry to over 35 per cent in biological sciences, physical sciences, social sciences and creative arts. The variation between subjects in the percentage of graduates obtaining permanent employment is also wide. Moreover, the broad categorization of subjects used in Table 8.3 conceals wide variations in the first destination of graduates between subjects within the same category. Within the social

Table 8.3   The first destination of UK graduates by subject, 1987/88

Subject group	EMPLOY	FURTHER	UNEMP
Medicine and dentistry	99.3	0.6	0.1
Studies allied to medicine	83.2	13.5	3.4
Biological sciences	51.2	35.9	12.9
Veterinary science, agriculture and related studies	77.2	14.4	8.4
Physical sciences	53.2	36.0	10.8
Mathematical sciences	72.7	20.1	7.2
Engineering and technology	83.3	11.6	5.1
Architecture and related studies	79.0	17.7	3.3
Social sciences	48.7	40.0	11.3
Business and financial studies	87.5	6.0	6.5
Librarianship and information science	66.3	14.5	19.3
Languages and related studies	54.5	13.7	31.7
Humanities	51.2	31.1	17.8
Creative arts	47.9	39.6	12.5
Education	87.9	5.9	6.1

Note:
See p. 125 for definitions of EMPLOY, FURTHER and UNEMP.
EMPLOY + FURTHER + UNEMP = 100. Errors in summation are due to rounding.
Source: Universities' Statistical Record, Cheltenham.

sciences category, for example, around 13 per cent of graduates proceeded to further education or training in economics compared with 78 per cent in law.

These variations in the first destination of graduates between subjects raise an interesting and important question: why do graduates in some subjects obtain a job more quickly than graduates in other subjects? One reason is that graduates with vocationally related degrees such as electrical engineering, accountancy and architecture are likely to take a job which is directly related to their degree subject and this will narrow the range of occupational opportunities which they are likely to consider. By contrast, graduates in subjects which are not so vocationally oriented (such as English, history, biology and geography) are more likely to undertake a wider search of the job market to find a satisfactory job. This could have the effect of lengthening the duration of the job search for graduates in non-vocational subjects. The high positive correlation between the degree of concentration of graduates in specific occupational categories and the proportion of graduates who obtain a permanent job (across degree subjects) confirms this explanation (see Taylor and Johnes 1989).

A second reason why graduates in vocationally related subjects obtain jobs more quickly than in other subjects is that they are likely to be of more immediate value to employers since they will require less training than graduates with degrees in less vocationally related subjects. This does not mean, of course, that graduates in less vocationally related subjects necessarily have poorer career prospects over the longer term. The labour market advantages possessed by graduates with vocationally related degrees may be temporary.

Whatever the reason for these differences between *subjects* in the first destination experience of graduates, it is clear that inter-university differences in *subject mix* are likely to play a considerable part in explaining inter-university differences in the first destination of graduates. The influence of each university's subject mix on the first destination of its graduates can be measured by calculating an *expected* value of EMPLOY and FURTHER (and hence UNEMP) for each university. An expected value of EMPLOY (i.e. EMPLOY^e), for example, can be calculated from two sets of information:

1. the subject mix of each institution
2. the national proportion of graduates obtaining a permanent job in each separately identifiable subject.

The *expected* value of EMPLOY is simply the proportion of graduates obtaining a permanent job which any given university would be *expected* to have, given each university's subject mix and national values of EMPLOY for each subject. A similar measure can be calculated for FURTHER. The calculation of these two measures is explained in the appendix to this chapter (pp. 143–4).

Once expected values have been calculated for EMPLOY and FURTHER (and hence UNEMP), it is then possible to examine the extent

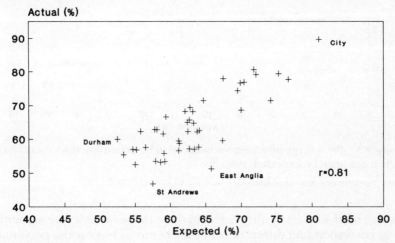

Figure 8.3 Percentage of graduates obtaining permanent employment: actual v. expected, 1985/86

Source: Universities' Statistical Record, Cheltenham (unpublished data).

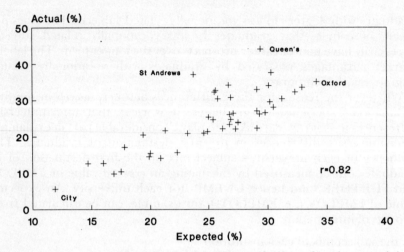

Figure 8.4   Percentage of graduates proceeding to further education or training: actual v. expected, 1985/86

Source: Universities' Statistical Record, Cheltenham (unpublished data).

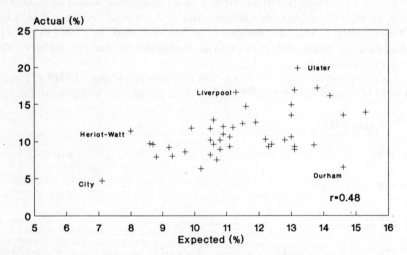

Figure 8.5   Percentage of graduates believed to be unemployed six months after graduation: actual v. expected, 1985/86

Source: Universities' Statistical Record, Cheltenham (unpublished data).

to which inter-university differences in these three variables are accounted for by corresponding differences in subject mix. Thus for the percentage of graduates obtaining a permanent job, Figure 8.3 shows that EMPLOY is highly positively correlated with EMPLOY^e ($r = 0.81$). Similar results are obtained by plotting the actual and expected values of FURTHER and

UNEMP (see Figures 8.4 and 8.5). Subject mix obviously plays a crucial role in determining the first destination experience of each university's graduates.

Further scrutiny of the relationship between the *actual* and the *expected* percentage of each university's graduates proceeding to a permanent job reveals that the ex-colleges of advanced technology have a favourable subject mix while the new greenfield universities have an unfavourable subject mix. This is not surprising since the ex-colleges of advanced technology tend to have a high proportion of vocationally related courses compared to the more academically oriented new universities. City, for example, had an extremely favourable subject mix as far as EMPLOY is concerned, whereas East Anglia had a very unfavourable subject mix.

Student-related factors

Many personal characteristics are likely to affect the first destination of individual graduates. These will include gender, personality, ambition, ability, social background and peer group influence. In investigating inter-university variations in the first destination of graduates, however, only a limited range of variables can be constructed which reflect inter-institutional differences in the personal characteristics of students. The dearth of information about the characteristics of graduates at the institutional level may not be a serious drawback since many of these personal factors are likely to be more important in explaining differences in first destination between *individuals* rather than differences in first destination between *institutions*. Some of the personality factors affecting individual behaviour may be expected to disappear in the averaging process.

Three student-related factors which are known to vary between universities and which may be expected to affect a graduate's first destination are

1. academic ability
2. social background
3. gender.

How is each of these three factors likely to affect the first destination of graduates? In particular, how are they likely to affect the proportion of graduates obtaining a permanent job or proceeding to further education and training?

The effect of the academic ability of students on the proportion of graduates obtaining a permanent job is expected to be positive since the most able students are likely to be more successful in the competition for permanent jobs. Using the average A level score of each institution and the percentage of firsts and upper seconds achieved by each university's graduates to measure the academic ability of each institution's graduates, we expect these two variables to be positively related to the proportion obtaining a permanent job. The expected relationship between these two variables and the proportion proceeding to further education or training is, however, ambiguous since not only will the best qualified tend to proceed to higher degrees but also those with the worst qualifications may have to undertake further education or training in order to improve their chances of obtaining a satisfactory job.

Social background can be expected to affect the first destination of graduates in so far as those graduates with a middle-class background are likely to have better contacts in the job market (or are able to draw upon better advice about opportunities in the job market from their parents). Although there is no direct measure of the social background of students at the institutional level, the percentage of each university's graduates who had previously attended either an independent school or a grammar school can be used as a proxy for social background. This variable is expected to be positively related to the proportion obtaining a permanent job but is not expected to have any effect on the proportion proceeding to further education or training.

Finally, the sex of graduates may influence their first destination. The male/female graduate ratio is therefore included as an explanatory variable.

University-related factors

Several factors relating to universities themselves may be expected to influence the first destination of their graduates. The most obvious of these factors is the efficiency of each university's careers advisory service. A well-run and well-funded careers advisory service should help to raise the proportion of graduates who obtain a satisfactory first destination. This is likely to be the case for FURTHER as well as EMPLOY since the careers service provides information about further education and training as well as about jobs. Two variables are used to measure the influence of the careers service: the student/careers staff ratio and the number of students per employer visit to each university on the annual 'milk-round'. The student/careers staff ratio is expected to have a negative effect on both EMPLOY and FURTHER. The effect of students per milk-round visitor, on the other hand, may have opposite effects on EMPLOY and FURTHER. The more students there are per milk-round visitor, the lower the chance of obtaining a job offer, hence giving rise to a negative relationship between this variable and EMPLOY. The effect of students per milk-round visitor on FURTHER is likely to be in the opposite direction to its effect on EMPLOY, however, since students who are not successful in obtaining permanent employment are likely to turn to the next best alternative – a place on a further education and training course (see Figure 8.6).

Other university-related factors which may have an effect upon the first

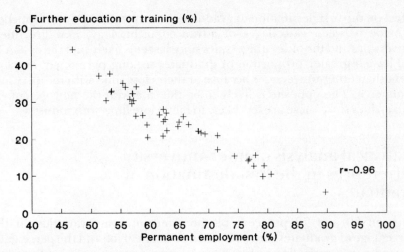

Figure 8.6 Graduates obtaining a permanent job v. graduates proceeding to further education or training, 1985/86

Note: Each point represents a university
Sources: Universities' Statistical Record, Cheltenham.

destination of graduates include age, size, location, research reputation (measured by the UFC research rating) and the student/staff ratio. In addition, universities can be characterized as belonging to several different general 'types': ex-colleges of advanced technology, new greenfield universities and the older civic universities. How are these various characteristics likely to affect inter-university variations in EMPLOY and FURTHER?

Two of these university-related factors are likely to be of particular significance in their effect on the first destination of graduates. First, the location of a university will affect the job prospects of graduates since those located in peripheral regions will be further away from the main job centres (particularly the south east) and will have fewer opportunities to visit employers before their final examinations. Moreover, graduates of universities located in regions of high unemployment will have fewer job opportunities 'on their doorstep' thus reducing the chances of finding a suitable job. EMPLOY can therefore be expected to be negatively affected by these two location factors while FURTHER will be affected in the opposite direction (since those graduates who fail to obtain a suitable job will have an incentive to find a place on a further education or training course). The influence of the location of a university is measured by two variables: the unemployment rate of the region in which a university is located and a binary variable to indicate whether or not a university is located in a peripheral geographical area (defined as Scotland, Wales or Northern Ireland in the empirical analysis in the next section).

The second important university-related factor which is likely to have an effect on the first destination of graduates is 'university type'. A distinction is made between ex-colleges of advanced technology, new greenfield universities and the older universities since it seems likely that the ex-CATs will have a greater proportion of graduates seeking permanent employment than other universities because of their close links with industry and commerce. The opposite is likely to be the case with the new greenfield universities since these are less likely to have close links with industry.

Statistical analysis of inter-university differences in the first destination of graduates

Between 60 and 70 per cent of the inter-university variation in the percentage of graduates who obtained a permanent job and the percentage of graduates proceeding to further education or training is explained by corresponding variations in subject mix (see Figures 8.3 and 8.4). The next step is to investigate the extent to which the remaining *unexplained* variation (of between 30 and 40 per cent) can be explained by other factors, such as those described as either student-related or university-related in the previous section. Since attention is now focused on the percentage of graduates who obtained a permanent job (EMPLOY) and the percentage who proceeded to further education or training (FURTHER), the two variables to be investigated in this section are:

$$EMP = EMPLOY - EMPLOY^e$$
$$\text{and} \quad FUR = FURTHER - FURTHER^e$$

where

EMPLOY   = percentage of graduates obtaining a permanent job
$EMPLOY^e$ = percentage of graduates *expected* to obtain a permanent job given each university's subject mix
FURTHER = percentage of graduates proceeding to further education or training
$FURTHER^e$ = percentage of graduates *expected* to proceed to further education or training given each university's subject mix.

Multiple regression analysis was used to test the extent to which EMP and FUR could be explained (statistically) by the student-related and university-related variables discussed in the previous section. These tests were carried out for four separate years during 1983–86 using only forty-three universities in the analysis (Belfast and Ulster were excluded because they were found to be having undue influence on the estimated coefficients). Since not all the variables specified in the previous section as potential determinants of EMP and FUR were found to be statistically significant in the regression analysis, only the most satisfactory results (from a statistical point of view) are given in the appendix (pp. 143–5). For example,

statistical testing indicated that the following variables were unrelated to
EMP and FUR: the male/female graduate ratio, the student/careers staff
ratio, the student/academic staff ratio, number of full-time students, and
the UFC research rating. The most surprising of these results is the lack of
any relationship between the student/careers staff ratio and the first
destinations of a university's graduates.

The regression equations given in the appendix indicate that three
variables are consistently associated with the difference between the *actual*
and the *expected* value of the proportion of graduates obtaining a
permanent job. These were whether a university was an ex-college of
advanced technology; whether a university was located in Wales or
Scotland; and the number of graduates per employer visit. Ex-colleges of
advanced technology were found to have a substantially higher proportion
of graduates obtaining a permanent job (by about four or five percentage
points on average). Universities located in Scotland and Wales appear to
have a significantly lower percentage of graduates obtaining a permanent
job (by as much as five or six percentage points on average). The number of
graduates per employer visit had the predicted negative effect on the
proportion of graduates proceeding to permanent employment.

There is some evidence that a university's mean A level score of
undergraduate entrants, the school background of its students and its age
also affect the proportion of graduates obtaining a permanent job.
Statistically significant results, however, were obtained only for one or two
of the four years included in the statistical analysis.

The results obtained in the statistical analysis of inter-university variations in FUR (see appendix) were generally more satisfactory than those in
the statistical analysis of EMP. Five of the explanatory variables had
estimated coefficients which were statistically significant in at least three of
the four years. These were graduates per employer visit, age of university,
regional unemployment rate, location (in Scotland or Wales) and whether a
university is an ex-college of advanced technology. All these explanatory
variables had the expected effect on the difference between the *actual* and
the *expected* proportion of graduates proceeding to further education or
training.

It has therefore been shown that

1. around 70 per cent of the inter-university variation in the proportion of
   graduates obtaining permanent jobs or proceeding to further education
   or training is explained by corresponding inter-university variations in
   subject mix (when Belfast and Ulster are excluded);
2. about 50 per cent of the remaining variation in inter-university
   variations in the proportion of graduates obtaining a permanent job
   which is *not* explained by subject mix is explained by other factors such
   as age of university and whether a university is an ex-college of
   advanced technology;
3. about 65 per cent of the remaining variation in inter-university

variations in the proportion of graduates proceeding to further education and training which is *not* explained by subject mix is explained by factors such as graduates per employer visit (on the annual milk-round), age of university, the regional unemployment rate, whether a university is located in Scotland or Wales, and whether it is an ex-college of advanced technology.

Hence around 90 per cent of the variation in the proportion of graduates obtaining a permanent job or proceeding to further education or training can be explained (statistically) by several of the variables suggested as possible determinants in the previous section.

Construction of a performance indicator based upon the first destination of graduates

In the previous two sections, it was shown that inter-university variations in the first destination of graduates can be explained (statistically) by several plausible explanatory variables, the main one being subject mix. Some universities have a subject mix which can be *expected* to lead to a very high proportion of its graduates obtaining a permanent job whereas other universities have a comparatively 'unfavourable' mix on this particular performance measure. Similarly some universities have a subject mix which can be *expected* to lead to a high proportion of its graduates proceeding to further education or training whereas exactly the opposite pertains in other universities. Subject mix therefore determines, to a very large extent, the first destination performance of each university's graduates. Even so, subject mix is not the only factor influencing inter-university differences in the first destination of graduates. This is clear from the results of the regression analysis reported in the previous section.

If a performance indicator is to be constructed on the basis of the first destination performance of each university's graduates, it is essential to take account of inter-university differences in the various explanatory variables. It would not be appropriate, for example, to compare the first destination of graduates between universities unless inter-university differences in subject mix were first taken into account. A similar argument holds for some of the other explanatory variables, such as the influence of the number of employers visiting a university on the proportion of graduates obtaining a permanent job, or the influence of job market opportunities (in the region in which a university is located) on the proportion of graduates proceeding to further education or training.

Thus if the performance of universities is to be assessed on the basis of the first destination of graduates, it is necessary to *standardize* for inter-university differences in factors such as subject mix. A set of standardized performance indicators based upon the first destination of graduates can be constructed by taking into account *all* the factors which are statistically significant in explaining inter-university variations in the first destination variables. A performance indicator based upon the proportion of graduates obtaining a permanent job can be constructed as follows:

1. Inter-university differences in subject mix have already been taken into account by calculating the *expected* proportion of graduates proceeding to a permanent job:

$$EMP = EMPLOY - EMPLOY^e$$

where

EMPLOY = proportion of graduates obtaining a permanent job
$EMPLOY^e$ = proportion of graduates *expected* to obtain a permanent job given each university's subject mix (see pp. 143–4).

2. Inter-university differences in EMP can be partly explained (statistically) by several explanatory variables. The estimated equation for 1986, for example, is as follows:

$$EMP^* = 5.35 - (0.30 \times MILKROUND) - (7.61 \times PERIPHERY) + (3.15 \times EXCAT)$$

where the explanatory variables are defined in the appendix to this chapter.

3. The above equation can now be used to compute a *standardized* value of EMP (i.e. EMP^*) for each university by substituting the actual values of each explanatory variable into the estimated equations.

4. Having calculated standardized values of EMP for each university, a performance indicator can be constructed by comparing the actual value of EMP with its standardized value (EMP^*), i.e. $EMP - EMP^*$.

5. Similarly a performance indicator based upon the proportion of graduates proceeding to further education or training is given by

$$FUR - FUR^*$$

where FUR^* is the standardized value of FUR for each university calculated by substituting the actual values of each explanatory variable into the appropriate regression equation. Thus for 1986, for example

$$FUR^* = 11.04 + (0.38 \times MILKROUND) - (0.12 \times AGE) + (0.43 \times UNEMPLOYMENT) + (3.70 \times EXCAT)$$

where the explanatory variables areas defined in the appendix.

These two performance indicators based upon the first destination of graduates are given for the years 1983 to 1986 in Table 8.4. The first point to note is the lack of correlation between the original variable (i.e. EMPLOY or FURTHER) and the associated performance indicator (i.e. $EMP - EMP^*$ or $FUR - FUR^*$ respectively) in all four years. Moreover, the inter-university variation in $EMP - EMP^*$ (and $FUR - FUR^*$) is very

Table 8.4   Performance indicators constructed from the first destination record

(a) A performance indicator constructed from the percentage of graduates obtaining a permanent job (EMP − EMP*),[1] 1983–86.

University	EMP − EMP*			
	1983	*1984*	*1985*	*1986*
Aston	−0.9	−3.3	−2.5	−5.6
Bath	−1.9	−0.4	4.7	−0.3
Birmingham	−0.2	0.0	−1.5	0.9
Bradford	−3.7	−2.7	−1.5	2.3
Bristol	−2.7	−1.0	−1.6	−0.8
Brunel	3.4	4.2	6.8	3.6
Cambridge	−2.2	−2.4	−2.3	−7.9
City	8.7	9.3	2.3	3.8
Durham	5.4	3.1	5.7	4.5
East Anglia	−3.0	−1.3	−3.3	−2.8
Essex	−6.8	−6.7	−1.1	−5.0
Exeter	6.8	4.6	6.0	2.0
Hull	−6.9	−3.5	0.4	4.1
Keele	−1.5	−0.9	−3.5	−6.1
Kent	4.6	2.7	0.3	5.0
Lancaster	1.3	4.4	6.2	5.9
Leeds	−0.4	−3.2	−2.7	−5.1
Leicester	1.9	1.5	1.1	0.4
Liverpool	−5.6	−4.0	−6.9	−4.5
London	1.0	−1.0	−2.6	0.7
Loughborough	0.8	−2.7	−1.5	0.4
Manchester	−3.2	−3.3	−5.9	−4.2
UMIST	−1.1	−3.2	−2.8	−1.7
Newcastle	4.3	4.4	2.7	4.6
Nottingham	−1.1	−2.0	−2.4	1.9
Oxford	3.5	0.9	2.1	−0.2
Reading	2.2	3.5	4.2	3.3
Salford	−4.2	−0.7	−4.1	−1.4
Sheffield	−4.8	−3.2	−2.7	−2.8
Southampton	4.8	3.5	2.3	2.8
Surrey	−0.7	−0.1	−0.8	0.3
Sussex	−5.4	−1.4	4.1	1.4
Warwick	4.9	1.9	−0.7	0.8
York	2.9	2.9	1.5	−0.1
Aberdeen	−0.5	1.4	0.4	2.3
Dundee	−1.6	−4.5	−2.8	−0.9
Edinburgh	1.6	0.8	0.6	0.6
Glasgow	0.4	0.5	−0.4	−0.1
Heriot-Watt	0.6	−0.4	0.5	−1.7
St Andrews	−4.6	−1.8	0.1	−5.7
Stirling	6.6	4.7	5.6	3.7
Strathclyde	−1.1	−0.0	−1.2	0.4
Queen's[2]	—	—	—	—
Ulster[2]	—	—	—	—
Wales	−1.4	−0.6	−2.8	1.4

Table 8.4 Continued

(b) A performance indicator constructed from the percentage of graduates proceeding to further education or training (FUR − FUR*),[1] 1983–86

University	FUR − FUR*			
	1983	*1984*	*1985*	*1986*
Aston	0.1	0.8	2.9	1.4
Bath	−0.9	1.6	−0.9	0.2
Birmingham	1.5	1.4	0.7	0.4
Bradford	0.9	−0.7	−1.2	−3.4
Bristol	0.4	1.5	1.4	1.3
Brunel	0.7	−1.2	−2.0	−0.4
Cambridge	3.7	2.9	1.8	2.9
City	−3.9	−4.5	−0.1	−2.6
Durham	1.0	−0.8	0.9	0.8
East Anglia	3.5	0.1	0.5	0.9
Essex	6.3	2.6	4.3	6.1
Exeter	−6.0	−2.3	−2.5	2.2
Hull	−3.7	−2.3	0.1	−0.1
Keele	6.7	4.6	2.9	7.0
Kent	−2.5	0.1	−1.7	−5.3
Lancaster	0.4	−0.8	−4.8	−2.7
Leeds	−3.7	0.3	0.5	1.2
Leicester	2.9	−0.7	1.1	2.7
Liverpool	1.4	0.5	0.6	−1.7
London	−1.8	−1.4	−0.2	−2.4
Loughborough	0.5	2.2	1.0	−2.3
Manchester	−1.7	−2.0	2.5	1.8
UMIST	−2.1	−0.1	−1.1	−1.0
Newcastle	0.2	−1.3	−1.5	−2.9
Nottingham	−0.5	2.5	1.4	0.2
Oxford	−2.5	−0.8	−0.3	−3.6
Reading	−1.1	−0.4	−3.9	1.7
Salford	1.2	0.4	−0.3	−1.5
Sheffield	−2.2	0.3	−2.4	−0.3
Southampton	1.5	0.2	2.5	0.4
Surrey	0.5	−1.6	−0.5	−0.9
Sussex	1.6	0.7	−0.9	−1.9
Warwick	−2.2	−3.2	−0.8	0.8
York	0.2	1.6	0.2	1.0
Aberdeen	−1.6	−5.2	−0.3	−3.5
Dundee	5.2	7.7	5.5	5.8
Edinburgh	−3.5	−1.7	−2.0	−2.5
Glasgow	1.0	−0.4	−0.7	−2.0
Heriot-Watt	2.2	3.8	2.1	−0.9
St Andrews	2.5	3.4	−0.2	7.2
Stirling	−4.3	−7.1	−5.1	−3.9
Strathclyde	1.0	−0.7	0.2	−0.7
Queen's[2]	—	—	—	—
Ulster[2]	—	—	—	—
Wales	−2.4	0.2	0.5	0.5

Notes:
1. Definitions of EMP − EMP* and FUR − FUR* are given on p. 139.
2. Queen's and Ulster were excluded from the regression analysis for reasons given in the appendix.

small compared to the inter-university variation in the proportion of graduates getting a permanent job or proceeding to further education or training. Once the various determinants of EMPLOY (and FURTHER) have been taken into account, inter-university variations are very small – and perhaps even too negligible to be regarded as being a useful measure of the performance of institutions based upon the first destination of their graduates. After all, around 90 per cent of the inter-university variation in EMPLOY and FURTHER has been explained (statistically) by the various explanatory variables specified on pp. 129–36. It is extremely questionable whether it is useful to use the remaining unexplained inter-university variation in these two variables as a performance indicator. It is nevertheless interesting to note that each performance indicator for any one year is highly correlated with itself for other years. There are a number of potential problems with using the unexplained residual as a performance indicator, however, and these were described in detail on pp. 77.

Conclusion

The purpose of this chapter was to investigate the value of data describing the first destination of graduates as a source of performance indicators. It is possible, for example, to measure the proportion of graduates from each institution who obtain a permanent job within six months of their graduation. The question this raises is whether such indicators should be used to measure the relative performance of different institutions. The answer given in this chapter is a categorical 'no'. At the very least, it is necessary to take inter-university differences in subject mix into account in constructing performance indicators based on the first destination data since about 70 per cent of inter-university variations in the first destination of graduates is explained by corresponding variations in subject mix.

Graduates with degrees in vocationally related subjects tend to obtain a permanent job more quickly after graduation than graduates with degrees in non-vocationally related subjects. Inevitably, then, universities with a high proportion of graduates in vocationally related subjects have a high proportion of their graduates obtaining permanent jobs within six months of their graduation. This means that if a first destination performance indicator is to be constructed in order to compare the performance of institutions, it is necessary to take into account any differences between institutions in their subject mix. If this is not done, the comparisons between institutions simply reflect differences in subject mix *as well as* differences in performance.

But taking the subject mix into account when constructing first destination indicators is not in itself sufficient since this implies that any differences in the first destination of graduates between institutions which are *not* explained by corresponding differences in subject mix must be due to differences in their 'performance'. The implication is that some universities produce less employable graduates than others. But this entirely ignores the possibility that some universities suffer from further disadvantages in addition to an unfavourable subject mix (compared to others). Indeed, an investigation of inter-university variations in the first destination of graduates revealed that around 90 per cent of the variation could be statistically explained. In addition to subject mix, these factors included the age of each university, the number of students per employer visit on the annual milk-round, whether a university is located on the geographical periphery of the UK labour market, whether a university is an ex-college of advanced technology, and the unemployment rate of the region in which each university is located. Since none of these variables can be regarded as a measure of the performance of each institution, it is tempting to attribute the *unexplained* inter-university variation in first destinations to inter-university differences in their performance. An investigation of the unexplained residual did, in fact, reveal a good deal of stability over several years.

But this stability in the residuals is not in itself sufficient to justify using these residuals as a performance indicator. One point in particular needs to be kept in mind. Once subject mix and several other factors have been taken into account, the residual differences in the first destination of graduates between universities is extremely small. In other words, the differences between institutions are too small in the main to have any relevance for the measurement of performance.

Finally, although this chapter has shown that a large proportion of the inter-university variation in the first destination of graduates can be explained by factors which are apparently unrelated to the performance of each institution, the fact that inter-institutional differences in subject mix are so important raises the further question as to whether those universities with an unfavourable subject mix should be planning to change it in the direction of those universities which have a favourable subject mix. This question cannot be answered here since it raises fundamental questions about the purpose of higher education and the relative value (ultimately to society as a whole) of graduates in different degree subjects.

Appendix to Chapter 8

Graduates proceeding to permanent employment or further education

The expected values of the percentage of graduates proceeding to permanent employment and the percentage of graduates proceeding to further education and training are calculated for each university as follows:

$$\text{EMPLOY}^e_i = \frac{100}{G_i} \sum_j G_{ij} \left(\frac{E_j}{G_j} \right) \qquad \begin{array}{l} i = \text{university} \\ j = \text{subject} \end{array}$$

$$\text{FURTHER}^e_i = \frac{100}{G_i} \sum_j G_{ij} \left(\frac{F_j}{G_j} \right)$$

where

E_j = graduates in subject j (all UK universities) who obtained a permanent job
F_j = graduates in subject j (all UK universities) who proceeded to further education and training
G_j = graduates in subject j (all UK universities)
G_i = graduates in university i (all subjects)
G_{ij} = graduates at university i in subject j.

Note also that since

$$\text{UNEMP}_i = 100 - \text{EMPLOY}_i - \text{FURTHER}_i$$

then

$$\text{UNEMP}^e_i = 100 - \text{EMPLOY}^e_i - \text{FURTHER}^e_i$$

Estimated regression equations: dependent variable = EMPLOY − EMPLOY^e

Explanatory variables	1983	1983	1984	1984	1985	1985	1986
CONSTANT	7.78	−8.09	8.71	−11.22	5.81	−36.73	5.35
	(2.99)	(−1.99)	(4.82)	(−1.99)	(2.86)	(−3.56)	(2.51)
ALEVEL		0.92*				1.80**	
		(2.29)				(3.58)	
SCHOOL				0.17**			
				(3.96)			
MILKROUND	−0.50*		−0.59**	−0.45**	−0.32*		−0.30*
	(−2.71)		(−4.55)	(−3.37)	(−2.01)		(−1.67)
AGE			0.006*			0.010**	
			(2.27)			(2.98)	
PERIPHERY	−6.71**	−5.63**	−4.99**			−4.67**	−7.61**
	(−4.51)	(−3.67)	(−4.02)			(−3.59)	(−5.79)
EXCAT	2.81*	6.18**	2.68*	3.84**	3.51**	5.20**	3.15**
	(1.77)	(4.10)	(2.10)	(2.79)	(2.44)	(4.02)	(2.22)
$\bar{R}^2$	0.46	0.44	0.56	0.57	0.43	0.41	0.53

Notes:
1. ( ) = t-ratios, ** = significant at 1%, * = significant at 5%. A one-tailed test is used for those variables for which the expected sign has been specified.
2. Spuriously high significance levels were obtained on some of the explanatory variables when Queen's and Ulster were included in the regression analysis. These two Northern Ireland universities were therefore excluded from the analysis.
3. Definition of variables
   EMPLOY = percentage of graduates obtaining permanent employment
   EMPLOY^e = percentage of graduates expected to obtain permanent employment given each university's subject mix
   ALEVEL = average A level score of each university's undergraduate entrants: A = 5, B = 4, C = 3, D = 2, E = 1
   SCHOOL = percentage of graduates who attended a grammar or independent school
   MILKROUND = graduates per employer visitor (on the annual 'milk-round')
   AGE = foundation year of university
   PERIPHERY = 1 if university is located in Scotland or Wales and 0 otherwise
   EXCAT = 1 if university is an ex-college of advanced technology and 0 otherwise.

Source: J. Johnes and Taylor 1989b.

Estimated regression equations: dependent variable = FURTHER − FURTHER'

Explanatory variables	1983	1984	1985	1986
CONSTANT	5.14	6.03	4.59	11.04
	(1.02)	(1.29)	(1.19)	(2.13)
MILKROUND	0.30*	0.32**	0.29**	0.38**
	(2.14)	(2.90)	(2.78)	(2.79)
AGE	−0.009**	−0.008**	−0.007**	−0.012**
	(−3.31)	(−3.28)	(−3.62)	(−4.75)
UNEMPLOYMENT	0.52**	0.30*	0.27*	0.43**
	(2.85)	(1.74)	(1.89)	(2.21)
PERIPHERY	3.07*	3.43**	4.17**	3.70**
	(2.40)	(2.87)	(4.21)	(2.82)
EXCAT	−2.63*	−2.85**	−2.33*	
	(−2.06)	(−2.51)	(−2.33)	
$\bar{R}^2$	0.60	0.62	0.70	0.60

Notes:
1. ( ) = *t*-ratios, ** = significant at 1%, * = significant at 5%. A one-tailed test is used for those variables for which the expected sign has been specified.
2. Queen's and Ulster were omitted. See note 2 to previous table.
3. Definition of variables
   FURTHER   = percentage of graduates proceeding to further education or training
   FURTHER'   = percentage of graduates expected to proceed to further education or training given each university's subject mix
   UNEMPLOYMENT = percentage unemployed in regions in which university is located.

Source: J. Johnes and Taylor 1989b.

9

The Evaluation of Research Output in the Higher Education Sector

Introduction

The perceived quality of each university's research has for some time featured prominently in the process of allocating resources to the university sector in the UK. This does not mean, however, that methods for the evaluation of either research output or research performance are highly advanced. On the contrary, the assessment of both is still highly controversial, as this chapter will demonstrate.

It is the purpose of this chapter to critically examine a number of measures of research output and to consider the possibility of constructing a research performance indicator for entire institutions. A vital step in any attempt to measure research performance is an investigation into factors likely to affect each university's level of research output. The remainder of this chapter is in six sections. The first section briefly describes the growing importance of the evaluation of research in the process of allocating resources to the university sector in the UK. The second section critically appraises several methods which have been used to assess research output. This is followed in the third section by a discussion of the 1989 Research Selectivity Exercise undertaken by the Universities Funding Council. The fourth section then uses the results of this exercise in an attempt to identify the factors that may have influenced the research performance of each institution. The relative importance of each of these factors is tested statistically, using regression analysis, in the fifth section. The sixth section examines the possibility of developing a performance indicator based on research output.

The role of the evaluation of research in resource allocation

As early as 1981, perceptions of each university's research strengths and weaknesses were amongst the criteria upon which the selective cuts in the funding of the university sector were based (see Chapter 3). By 1984, however, it was clear that the evaluation of research output would play an even greater role in the resource allocation process:

> We propose to adopt a more selective approach in the allocation of research support among universities in order to ensure that resources for research are used to the best advantage.
>
> (UGC 1984: 5)

During 1985 a new framework for allocating resources was developed. The new model was used to aid the allocation of resources in the university sector from 1986/87 to 1989/90. The model consists of three components, namely

1. teaching
2. research
3. special factors.

The teaching component is approximately 60 per cent of the total allocation (though this varies between subjects) while the research component is roughly 35 per cent. The precise amount received by each university for research, however, is variable and depends on a number of criteria:

1. student numbers
2. income from research grants awarded by research councils
3. income from research contracts
4. selectivity.

The proposed breakdown of the allocation for 1989/90 (which is typical of the previous two years) is displayed in Table 9.1. Student numbers and the ability to attract research grants and contracts determine around 43 per cent and 17 per cent of the total research allocation respectively. Just over 40 per cent of the research allocation, however, depends on perceived research performance. The appraisal of research is therefore a highly

Table 9.1 Allocation of resources by the UGC, 1989/90

	% of total allocation
Teaching	61.2
Research	
– student-number related	14.8
– grant-related	5.2
– contract income related	0.7
– selective	14.1
Special factors	4.0

Source: Clayton 1988.

important determinant of the amount of funds awarded to each university. In addition, the Universities Funding Council has made it clear that it expects universities to take research performance into account in allocating funds between departments within institutions. It is also stressed, however, that the appraisal of research output will have no bearing on the allocation of funds set aside to support the teaching activities of universities.

Measuring research output

The measurement of research output is a difficult task both in principle and in practice (Lloyd 1987; G. Johnes 1988). This section demonstrates these difficulties by critically appraising four alternative measures of research output: peer review, publications, citations and research income.

Peer review

In theory, the advantage of peer review of the research output of departments is that the evaluation can take into account all aspects of research activity (e.g. productivity, quality and impact). In practice, however, any measure based on the opinions of others in the field will inevitably be highly subjective: ratings are likely to be heavily influenced by the individual reviewer's personal research interests and by his or her loyalties and affiliations to particular institutions (R. Smith and Fielder 1971; Dean 1976; Webster 1981; Martin and Irvine 1983).

Ratings based on peer review are also influenced by 'halo effects' (R. Smith and Fielder 1971; Anderson *et al.* 1978; Webster 1981; Cave *et al.* 1988) whereby the individual department acquires benefits from the overall reputation of the institution as a whole (see Anderson *et al.* 1978 for evidence). There is also a danger that a judgement derived from peer review may be out of date (R. Smith and Fielder 1971; Webster 1981). The reputation of a department can be considerably boosted by the presence of one highly productive and eminent researcher. The department may retain this reputation long after the eminent researcher has left and may no longer be deserved.

Large departments have an undoubted advantage over smaller departments when evaluation is based on peer review (R. Smith and Fielder 1971; G. Johnes 1989). A large department is more visible than a small one, and there is more chance that someone on the review panel will know the work of at least one of its members.

Finally, it is worth considering the implications for resource allocation of using peer review to evaluate research output. Such a practice is likely to encourage departments to spend more on enhancing their image outside their university in an effort to increase their ranking (Harris 1988). This may result in an inefficient use of resources.

Publications

Publications are the most obvious evidence of research activity. Moreover, measures of research outputs based on publications are considered to be more objective than measures based on peer review.

In general, a publications count is based on refereed publications in academic journals. Any count derived using all forms of publication (e.g. books as well as papers) requires a weighting system to reflect the relative merits of the various forms of publication (Meltzer 1949; Manis 1951; R. Smith and Fielder 1971; Niemi 1975). The suggestions for the weighting of journal articles to books have ranged from 1:4 (Crane 1965) to 1:18 (Meltzer 1949; Manis 1951).

A count of publications which is confined only to refereed journal articles can be performed either by obtaining a publications list from each department or by referring to the journals themselves. The success of the former method clearly depends on the degree of co-operation from individual departments. The latter method, on the other hand, encounters the problem of choosing an appropriate set of journals from which to derive a count of publications which adequately reflects the research activities of a specific subject area (since to cover all journals would be an impossible task).

The choice of journals to be used in the count will inevitably introduce biases. For example, the selection of journals in a specific subject area on the basis that they are generally considered to be of high quality and of general interest would produce a publications count biased against highly specialized research areas (G. Johnes 1988). In addition, departments whose members publish 'outside' their own specific subject will be disadvantaged by such a method.

Journal articles vary in length and it could be argued that a publications count should take this factor into account (see House and Yeager 1978; Hirsch *et al.* 1984). The introduction of a publications count to measure research output which took no account of article length could lead to a proliferation of short papers in order to boost research 'output' and hence the ranking of departments. The major criticism of using a publications count to reflect research output (regardless of whether or not article length has been taken into account) is that it reflects quantity rather than quality (Bayer and Folger 1966; R. Smith and Fielder 1971; Whitley and Frost 1971; King 1987). Papers vary in quality and in what they contribute to a subject. Thus a theoretical paper and a survey of the literature make different contributions to the field of research. One possible solution in principle is to use weights to reflect the relative quality and contribution of each paper. Such a system, however, requires a consensus of opinion on an appropriate weighting system and necessitates a (subjective) judgement of each paper's relative quality. This would be both time-consuming and beset by similar problems to measures of research output based on peer review.

Alternative methods include using a weight derived from the relative quality index (or impact factor) of the journal in which the article appeared (Martin and Irvine 1983), or using a weight to reflect the *type* of publication (G. Johnes 1990). It is important that some weighting system to reflect relative quality should be devised if a publications count is to become the standard measure of research output. The danger of not doing so is that it may lead to a lowering in the quality of research if researchers begin to sacrifice quality for quantity in order to boost their research rating.

The major problem with using a weighting system to reflect the quality of publications, however, is that it is first necessary to reach a consensus on the relative weights to be attached to each publication. Recent work by Geraint Johnes (1990) shows that the ranking of economics departments in UK universities is extremely sensitive to the weights attached to each of eleven different types of publications. These are as follows:

1. Papers in academic journals
2. Letters in academic journals
3. Articles in professional journals
4. Articles in popular journals
5. Authored books
6. Edited books
7. Published official reports
8. Contributions to edited works
9. Contributions to edited proceedings
10. Other publications
11. Other media.

The best and worst ranks obtained by G. Johnes for each economics department in the sample (using 120 different weighting schemes) are given in Table 9.2. In addition, the mean rank can be compared with the UFC's research rating for each university since these two sets of research ratings covered the same period (1984–88 inclusive). Figure 9.1 shows that there is little relationship between these two measures of research performance. This suggests that the judgemental factor figured prominently in the UFC's selectivity exercise.

Further problems with a publications count emerge as a consequence of the time lag between completing a piece of research and its publication. If the author moves to a different institution, the question arises as to whether the publication should be credited to the institution where the research was done or the researcher's current institution. It has been argued that the latter is more appropriate since a publications count should be a reflection of research *potential* rather than *past* research activity (Bell and Seater 1978; Hogan 1984).

Multiple-authored papers also pose a problem. In the absence of any firm evidence of relative contributions to a paper, the credit for a publication with more than one author should be divided equally between each author (Bell and Seater 1978; House and Yeager 1978; Graves *et al.* 1984; Hirsch *et al.* 1984). The alternative of giving full credit to each author

Table 9.2 University research rankings: publications per capita in departments of economics in UK universities

| University | Rank | | | UFC score |
	Best	Worst	Mean	
Aston	—	—	—	—
Bath	7	27	15.5	3
Birmingham	12	38	26.0	3
Bradford	—	—	—	—
Bristol	4	38	24.0	4
Brunel	4	39	22.6	1
Cambridge	6	23	14.8	4
City	11	39	26.6	1
Durham	5	23	12.8	2
East Anglia	16	30	20.7	3
Essex	—	—	—	5
Exeter	24	36	32.6	2
Hull	18	40	32.3	3
Keele	1	23	8.0	1
Kent	17	33	25.7	3
Lancaster	12	28	20.3	—
Leeds	—	—	—	2
Leicester	—	—	—	2
Liverpool	5	22	12.6	3
London (Birkbeck)	1	12	2.5	5
London (LSE)	—	—	—	5
London (QMC)	15	35	24.2	3
London (UCL)	2	24	9.9	4
Loughborough	1	11	3.3	2
Manchester	—	—	—	3
UMIST	—	—	—	—
Newcastle	—	—	—	4
Nottingham	2	13	6.2	3
Oxford	2	19	8.4	5
Reading	5	21	11.0	4
Salford	12	40	34.0	1
Sheffield	24	34	29.7	2
Southampton	—	—	—	5
Surrey	1	9	2.9	2
Sussex	15	36	25.8	3
Warwick	4	37	18.4	5
York	1	37	13.1	5
Aberystwyth	13	24	19.6	2
Bangor	5	31	16.0	—
Cardiff	22	38	31.4	—
Lampeter	—	—	—	—
Swansea	—	—	—	1
UWIST	—	—	—	—
Aberdeen	2	11	6.3	3
Dundee	10	24	14.2	1
Edinburgh	30	40	37.2	2
Glasgow	30	40	37.7	2
Heriot-Watt	32	40	38.0	1
St Andrews	7	39	20.1	2
Stirling	5	30	18.8	2
Strathclyde	23	39	33.3	2
Queen's	29	38	34.6	2
Ulster	—	—	—	1

Note:
The mean research rank is the mean of 120 ranks, each of which used a different weighting system for 11 different types of publications

Sources: G. Johnes (1990); *Research Selectivity Exercise 1989: The Outcome*, UFC.

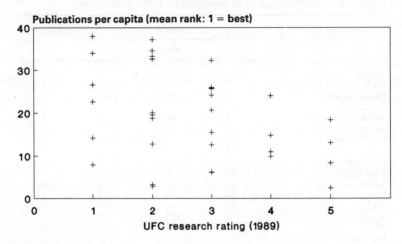

Figure 9.1   Publications per capita (mean rank) v. UFC research rating: economics departments in UK universities

Source: See Table 9.3.

or full credit to the first-named author only are likely to introduce serious biases into any publications count (Lindsey 1980).

Finally, publication is not the only method of disseminating research. Alternative means of dissemination include lectures, seminars, conferences, departmental discussion papers and informal correspondence. Unless work transmitted in these forms is subsequently published, a large chunk of research may be omitted from any measure based on publications. This would introduce serious biases if the propensity to disseminate knowledge through alternative methods to publishing in journals differed not only between subjects (for which some correction could be made) but also between departments within a specific discipline.

Citations

The attraction of a measure of research output based on citations is that it appears not only to be objective but also to reflect quality (evidence to support the latter contention is supplied by S. Cole and J. R. Cole 1967, and Garfield 1970).

The major criticism of using citations to measure the quality of research is that references to published work are not necessarily complimentary and may even point out serious flaws (Margolis 1967; Croom 1970; Moravcsik 1973; Goudsmit 1974; Yaes 1974; Wade 1975; Porter 1977; Webster 1981; King 1987). An alternative point of view holds that differences in type of citation may not be a serious problem as few would take the trouble to criticize or correct something trivial (J. R. Cole and S. Cole 1974). It is perhaps reassuring that there is evidence to suggest that uncomplimentary citations are relatively uncommon (MacRoberts and MacRoberts 1984).

Other suggestions for making a citations count a truer reflection of quality have been to weight each citation according to either the reputation of the citer or the prestige of the journal in which the citation was made. This would inevitably lead to immense problems concerning the derivation of an acceptable weighting scheme.

Perhaps a more serious criticism of a citations count is the assertion that there are errors (possibly substantial) in the citations practices of authors. Such errors include the omission of a large chunk of literature owing to ignorance of its existence (Janke 1967; Goudsmit 1974; Cave *et al.* 1988); the 'plagiarism' of citations without having read the cited work (May 1967); the practice of citing literature reviews rather than the original work (MacRoberts and MacRoberts 1987b); the omission of citations to very well-known works (May 1967; Croom 1970; R. Smith and Fielder 1971; Moravcsik 1973; Goudsmit 1974; Porter 1977); the citation of work by eminent researchers at the expense of work by little-known researchers, even though the latter may be more appropriate, i.e. 'persuasive citing' (R. Smith and Fielder 1971; J. R. Cole and S. Cole 1972); citation of one's own or a colleague's work, although self-citations can be, and often are, excluded from citation counts (Whitley and Frost 1971; J. R. Cole and S. Cole 1972; Porter 1977; Davis and Papanek 1984; King 1987). It is also the case that researchers who have established their reputations with a particular piece of work will continue to receive large numbers of citations for subsequent work simply because their names are well known, i.e. the 'halo effect' (Whitley and Frost 1971; J. R. Cole and S. Cole 1972).

Recent studies of citation practices indicate the existence of many of the problems referred to above (MacRoberts and MacRoberts 1987a; 1987b). Before a citations count is seriously considered for use in the evaluation of research output, there is clearly a need for more work to determine the extent of the bias in ranking caused by the numerous peculiarities in citation practices.

There are several additional problems with citations which need to be overcome. The simplest way of performing a citations count is to use a citations index. There are errors of record in such indices, however. Citations to a paper written by more than one author are recorded under the first author's name only (Bayer and Folger 1966; Croom 1970). Other joint authors receive no credit whatsoever. Another problem is that changes in name (for example by marriage or simply by the inclusion or exclusion of an initial) will cause citations to be attributed to two different people (Croom 1970). Conversely, citations to people with a common name will be attributed to one person if they all have the same initials (Wallmark and Sedig 1986).

A further difficulty with a citations count in general is the choice of an appropriate time period for the count (Phillimore 1989). It may be tempting to use a short time period in order to make the measure as accurate a reflection of current research output as possible. This would discriminate against authors whose work increases in importance over time (Janke 1967; R. Smith and Fielder 1971; Lawani 1977; Porter 1977).

As with measures based on publications, there are difficulties arising from the mobility of academics and the necessary time lag over which citations are counted. Thus a consensus view needs to be established concerning the best way of allocating citations between the institution where the research was done, where the researcher was when it was published, and the researcher's location at the time of citation.

A citations count will be biased if citations practices vary by area of research. In addition, some areas within a particular discipline may be more popular than others and researchers in this field will therefore receive more citations (Margolis 1967; McGervey 1974; Webster 1981). A further problem is that a citations count will discriminate against the department whose members are relatively young with few publications to be cited (Davis and Papanek 1984).

Finally, the widespread use of citations to measure research output could be expected to alter the citation habits of academics (May 1967; Webster 1981; Harris 1988). The likely consequences are an increase in self-citations (if self-citations are to count) and in citations of the work of colleagues within the same department. Such changes would render a citations count meaningless (May 1967; Webster 1981; Harris 1988).

Research income

Unlike publications or citations, which necessarily require a time lag over which to perform the count, measures based on research income are considered to give a more up-to-date picture of the research output of departments (Webster 1981). An even stronger attraction of using research income is that the data are already published at both university and cost centre level for the UK university sector.

The main criticism of measuring research output using income data is that the latter is an input into, not an output of, the research production process (D. M. Smith 1986; Gillett 1987a; 1987b; Gillett and Aitkenhead 1987; Hare and Wyatt 1988; Harris 1989). The receipt of a grant, it is argued, indicates nothing about the quality or even quantity of research produced from the input (Gillett 1987a; 1987b; Gillett and Aitkenhead 1987). Moreover, fields of research where grants are in short supply would be disadvantaged by such a measure (Gillett 1987a; 1987b). An alternative view is that research grants and contracts can be used to reflect the market value of the research being undertaken since they are awarded for a specific package of research, proposed and approved at the outset.

There are several further problems however with using research income as a measure of research output. There are well-known differences for example in the input requirements for research in different subjects (Cave *et al.* 1988). If the differences were simply between subjects then they would be relatively simple to take into account (i.e. evaluation could either be carried out at subject level, or if carried out at university level, methods could be devised to take into account subject mix). There can be large differences, however, in the input requirements in different areas of the same discipline. Within economics, for example, applied researchers are likely to require more expensive resources to carry out their research than theoreticians, who require little more than paper, pen and time to think. Any disregard for these differences would mean that a measure of research output based on research income would value the research of departments requiring expensive resources more highly than the research of departments able to produce useful results from relatively fewer resources (D. M. Smith 1986).

A much more serious problem with measures based on research income is the question of whether the market value of research is the appropriate yardstick by which to measure its social value. Research may be considered to be a public good (Brandl 1970) and valuation based on its market value will consequently result in a lower level of research output than is socially optimal. The intervention of grant-awarding bodies is unlikely to be able to correct this problem entirely.

A further problem is that the nature of research will undoubtedly change if its market value is used to reflect its true value to society. The research most likely to attract funding will be that which has the most obvious relevance to the buyer. Applied research, in particular, will be highly 'marketable'. The basic aim of research, however, is to increase the stock of knowledge, and the widespread encouragement of 'marketable' research may not be the best way of achieving this.

Finally, there are serious implications of using research income to measure output. There will be an incentive for academics who could perform a piece of research adequately on a very low budget to over-fund their research grant applications in order to boost the ranking of their department.

The 1989 research selectivity exercise of UK universities

Two separate research assessment exercises have now been undertaken, one by the University Grants Committee in 1985/86 and one by the Universities Funding Council in 1989. The results of the first exercise came in for very heavy criticism from many quarters (see Moore 1987; DES 1987c) and it was consequently decided that a more thorough and more comprehensive exercise would be undertaken in 1989. The 1986 exercise was based upon peer review with little emphasis being placed on the actual research output produced by universities. Subject panels consulted well-known academics in each subject area and research councils provided information about research grants awarded during the previous five years. In addition, each university or cost centre was asked to submit an extremely brief account of its research performance and future research plans and to select five recent publications which accurately reflected the research work being undertaken in each cost centre (or department in many cases).

The very limited approach adopted in the 1986 exercise was criticized on several grounds. The main criticisms were as follows (Gillett 1987a; 1987b; Gillett and Aitkenhead 1987; P. K. Jones 1989):

1. the criteria for assessing research quality had not been made clear to universities
2. the identity of the assessors was confidential
3. the ultimate rankings appeared to be strongly influenced by the ability of universities to attract research grants, particularly from the research councils (thus favouring large departments)
4. there was insufficient consultation with professional bodies about the appropriate methods of assessment to be used
5. different assessment standards were used for different subjects.

The UFC responded to these criticisms in the preparation of the 1989 exercise by accepting the need for openness in its deliberations and for improving the evaluation methodology. As with the 1986 exercise, evaluation was based upon *informed peer review* but the UFC adopted a more comprehensive and more formal approach to its 1989 exercise. In particular, more data describing research *output* were collected and used in the 1989 exercise. The UFC was keen to stress that the assessments made by advisory groups and panels were 'output led' (rather than 'income led' as in the 1986 exercise). The method of assessment was broadly as follows:

1. Around 70 advisory groups and panels were set up involving 300 members and covering 152 subject units of assessment. In addition, about 100 outside advisers were consulted in confidence.
2. Each advisory group or panel was provided with information obtained from each institution describing the research output in each identifiable subject area over the period 1984–88 inclusive. This included a brief description of each department's research accomplishments and future plans as well as a numerical summary of publications and research reports. In addition, up to two publications were listed for each full-time member of the academic staff in post during 1984–88.
3. The advisory groups and panels were then asked to rate each department on a five-point scale common to all subject areas. The ratings of different subjects were intended to be directly comparable and this was to be achieved by using the concept of 'attainable levels of excellence' in each subject area. In effect, this meant that research output was compared against an international standard. Each department's research output was therefore measured against this benchmark. The rating scale is given in Table 9.3 together with a definition of 'research'.

Six main criticisms have been directed at the 1989 research selectivity exercise. First, there was inadequate consultation in the design of the questionnaire. This led to criticisms of the assessment exercise itself since it was widely felt that a more carefully prepared questionnaire would have produced better information about research performance in individual assessment units.

Second, the process of evaluation was undertaken too hurriedly. The advisory group and subject panels had only three months to evaluate the research output of the entire UK university sector in their respective subject areas. This typically involved an initial meeting of the advisory group, followed by three meetings of the subject panels and ending with a meeting of the advisory group to agree the final ratings.

Third, the definition of the unit which was assessed is open to criticism. Assessment was based on the research output of all full-time academic staff in post during the assessment period. Since staff turnover has been high in

Table 9.3   The Research Selectivity Exercise 1989: The Rating Scale

Five-point scale

The Universities Funding Council's advisory groups and panels used the following five-point scale:

5 = Research quality that equates to attainable levels of international excellence in some sub-areas of activity and to attainable levels of national excellence in virtually all others.

4 = Research quality that equates to attainable levels of national excellence in virtually all sub-areas of activity, possibly showing some evidence of international excellence, or to international excellence in some and at least national level in a majority.

3 = Research quality that equates to attainable levels of national excellence in a majority of the sub-areas of activity, or to international levels in some.

2 = Research quality that equates to attainable levels of national excellence in up to half of the sub-areas of activity.

1 = Research selectivity that equates to attainable levels of national excellence in none, or virtually none, of the sub-areas of activity.

Definition of research

'Research' for the purposes of the Council's review is to be understood as original investigation undertaken in order to gain knowledge and understanding. In the humanities it includes scholarship which leads to new or substantially improved insights. In science and technology it includes the use of existing knowledge in experimental development to produce new or substantially improved materials, devices, products and processes, including design and construction. It excludes routine testing and analysis of materials, components and processes – e.g. for the maintenance of national standards – as distinct from the development of new analytical techniques.

Source: P. K. Jones 1989.

some departments, it could be argued that a far better indicator of research potential would be the research record of staff in post at a given census date. A related problem concerns the research undertaken by staff financed by research grants (which may or may not have been funded by the UFC or the research councils). Should this research output be attributed to the relevant cognate department even if it is undertaken in an entirely separate and independent organizational unit, such as a research institute? Attribution of this research output to the nearest cognate department could have resulted in an over-estimation of the research output of some assessment units.

Fourth, several problems were encountered in defining research output. In some cases, edited books were counted as authored books; book reviews were included as articles; unpublished research reports were included as books; co-authored books were included twice (or more) under separate authors; no distinction was made between articles published in non-refereed journals and articles published in refereed journals, and so on. Assessment of research will obviously be seriously impeded unless a common set of definitions is used by all assessment units.

Fifth, there is still no consensus on whether the five-point rating scale allows accurate comparisons to be made between different subjects. The adoption of 'attainable levels of excellence' in each subject area was intended to achieve comparability between subjects, as indeed is essential if the research ratings are to be used to allocate resources between departments within institutions. Nevertheless, there has been some dissatisfaction about the substantial inter-subject differences in the mean score (see Tables 9.4 and 9.5). For example, the mean scores in pharmacology (3.6), history (3.4), social policy (3.4) and law (3.3) compare very favourably to the mean scores in veterinary science (2.7), economics (2.7) and German (2.7). Since the purpose of the research exercise was to help in the allocation of research funds between subject areas, we can expect to see a shift of resources away from low-score subjects towards high-score subjects. But this would be efficient only if the scores were comparable between subjects. It must be seriously doubted whether this is the case and it would therefore be wise for universities to be cautious in shifting resources between subjects. This problem has been acknowledged by the UFC but was not regarded as being of any great significance:

> Anxieties were expressed in some panels that they were being 'tougher' than others but Executive monitoring and guidance seems to have avoided this.
>
> (P. K. Jones 1989: 17)

Finally, there was some evidence of cheating in the 1989 research assessment exercise. In some cases, inaccurate publication dates were included in order to gain advantage and publications were included when they should have been attributed to another institution. It has therefore been suggested that penalties (i.e. automatic lower rating) will be imposed

Table 9.4 University Funding Council research ratings for selected subjects in the 1989 Research Selectivity Exercise

Subject	Mean score (all universities)
Clinical medicine	3.3
Clinical dentistry	2.4
Pre-clinical studies	3.3
Anatomy	2.5
Physiology	3.3
Pharmacy	3.4
Pharmacology	3.6
Biochemistry	3.4
Psychology	3.1
Biotechnology	3.0
Botany	2.9
Genetics	3.4
Zoology	3.1
Agriculture	3.0
Clinical veterinary science	2.7
Chemistry	3.0
Physics	3.3
Mathematics	3.1
Computer science	3.2
Civil engineering	2.9
Electrical and electronic engineering	2.9
General engineering	3.3
Chemical engineering	3.3
Mechanical engineering	3.4
Metallurgy and materials	3.7
Architecture	2.8
Town and country planning	3.0
Geography	3.2
Law	3.3
Economics	2.7
Politics	3.0
Sociology	3.2
Social policy and administration	3.4
Business and management	2.4
Classics	3.3
English language and literature	3.2
French	3.0
German	2.7
Italian	2.7
Linguistics	3.2
Archaeology	3.3
History	3.4
Philosophy	3.3
Theology	3.6
Music	3.3
Education	2.5

Note: 152 separate subjects (i.e. units of assessment) were assessed by the UFC's sub-committees.

Source: UFC 1989c.

Table 9.5 Research ratings for each cost centre, 1989 Research
Selectivity Exercise: UK averages

Cost centre	Mean rating	Number of cost centres
Clinical medicine	3.1	17
Clinical dentistry	2.1	11
Pre-clinical studies	3.0	5
Anatomy and physiology	2.7	15
Pharmacology	3.5	14
Pharmacy	3.4	9
Nursing	2.4	8
Other studies allied to medicine	2.4	13
Biochemistry	3.3	23
Psychology	3.2	37
Other biological sciences	3.0	42
Agriculture and forestry	3.2	9
Veterinary science	2.8	5
Chemistry	3.0	44
Physics	3.2	41
Other physical sciences	3.1	33
Mathematics	3.1	46
Computing	3.2	45
General engineering	3.1	13
Chemical engineering	3.1	17
Civil engineering	2.1	26
Electrical and electronic engineering	3.0	34
Mechanical, aero and production engineering	2.7	28
Mineral engineering	3.5	6
Metallurgy and materials	3.4	15
Architecture	2.4	12
Other technologies	2.4	8
Planning	3.3	13
Geography	3.2	31
Law	3.0	33
Other social studies (economics, sociology, etc.)	3.2	45
Business and management studies	2.8	28
Accountancy	3.0	25
Language-based studies	3.2	45
Humanities	3.1	39
Creative arts	3.1	32
Education	3.1	37
All cost centres	3.0	—

Note: London University is excluded from the analysis.
Source: UFC 1989c.

after the 1993/94 exercise if any department is found guilty of deliberate misrepresentation.

It is problems such as these which have undermined confidence, at least to some extent, in the outcome of the 1989 research assessment exercise with the result that the 1993/94 exercise is likely to be more carefully prepared.

Some explanations of inter-university variations in research performance

The wide variations in the UFC's average rating of research performance in different *subjects* have already been noted. Table 9.6 indicates a large disparity in the UFC's average rating of research performance in different *universities*. Two measures of average rating have been calculated and are displayed in Table 9.6, the latter measure being a weighted average. Thus the ratings of large cost centres carry more weight than those of small cost centres in the weighted average (precise definitions of both measures are given in the appendix to this chapter: pp. 170–2). In practice, there is a strong degree of correlation between these two measures ($r = 0.98$). In both cases, the mean research rating varies from around 2 at Keele, City and Salford to around 4.8 at Oxford and Cambridge.

Such vast differences in the research performance of universities are clearly worthy of closer examination and investigation. In particular, can inter-university differences in research performance be explained by inter-university differences in the inputs available to individual institutions? Earlier studies indicate that factors such as the characteristics of the staff, facilities available and characteristics of the university are highly influential in determining the research performance of *individual departments* (Graves *et al.* 1982; G. Johnes 1988; 1989). In this section we investigate the factors most likely to cause the observed variations in research performance of *UK universities* as reflected by the UFC's 1989 research ratings. The discussion is limited to those factors for which quantitative measures can be constructed.

Universities with the greatest financial resources available to spend on research activities are expected to produce the highest levels of research output. Moreover, close inspection of universities' expenditure data reveals a substantial inter-university variation in research expenditure per member of academic staff (see Table 9.7). In 1986/87, for example, the amount varied from below £6,000 at East Anglia, Exeter, Hull, Lancaster and Ulster to over £12,000 at Cambridge, London, UMIST, Oxford, Southampton, Surrey, Dundee and Heriot-Watt. This degree of variation is typical of other years. However, part of this variation in research expenditure per member of staff is a consequence of the fact that research in some subjects requires greater financial resources than in others, and subject mix varies across universities. By calculating for each university the

Table 9.6   Research performance ratings of UK universities calculated from the UFC's 1989 research ratings of each cost centre

University	Average research rating	Weighted average research rating
Aston	2.6	2.5
Bath	2.8	2.9
Birmingham	3.1	3.3
Bradford	2.4	2.6
Bristol	3.8	3.8
Brunel	2.1	2.3
Cambridge	4.7	4.8
City	2.0	2.1
Durham	3.2	3.2
East Anglia	3.1	3.3
Essex	3.4	3.7
Exeter	2.9	3.1
Hull	2.5	2.7
Keele	2.0	2.1
Kent	2.7	2.9
Lancaster	3.2	3.3
Leeds	3.1	3.1
Leicester	2.8	2.9
Liverpool	3.3	3.2
London	3.5	3.4
Loughborough	2.6	2.7
Manchester	3.6	3.6
UMIST	3.7	3.7
Newcastle	3.1	3.5
Nottingham	3.1	3.4
Oxford	4.6	4.8
Reading	2.9	2.9
Salford	2.0	2.2
Sheffield	3.2	3.3
Southampton	3.3	3.7
Surrey	3.0	3.3
Sussex	3.4	3.4
Warwick	4.1	4.2
York	3.7	3.8
Aberdeen	2.7	2.8
Dundee	2.5	2.7
Edinburgh	3.3	3.3
Glasgow	2.9	3.3
Heriot-Watt	2.3	2.3
St Andrews	2.9	3.1
Stirling	2.2	2.4
Strathclyde	2.4	2.9
Queen's	2.3	2.6
Ulster	2.1	2.2
Wales	2.8	2.7

Note: See pp. 170–2 for details on how the two ratings were calculated.

Table 9.7   Research expenditure per full-time
member of academic staff

University	Research expenditure per full-time academic	
	1986/87	*1987/88*
Aston	8393	7306
Bath	8351	8815
Birmingham	8482	9282
Bradford	5773	6133
Bristol	9390	10022
Brunel	12226	11595
Cambridge	11212	12406
City	6573	6204
Durham	6400	6693
East Anglia	5924	5691
Essex	6531	6939
Exeter	3750	5184
Hull	5677	4265
Keele	6028	6435
Kent	6184	8564
Lancaster	5164	5758
Leeds	6954	7403
Leicester	8445	8939
Liverpool	8395	9551
London	14892	16059
Loughborough	10900	11266
Manchester	7663	8142
UMIST	15020	13738
Newcastle	8286	9264
Nottingham	9049	9157
Oxford	13816	15746
Reading	7555	9120
Salford	6015	6936
Sheffield	7181	8522
Southampton	12297	12177
Surrey	11662	12656
Sussex	9175	9808
Warwick	9829	11405
York	9863	10061
Aberdeen	5958	6787
Dundee	11505	12077
Edinburgh	10679	11838
Glasgow	10228	11756
Heriot-Watt	11500	15724
St Andrews	6172	6238
Stirling	5690	6414
Strathclyde	9707	9507
Queen's	4774	6138
Ulster	2636	3131
Wales	9125	8373

Source: University Statistics: Finance, 1986/87 and 1987/88.

expenditure on research per member of staff which could be *expected* given its subject mix (see appendix for details pp. 170–2) it can be shown that around 46 per cent of the inter-university variation in research expenditure per member of staff is accounted for by variations in subject mix. Figure 9.2 indicates that several universities have considerably greater research expenditure per member of staff than others; UMIST, London, York and Warwick, are much better placed than Ulster, Aberdeen, Salford and Exeter. The former group of universities may therefore be expected to have a greater research output than the latter group.

The composition of staff at each university is also likely to affect its research performance. First, universities employ a certain number of staff solely to do research. The percentage of 'research only' academic staff varies widely from under 16 per cent at Exeter, Hull, Keele and Ulster to over 35 per cent at Bristol, Cambridge, London, UMIST, Southampton and Surrey. This is likely to have a positive effect on research performance. Second, older and more experienced members of staff who have established reputations in research may be expected to contribute more to a university's research output than their junior colleagues.

The composition and number of students (relative to staff) may also affect research performance. A university's research output may be expected to be boosted by the presence of a large number of research students. First, research students may contribute directly to the research effort of a department. Second, research students are often hired to teach, leaving more time for staff to undertake research.

Staff time is devoted to teaching (and administration) as well as research.

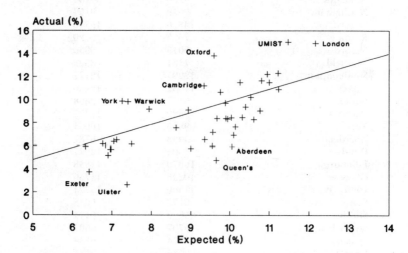

Figure 9.2 Research expenditure per member of academic staff: actual v. expected, 1986/87

Source: University Statistics, Finance, 1986/87 and own calculations.

The amount of time spent on teaching can be proxied using the student/staff ratio which has been shown to vary substantially between universities (see Chapter 2). Part of this inter-university variation can be explained by subject mix (i.e. the optimal student/staff ratio clearly varies between subjects). Even when subject mix has been taken into account, however, some universities have a more favourable student/staff ratio than others, and these universities can therefore be expected to have a greater research output.

Another factor which may influence research output is a university's geographical location. Universities located close to London have access to superior facilities and can reap the benefits which accrue from the high concentration of research facilities in a single region (i.e. the South East). This effect may be proxied by using the distance (in miles) of each university from London or by distinguishing universities on the geographical periphery of the UK (i.e. those in Wales, Scotland and Northern Ireland) from the rest.

Research performance may vary between different types of institutions. Oxford and Cambridge can be singled out because of their established reputations in research. These two universities are likely to attract some of the highest calibre staff available (including those from overseas). Two other groups of universities may be distinguished from the rest: the new greenfield universities and the ex-CATs.

Finally, several other factors which may have an effect on research output are included in the statistical analysis reported in the next section. These include the age of a university, its size, its library stock and expenditure on central computing facilities (as measured by Computer Board grants as a percentage of total recurrent income).

Statistical analysis of inter-university differences in UFC research rating

Multiple regression techniques were used to estimate the extent to which differences between universities in the UFC's rating of their research performance during 1984–88 could be explained statistically by the factors identified in the previous section. A selection of estimated regression equations (with the weighted average UFC rating as the dependent variable) is given in the appendix to this chapter. Also shown is the same set of estimated equations with the *logit* of the weighted average UFC rating as the dependent variable. The logit transformation is used because the UFC rating has a restricted range of between 1 and 5. Both sets of results are broadly similar and the same explanatory variables are found to be significant in each case. These are

1. the student/staff ratio (having taken into account the variation in this variable due to subject mix)

2. 'research only' staff as a percentage of all full-time academic staff
3. research expenditure per full-time academic (having taken into account the variation in this variable due to subject mix)
4. whether or not a university is located on the periphery of the UK (i.e. in Wales, Scotland and Northern Ireland)
5. whether or not the university is an ex-CAT.

An unfavourable student/staff ratio (i.e. one which exceeds that which could be expected on the basis of subject mix) has a significantly negative effect on research performance. There is evidence to suggest, however, that the decrease in research performance caused by successive increases in the student/staff ratio occurs at a decreasing rate (i.e. the relationship is non-linear).

There is a strong positive correlation between two explanatory variables:

1. 'research only' staff as a percentage of total staff
2. the ratio of actual to expected research expenditure per member of staff.

It is therefore impossible to include these two variables in the estimated equations at the same time. The results obtained when these two variables are included in separate equations indicate that each has a positive effect on research performance. Thus the presence of a substantial number of 'research only' staff (relative to all academic staff) increases research output. A 20 percentage point increase in 'research only' staff as a percentage of all academic staff (this is approximately equivalent to the difference in the value of this variable between City and Surrey) results in an increase in the university's research rating by about 0.5 (e.g. from 3 to 3.5).

Geographical location on the periphery of the UK (i.e. Northern Ireland, Scotland and Wales) has a detrimental effect on research rating. Universities located in these geographically peripheral areas can expect a research rating which is approximately 0.3 points lower (on average) than universities located in England.

Universities which were formerly colleges of advanced technology were found to have research ratings around 0.4 points lower (on average) than those obtained by other universities. This may be because the ex-CATs are more oriented towards applied research, which generally has lower kudos than theoretical research (see the UFC's definition of research in Table 9.3).

Finally, there was clearly a highly significant 'Oxbridge' effect. The research ratings of Oxford and Cambridge were so exceptional (even taking into account the factors described above) that all equations were re-estimated without these two universities. The estimated coefficients on the explanatory variables remained very stable.

Variables which proved not to be significant determinants of a university's research performance (as reflected by its UFC rating) include the average age of a university's staff; the percentage of its staff who are professors; the percentage of students undertaking research; expenditure on computing services as a percentage of total recurrent income; the stock of books held in its library; its age; and its size (reflected by the number of staff).

Construction of a performance indicator based upon research

The statistical results reported in the previous section indicate that around 60 per cent of the variation in the research performance of UK universities (excluding Oxford and Cambridge) can be explained by inter-university variations in the inputs available to institutions. It is therefore clear that a reliable indicator of the research performance of universities should take into account the factors which influence the ability of each university to produce research output.

Thus in evaluating the research performance of a university, the UFC's research rating should be compared not to the ratings obtained by other universities but to the rating which it could have been *expected* to achieve given its particular inputs and specific characteristics. An indicator of each university's research performance could therefore be defined as follows:

$$\text{RESEARCH} - \text{RESEARCH*}$$

where RESEARCH* is the *expected* UFC rating calculated for each university by substituting the actual values of each explanatory variable into the appropriate regression equation. Specifically

$$\text{RESEARCH*} = 2.56 - (0.49 \times \text{EXCAT}) + (0.028 \times \text{RESSTAFF}) - (1.55 \times \text{lnSTUDSTAFF}) - (0.29 \times \text{PERIPHERY})$$

All the explanatory variables are defined in the appendix to this chapter, pp. 170–2.

There is a problem in using this equation to construct a research performance indicator since it is not immediately obvious whether the two binary variables, EXCAT and PERIPHERY, should be included in estimating the expected value of each university's research rating. Leaving these two binary variables in the estimating equation acknowledges that the ex-colleges of advanced technology and the universities located on the geographical periphery of the UK have experienced specific problems which have led to a worse research performance than universities not in these two categories. It could be argued, however, that no allowance should be made for these specific problems (whatever they may be) in estimating the *expected* UFC research rating for each university. If EXCAT and PERIPHERY are excluded from the estimate of RESEARCH*, this has a considerable adverse effect on the estimated research performance of these two groups of universities (particularly the ex-colleges of advanced

Table 9.8 A performance indicator based on the UFC's 1989 research ratings

University	RESEARCH − RESEARCH*[1]			
	1^2	Rank (1 = best)	2^2	Rank (1 = best)
Aston	0.27	8	−0.21	22
Bath	0.10	19	−0.39	30
Birmingham	−0.26	35	−0.26	25
Bradford	0.18	11	−0.31	27
Bristol	0.12	17	0.12	12
Brunel	−0.39	37	−0.88	41
Cambridge[3]	—	—	—	—
City	−0.44	40	−0.93	42
Durham	−0.03	24	−0.03	15
East Anglia	0.17	15	0.17	11
Essex	0.38	4	0.38	2
Exeter	0.17	14	0.17	10
Hull	−0.12	29	−0.12	17
Keele	−0.58	43	−0.58	37
Kent	−0.28	36	−0.28	26
Lancaster	−0.12	30	−0.12	18
Leeds	−0.10	27	−0.10	16
Leicester	−0.47	41	−0.47	33
Liverpool	0.18	12	0.18	8
London	−0.24	33	−0.24	23
Loughborough	−0.11	28	−0.60	38
Manchester	0.32	6	0.32	3
UMIST	0.36	5	−0.13	19
Newcastle	0.18	13	0.18	9
Nottingham	−0.02	22	−0.02	14
Oxford[3]	—	—	—	—
Reading	−0.44	39	−0.44	31
Salford	0.02	21	−0.47	32
Sheffield	0.30	7	0.30	4
Southampton	0.10	18	0.10	13
Surrey	−0.02	23	−0.50	35
Sussex	−0.18	31	−0.18	21
Warwick	0.73	1	0.73	1
York	0.19	10	0.19	7
Aberdeen	−0.08	26	−0.38	29
Dundee	−0.41	38	−0.70	39
Edinburgh	0.05	20	−0.24	24
Glasgow	0.54	2	0.25	5
Heriot-Watt	−0.24	34	−1.02	43
St Andrews	0.50	3	0.21	6
Stirling	−0.49	42	−0.78	40
Strathclyde	0.27	9	−0.51	36
Queen's	−0.20	32	−0.50	34
Ulster	0.15	16	−0.14	20
Wales	−0.08	25	−0.37	28

Notes:
1. See p. 167 for definition of RESEARCH − RESEARCH*.
2. Research performance indicator 1 includes EXCAT and PERIPHERY in the calculation of RESEARCH*. Indicator 2 excludes EXCAT and PERIPHERY in the calculation of RESEARCH*.
3. Values for Cambridge and Oxford have been excluded from the table. If performance values are calculated without incorporating the binary variable OXBRIDGE in the computation of RESEARCH*, they obtain 1.13 and 1.14 respectively. Clearly if the binary variable OXBRIDGE is included in the computation of RESEARCH*, these performance values fall to zero (since the coefficient on OXBRIDGE is 1.13).

technology located on the geographical periphery of the UK). The effect of excluding EXCAT and PERIPHERY from the equation used to estimate RESEARCH* can be seen from Table 9.8.

A further problem arises as a result of the fact that some of the 'independent' variables in the estimated equations may themselves be dependent upon research output. Research funds per member of staff and the student/staff ratio may both be affected by a university's research record. It may be easier to attract research funding, for example, to universities which have a good research record. Research funds will therefore not only be a determinant of each university's research rating but also be determined by it. More advanced statistical methods should be used in such cases since there is an 'identification' problem.

Finally, the danger of using the residual of a regression equation as a performance indicator must once more be stressed (see p. 77).

Conclusion

The perceived quality of each university's research output has for some time been a determinant of the amount of funds it receives. Perceptions of research performance therefore already play a crucial role in the resource allocation process. Yet methods for evaluating research performance are still relatively undeveloped. There have been two serious attempts at evaluating the research performance of UK universities. The first, undertaken by the UGC in 1985/86, was roundly criticized. The methodology used in the second exercise (undertaken by the UFC in 1989) was developed in the light of these criticisms. Even so, a number of weaknesses rapidly became apparent

The main purpose of this chapter was to consider whether the research performance of entire institutions could be evaluated. The UFC's research rating of each cost centre was used to produce an average rating of the research performance of each university. We then investigated the extent to which inter-university variations in the inputs available to institutions were responsible for the apparent variations in their research performance, as reflected by the UFC's research selectivity exercise.

A number of factors could potentially affect a university's research output. The statistical analysis undertaken in this chapter indicates that a university's research output is significantly related to four main factors: its student/staff ratio; the resources devoted to research (e.g. expenditure on research or the number of 'research only' staff relative to all academic staff); being located on the geographical periphery of the UK; and whether or not a university is an ex-CAT. In addition, a significant 'Oxbridge' effect was found. The research performance of Oxford and Cambridge was exceptional even when input factors were taken into consideration.

The final section of this chapter focused attention on the possibility of creating an indicator of each university's research performance taking into account not only the quality of its research output (as reflected by the UFC rating) but also the quantity and quality of the inputs at its disposal. Regression analysis was used to produce such an indicator. Specifically the UFC rating which each university could have *expected* (given its particular array of inputs) was computed and compared with the actual UFC rating received. The resulting variable was only weakly correlated with the UFC's research rating. *It is therefore vitally important to take input variations into consideration when evaluating research output.*

Appendix to Chapter 9

UFC research rating

The unweighted mean UFC research rating for each university is simply the sum of the rating received for each cost centre divided by the number of cost centres receiving a rating. The weighted mean UFC research rating for a university is calculated as follows:

$$\text{RESEARCH}_i = \frac{\sum_j (\text{STAFF}_{ij} \times \text{RATING}_{ij})}{\sum \text{STAFF}_{ij}}$$

i = university
j = cost centre

where

STAFF_{ij} = number of full-time academic staff in cost centre j of university i
RATING_{ij} = UFC research rating for cost centre j of university i

Notes:
1. Only those cost centres which obtained a research rating were included in the calculation.
2. For London University, the cost centre rating was an average of the rating received by each constituent college for that cost centre.
3. In the case of Wales, a weighted average rating was calculated for each Welsh University College separately. A weighted average was then calculated to obtain the value for Wales as a whole.
4. Source of data: UFC 1989c.

Research expenditure per member of staff

The expected value of the research expenditure per member of staff is calculated for each university as follows:

$$\text{RESEXP}^e_i = \frac{1}{\text{STAFF}_i} \sum_j \text{STAFF}_{ij} \left(\frac{\text{RESEXP}_j}{\text{STAFF}_j} \right)$$

i = university
j = cost centre

where

RESEXP$_j$ = research expenditure per full-time member of academic staff in cost-centre j (all UK universities)
STAFF$_i$ = full-time academic staff in university i
STAFF$_j$ = full-time academic staff in cost centre j (all UK universities)
STAFF$_{ij}$ = full-time academic staff in university i, cost centre j.

Estimated regression equations: dependent variable = RESEARCH

Explanatory variables	Estimated coefficients					
			Equation number			
	(1)	*(2)*	*(3)*	*(4)*	*(5)*	*(6)*
CONSTANT	2.56	2.69	4.56	2.56	2.68	4.54
	(10.02)	(10.55)	(6.24)	(9.84)	(10.35)	(6.15)
EXCAT	−0.49	−0.42	−0.42	−0.49	−0.42	−0.43
	(−3.91)	(−3.45)	(−3.43)	(−3.86)	(−3.42)	(−3.40)
RESSTAFF	0.028				0.028	
	(2.90)				(2.85)	
STUDSTAFF			−1.88			−1.88
			(−3.34)			(−3.30)
lnSTUDSTAFF	−1.55	−2.05		−1.55	−2.05	
	(−2.38)	(−3.43)		(−2.33)	(−3.39)	
RESEXP		0.65	0.67		0.66	0.69
		(2.35)	(2.44)		(2.37)	(2.45)
PERIPHERY	−0.29	−0.27	−0.28	−0.29	−0.27	−0.28
	(−2.55)	(−2.32)	(−2.35)	(−2.52)	(−2.29)	(−2.32)
OXBRIDGE	1.13	1.10	1.10			
	(4.65)	(4.26)	(4.23)			
$\bar{R}^2$	0.75	0.73	0.73	0.62	0.60	0.60
n	45	45	45	43	43	43

Notes:
1. ( ) = t-ratios
2. A t-ratio $\geq$ 1.96 indicates significance at the 5% level or less; a t-ratio $\geq$ 2.58 indicates significance at the 1% level or less (using two-tailed test)
3. Equations *(1)*, *(2)* and *(3)* are estimated using all 45 UK universities
   Equations *(4)*, *(5)* and *(6)* exclude Oxford and Cambridge
4. Definition of variables
   EXCAT = 1 if a university is an ex-CAT and 0 otherwise
   RESSTAFF = 'research only' staff as a percentage of full-time academic staff
   STUDSTAFF = actual ratio of full-time equivalent students to full-time academic staff divided by expected ratio of full-time equivalent students to full-time academic staff
   lnSTUDSTAFF = natural logarithm of STUDSTAFF
   RESEXP = actual research expenditure per full-time member of academic staff divided by expected research expenditure per full-time member of academic staff
   PERIPHERY = 1 if a university is located in Scotland, Wales or Northern Ireland and 0 otherwise
   OXBRIDGE = 1 if university is Oxford or Cambridge.

Estimated regression equations: dependent variable = logit (RESEARCH)

Explanatory variables	Estimated coefficients					
	Equation number					
	(1)	(2)	(3)	(4)	(5)	(6)
CONSTANT	0.06	0.10	1.66	0.06	0.09	1.66
	(0.27)	(0.44)	(2.57)	(0.24)	(0.40)	(2.52)
EXCAT	−0.41	−0.37	−0.37	−0.41	−0.37	−0.37
	(−3.63)	(−3.38)	(−3.36)	(−3.60)	(−3.34)	(−3.33)
RESSTAFF	0.023			0.023		
	(2.68)			(2.66)		
STUDSTAFF			−1.58			−1.57
			(−3.16)			(−3.11)
lnSTUDSTAFF	−1.41	−1.73		−1.39	−1.73	
	(−2.38)	(−3.26)		(−2.31)	(−3.22)	
RESEXP		0.63	0.65		0.64	0.66
		(2.58)	(2.67)		(2.57)	(2.65)
PERIPHERY	−0.26	−0.24	−0.25	−0.26	−0.24	−0.25
	(−2.47)	(−2.32)	(−2.35)	(−2.44)	(−2.29)	(−2.32)
OXBRIDGE	2.09	2.04	2.04			
	(9.46)	(8.88)	(8.81)			
$\bar{R}^2$	0.84	0.84	0.83	0.60	0.60	0.59
n	45	45	45	43	43	43

Notes:
1. See notes to previous table
2. logit (RESEARCH) = ln $\left[\dfrac{\text{RESEARCH}}{5 - \text{RESEARCH}} \right]$

10

The Performance of UK Universities across Five Indicators

Introduction

Chapters 6 to 9 focused upon several measures of the output of the university sector. Teaching output was assumed to be reflected by non-completion rates, degree results and the first destination of graduates; and research output was measured by using the results of the 1989 Research Selectivity Exercise undertaken by the Universities Funding Council. The principal finding in each of these earlier chapters was that a large proportion of the differences between universities in their teaching and research output can be explained (statistically) by a set of plausible explanatory variables. It has been demonstrated that it is important to take account of the particular circumstances of each university when attempting to evaluate the performance of individual institutions. Hence there is little point in making direct comparisons between institutions of their *actual* output since a large proportion of the variation between universities in their outputs (however measured) was shown to be accounted for by corresponding variations in the inputs used.

The main conclusion to be drawn from Chapters 6 to 9 is that inter-university comparisons of outputs are of little value unless the inputs used to produce those outputs are explicitly taken into account. This can be done by using regression models to estimate the output that each university *could be expected to produce given the inputs available to it*. Doubts were raised, however, in each of the previous chapters about the value of using regression residuals (i.e. the actual value minus the predicted value of each output) to measure performance (see p. 77). In particular, it was shown that once inter-university variations in the inputs used were taken into account, the remaining 'unexplained' variation in each of the output measures was relatively small (under 20 per cent for the measures of teaching output).

A further problem with these indicators concerns the use of variables reflecting particular characteristics of universities (e.g. whether or not a university is located in Scotland and whether or not it is an ex-college of advanced technology). In previous chapters, if a particular sub-group of universities with a common characteristic was found to be performing significantly differently (on average) from other UK universities, this difference was 'allowed for' in the computation of the specific performance indicator. This method favours sub-groups which are found to be performing differently from others. This chapter investigates the extent to which each of the performance indicators constructed in previous chapters is sensitive to changes in the assumptions underlying its calculation.

Any investigation into university performance would not be complete if universities were judged on the basis of only one of the many activities in which they are involved. Universities are multi-product organizations and as such may well perform better on some indicators than they do on others. It is important that this fact should be recognized and incorporated into any appraisal of university performance. This chapter uses the performance indicators constructed in previous chapters to illustrate the problems which are likely to be encountered when attempting to assess performance across several indicators simultaneously.

The remainder of this chapter is in three sections. The first section brings together the performance indicators constructed in Chapters 6 to 9. The second section investigates the sensitivity of each of these performance indicators to changes in its specification. The third section discusses the possibility of measuring the performance of universities across all indicators simultaneously.

Five indicators of the performance of universities

Five quantitative measures of output have been defined and evaluated over several years in earlier chapters. These measures are

1. the non-completion rate (NCR)
2. the percentage of graduates obtaining a first or upper second class honours degree (DEGREE RESULT)
3. the percentage of graduates obtaining permanent employment (EMPLOY)
4. the percentage of graduates proceeding to further education or training (FURTHER)
5. the average research rating obtained by each university in the UFC's 1989 Research Selectivity Exercise (RESEARCH).

The results of the regression analyses reported in Chapters 6 to 9 are now used to estimate the value of output that each university would have been expected to achieve given its particular inputs and characteristics. The equations for estimating these expected values for all five outputs are given in the appendix to this chapter (pp. 179–80). Thus the *expected* non-completion rate is calculated for each university by substituting actual values of ALEVEL, BUS + LANG, HALL and SCOTTISH into the first equation given in the appendix. Having obtained the *expected* non-completion rate for each university, this is then subtracted from the *actual* non-completion rate. A similar exercise has been undertaken for the other four output measures in order to construct a set of performance indicators for all UK universities. (The two Northern Ireland universities had to be excluded since they were not included in the first destinations analysis in Chapter 8.)

Two questions concerning these performance indicators are addressed in the remainder of this chapter. First, how sensitive are the performance indicators to changes in the method of calculating the expected value? Second, what difficulties are likely to be encountered in any attempt to carry out an assessment of university performance based upon several performance indicators simultaneously?

Sensitivity analysis

Although the equations given in the appendix to this chapter can be used to calculate performance indicators for each of the five measures of university output, a problem arises concerning whether all explanatory variables should be included as inputs into the production process. The problem concerns the inclusion (or otherwise) of variables used in the regression analysis to distinguish between different types of universities.

Several sub-groups of universities have been identified as performing significantly differently from other universities on each of the five output measures. Universities located in Scotland, for example have a higher non-completion rate by about four percentage points (on average) than other universities even after other factors have been taken into account. Thus the *expected* non-completion rate in Scottish universities is four percentage points higher than in non-Scottish universities. Several possible reasons have been suggested as to why the non-completion rate is higher on average in Scottish universities – such as the higher percentage of students on four-year degree courses and the far higher proportion of 17- and 18-year-olds in total entrants compared to the rest of the UK.

The question to which we need an answer is whether any allowance should be made for the poorer performance of Scottish universities compared to their non-Scottish counterparts. If such an allowance is made (by including SCOTTISH in the equation used to estimate the *expected* non-completion rate) this has the effect of boosting the performance of Scottish universities by four percentage points. Whether such an allowance should be made, however, is unclear. This is because the reasons for the higher non-completion rates in Scottish universities (when considered as a group) are not yet known.

A similar argument applies to other variables which have been included to reflect different types of universities. Thus the ex-colleges of advanced

Table 10.1   A comparison of the rankings of universities derived from various performance indicators

University	Non-completion rate		Degree results		Employability of new graduates		Further education or training		Research rating	
	1	*2*	*1*	*2*	*1*	*2*	*1*	*2*	*1*	*2*
Aston	14	13	9	1	40	26	10	14	8	23
Bath	36	30	12	3	28	13	20	24	18	31
Birmingham	13	12	18	23	17	19	18	22	35	26
Bradford	10	9	36	16	11	4	39	41	11	28
Bristol	16	14	4	12	29	25	11	15	16	14
Brunel	42	39	15	5	8	2	24	30	37	41
Cambridge	18	16	6	15	43	41	5	7	22	2
City	38	32	22	8	6	1	36	38	40	42
Durham	12	11	37	35	4	7	16	21	25	17
East Anglia	6	5	24	21	34	27	14	19	15	13
Essex	19	17	11	13	38	33	3	4	4	4
Exeter	21	18	38	36	13	14	7	10	14	12
Hull	37	31	19	26	5	8	22	27	30	19
Keele	43	42	20	18	42	36	2	3	43	37
Kent	34	28	33	25	2	5	43	43	36	27
Lancaster	4	3	23	20	1	3	37	39	31	20
Leeds	5	4	28	30	39	34	12	16	28	18
Leicester	8	7	21	27	22	22	6	9	41	34
Liverpool	30	25	35	33	37	32	30	34	12	10
London	39	33	10	19	19	21	34	37	33	24
Loughborough	3	2	34	14	21	9	33	36	29	38
Manchester	28	23	26	28	36	31	8	11	6	5
UMIST	11	10	29	9	33	18	28	32	5	21
Newcastle	33	27	42	37	3	6	38	40	13	11
Nottingham	7	6	7	17	14	15	21	26	23	16
Oxford	40	34	43	39	27	24	41	42	21	1
Reading	26	21	1	2	9	11	9	13	39	32
Salford	31	26	14	4	31	16	29	33	20	33
Sheffield	9	8	31	32	35	28	23	29	7	6
Southampton	17	15	27	29	10	12	19	23	17	15
Surrey	1	1	30	11	24	10	27	31	24	35
Sussex	24	19	32	24	15	17	31	35	32	22
Warwick	29	24	8	10	18	20	15	20	1	3
York	27	22	5	6	26	23	13	18	10	9
Aberdeen	35	41	16	40	12	35	40	25	27	30
Dundee	41	43	25	38	30	42	4	2	38	39
Edinburgh	20	36	17	41	20	39	35	17	19	25
Glasgow	32	40	40	43	25	40	32	12	2	7
Heriot-Watt	23	38	39	34	32	37	26	8	34	43
St Andrews	22	37	3	31	41	43	1	1	3	8
Stirling	2	29	41	42	7	29	42	28	42	40
Strathclyde	15	35	2	7	23	30	25	6	9	36
Wales	25	20	13	22	16	38	17	5	26	29

Notes:
Definitions of the two indicators for each performance measure are given on p. 177.
The two Northern Ireland universities (Belfast and Queen's) are not included because a complete set of performance values was not available for these two universities.
All four indicators of teaching output refer to 1985/86; the research indicator covers the period 1984–88.

technology (ex-CATs) perform better as a group in getting their graduates into permanent jobs (even after allowing for factors such as differences in subject mix between ex-CATs and other types of universities). On the other hand, the ex-CATs have a lower research rating (on average) than other types of universities. Once again, we face the problem of deciding whether the variables included to reflect different types of institutions should themselves be included in calculating a performance indicator. In view of the uncertainty about whether these variables should be included or excluded in calculating the expected value of each output indicator, this section undertakes a sensitivity analysis on all five performance indicators.

Two sets of performance indicators have been constructed for all five measures of university output. The rank of each university (1 = best performer) is given for each performance indicator in Table 10.1. In all cases, indicator 1 includes all explanatory variables whereas indicator 2 excludes the variables which distinguish between different types of universities (i.e. EXCAT, SCOTTISH, etc.). The primary purpose of this exercise is to test the sensitivity of each performance indicator to the inclusion (or exclusion) of these variables. The main result is that the two performance indicators for each measure of university output are significantly positively correlated: the correlation coefficient ranges from 0.62 for the two performance indicators based on degree results to 0.88 for the two performance indicators based on graduates proceeding to further education or training. Although the correlation between indicator 1 and indicator 2 is significant for all five output measures, there are substantial changes in the rank of several universities. Even in the case of the most highly correlated pair of performance indicators (i.e. graduates proceeding to further education or training) five universities experience a change in their rank of at least 15 places. Thus Aberdeen, Heriot-Watt, Edinburgh, Glasgow and Strathclyde all achieve a substantially better rank when their geographical location is not included as an explanatory variable (i.e. PERIPHERY is omitted from the calculation of the expected percentage of graduates proceeding to further education or training). The opposite result is obtained when geographical location is excluded from the indicator based upon the proportion of graduates obtaining a permanent job.

The results given in Table 10.1 clearly indicate that the performance indicators are very sensitive to the inclusion (or exclusion) of variables used to identify different types of universities. This is particularly true for the ex-CATs and for Scottish universities. The implication of this high degree of sensitivity in the rank of institutions which belong to particular sub-groups of universities is that we need to know more about why such sub-groups behave in the way they do if further progress is to be made in constructing adequate performance indicators at the institutional level.

Constructing an overall performance indicator: is this possible?

The importance of considering the performance of a university across several indicators is vividly demonstrated in Table 10.1. Taking any individual university, we can see that its relative performance varies considerably depending upon which indicator is selected. The variation in each university's performance between the five indicators is substantial for *all* universities. No university has performed either consistently well or consistently badly across all indicators.

Further evidence of the lack of consistency in performance across all five indicators is provided by Table 10.2, which gives the correlation coefficient between each pair of indicators. In all cases, there is very little correlation between the indicators. The obvious conclusion to be drawn is that it would be pointless to attempt to construct a composite performance indicator which attempted to measure the overall performance of each university across several indicators simultaneously. This could be done only if a weight could be attached to each indicator to reflect the relative worth of the various outputs produced by the university sector. Is it more important

Table 10.2   The correlation between each pair of performance indicators

Variables correlated	Correlation coefficients	
	Indicator 1	*Indicator 2*
Non-completion rate v. degree results	−0.04	0.31
Non-completion rate v. graduate employability	0.00	0.41**
Non-completion rate v. further education or training	−0.15	−0.37*
Non-completion rate v. research rating	0.29*	0.25
Degree results v. graduate employability	−0.20	−0.12
Degree results v. further education or training	0.42**	−0.09
Degree results v. research rating	0.08	−0.15
Graduate employability v. further education or training	−0.59**	−0.73**
Graduate employability v. research rating	−0.31*	−0.20
Further education or training v. research rating	0.09	−0.01

Notes:
* = significant at 5%; ** = significant at 1%
The variables are the performance indicators from which the ranks given in Table 10.1 were derived.

to produce high-quality research output or to provide students with excellent tuition? Is it more important to reduce the non-completion rate or to improve degree results? Is it more important to increase the proportion of graduates obtaining permanent employment or to improve degree results? Since we can provide no answers to such fundamental questions, there is little point in even attempting to construct an overall measure of performance for each individual institution.

Conclusion

The primary purpose of this chapter has been to investigate the performance of each university across a range of indicators in order to discover whether any individual institutions have performed consistently well or consistently badly. This was done by comparing the performance of each university across the four teaching indicators constructed in Chapters 6 to 8 and the research indicator constructed in Chapter 9. Our main finding was that all universities performed relatively well on some indicators while simultaneously performing relatively badly on others. Perhaps this is only to be expected, however, since these indicators reflect different aspects of the output produced by universities.

A further finding of some interest concerns the performance of universities which belong to identifiable sub-groups, such as Scottish universities and the ex-CATs. The estimated performance of Scottish universities, for example, deteriorates for most indicators when Scottish universities are not separately identified. The same is true for the ex-CATs. But why do universities in these two sub-groups generally perform differently from universities which do not belong to these sub-groups? Convincing answers to this question have not yet been provided.

Appendix to Chapter 10

Equations used to construct five performance indicators

Non-completion rate
$NCR^* = 36.46 - (1.59 \times ALEVEL) - (0.14 \times BUS + LANG) - (0.063 \times HALL) + (4.05\ SCOTTISH)$

Degree results
$DEGREE\ RESULT^* = -3.26 + (3.26 \times ALEVEL) - (0.05 \times LIVEHOME) + (2.94 \times LIBRARY) + (7.05 \times EXCAT) + (2.88 \times NEW) - (6.85 \times SCOTTISH)$

Employability

EMP* = 5.35 − (0.30 × MILKROUND) − (7.61 × PERIPHERY) + (3.15 × EXCAT)

Further education or training

FUR* = 11.04 + (0.38 × MILKROUND) + (0.43 × UNEMPLOYMENT) − (0.12 × AGE) + (3.70 × PERIPHERY)

Research performance

RESEARCH* = 2.56 + (0.028 × RESSTAFF) − (1.55 × lnSTUDSTAFF) − (0.49 × EXCAT) − (0.29 × PERIPHERY) + (1.13 × OXBRIDGE)

Notes:

1. *Definition of variables*

ALEVEL	= average A level score of undergraduate entrants
BUS + LANG	= percentage of undergraduate entrants undertaking business, social science or language courses
HALL	= percentage of full-time students living in halls of residence
LIVEHOME	= percentage of full-time students living at home
LIBRARY	= library expenditure as a percentage of total recurrent expenditure
MILKROUND	= number of graduates per employer visit (to each university)
UNEMPLOYMENT	= percentage of unemployed in region in which university is located
AGE	= foundation year of university
RESSTAFF	= 'research only' staff as a percentage of all full-time academic staff
lnSTUDSTAFF	= natural logarithm of the student/staff ratio divided by the expected student/staff ratio (on the basis of subject mix)
SCOTTISH	= 1 if a university is located in Scotland, 0 otherwise
EXCAT	= 1 if a university is an ex-CAT, 0 otherwise
NEW	= 1 if a university is a new greenfield university
PERIPHERY	= 1 if a university is located outside England, 0 otherwise
OXBRIDGE	= 1 if university is Oxford or Cambridge, 0 otherwise
EMP	= actual minus expected (on the basis of subject mix) percentage of graduates obtaining permanent employment
FUR	= actual minus expected (on the basis of subject mix) percentage of graduates proceeding to further education or training.

2. All five performance indicators are for 1985/86 except RESEARCH, which covers the period 1984–88, and NCR which is based on 1980 entrants.

11

Performance Measurement in Universities: Some Conclusions

Introduction

The main aim of this book has been to take a critical look at the possibility of measuring the performance of UK universities. The need for such an assessment derives directly from the government's insistence that higher education must become more accountable to the taxpayer. This is part of a much broader policy requiring all publicly funded organizations to prove that they are worthy of support. The logic underlying this policy is that performance indicators are needed for those parts of the public sector in which normal commercial criteria (e.g. profitability) are not applicable. The non-marketability of much of the output of higher education and the nebulous nature of many of the benefits mean that its performance cannot be measured by examining the profit and loss accounts of each institution. More ingenious methods have to be devised for measuring performance in the public sector.

Despite the obvious distaste in academic circles for performance measurement, governments in many parts of the world are clearly determined to make the higher education sector more accountable to the taxpayer (Cave and Hanney 1990). It is therefore important for questions to be asked about the way in which the performance of higher education institutions should be measured and assessed. Indeed, there is now a substantial international literature which investigates the problems of performance measurement in higher education. Much of the work, however, concentrates on methodological issues and there have been few attempts so far to construct and evaluate specific performance indicators. The present book is an attempt to begin the process of filling this void.

Constructing performance indicators

Four specific indicators of the teaching and research activities of UK universities have been investigated in detail in this book. These are

1. undergraduate non-completion rates

2. degree results
3. the first destination of newly qualified graduates
4. the research rating of each university.

These four indicators were chosen for several reasons. First, they could all be regarded as measuring in some way the outcome of the activities of the university sector. In other words, they could be treated *as if* they were the outputs produced by universities. Second, data were available at the institutional level for all four variables. Third, the government itself has indicated that these four variables should be included in any performance measurement. Fourth, the university sector takes these four variables very seriously in discussions of performance.

It is our contention, however, that *none* of these variables is useful as a performance indicator *per se*. This is because variations in these various measures of output between institutions are only to be expected since outputs are *always* determined by inputs and since the type and quality of inputs available to universities varies enormously *between* universities. It is therefore hardly surprising that there are extremely wide variations between universities in variables such as non-completion rates, degree results, the first destination of graduates and research output. This means that it is pointless to compare the output of universities without taking into account differences in the inputs used up in producing these outputs.

The importance of inputs in determining outputs is easily demonstrated. Chapters 6 and 7 showed that inter-university differences in non-completion rates and degree results could be accounted for, to a substantial extent, by corresponding differences between universities in the ability of student entrants (as reflected by A level scores). The ability of students is not the only factor, of course, which affects non-completion rates and degree results but this example serves to demonstrate the importance of inputs in determining outputs. Similarly Chapter 8 showed that subject mix plays a major part in explaining inter-university differences in the percentage of each university's graduates who obtain a permanent job; Chapter 9 shows that differences in research rating between universities are highly significantly related to variables such as the student/staff ratio (negatively) and research income per member of staff (positively).

This brief summary of the results obtained from various statistical analyses of the relationship between inputs and outputs in the UK university sector is sufficient to demonstrate that it would be entirely misleading to compare the output of different universities without taking into account corresponding variations in the type and quality of the inputs used to produce those outputs. Our methodological approach has therefore been to compare inter-university differences in outputs *only after allowing for inter-university differences in the inputs actually used.* Thus for each measure of output, we identified what we believed to be the main explanatory variables (for which information was readily available or could be acquired). Multiple regression analysis was then used to estimate the relationship between each selected output variable and a set of explanatory variables (i.e. the inputs). These inputs were then substituted into the estimated regression equation in order to produce a *standardized* value for each university and this standardized value was then used as the benchmark against which each university's *actual* output was compared.

This approach has been used on all four measures of university output. Our main finding is that once inter-university differences in inputs available to each institution are taken into account, the remaining 'unexplained' variation between universities is relatively small – especially for the three indicators of teaching output (non-completion rates, degree results and first destinations of newly qualified graduates). In all three cases, over 80 per cent of the variation between universities can be explained by a set of plausible explanatory variables. With less than 20 per cent of the variation remaining unexplained after differences in inputs have been taken into account, this raises the question as to whether the unexplained variation is itself a useful indicator of performance. Our own view is that the indicators devised in this book are more acceptable as measures of performance than comparisons of the *actual* value of the four output indicators since they do at least take inputs into account. More rigorous tests would be required, however, before they could be regarded as sufficiently robust to be used for resource allocation purposes.

Problems to be overcome and possible ways forward

Several major practical and methodological problems still have to be overcome in performance measurement in the higher education sector. First, the types of performance indicators considered in the present book are too simplistic to be used with confidence for resource allocation purposes. To what extent can teaching quality be accurately reflected by variables such as non-completion rates, degree results and the first destination of newly qualified graduates – even allowing for inter-university differences in the inputs used? Would it not be more appropriate to assess teaching quality directly by continuous monitoring and appraisal of *all* teaching activities in *all* institutions? But this would require enormous amounts of time and energy if it were to be done properly. Would it be worth it? This question needs to be answered before large amounts of resources are committed to such an exercise.

A second problem with the types of indicators investigated in this book is that they are 'data driven'. Variables such as non-completion rates, degree results and those relating to the first destination of new graduates have been produced for administrative purposes and not with the construction of performance indicators in mind. The indicators are therefore motivated by data availability rather than by any attempt to define a set of objectives and then produce data which relates specifically to these objectives. It is far from clear, however, that the objectives of higher education could be specified in such a way that appropriate data could be collected for assessing the extent to which the objectives were being achieved (see Chapter 4). What types of data would be collected, for example, to measure whether any individual institution is 'preserving and disseminating cultural values' or 'cultivating talent for the sake of self-enrichment'?

Third, this book has focused almost entirely on whole institutions. This is fine for providing information about how one institution compares with another. This level of aggregation is inappropriate, however, for managing resources *within* institutions. Cost centres are more relevant for this purpose since they are increasingly being treated as accounting units. More attention should therefore be devoted to inter-university comparisons *at the cost centre level*.

Fourth, only one approach to measuring the performance of institutions has been explored in this book. Regression methods have been used to estimate the relationship between inputs and outputs and these estimated relationships have then been used to produce performance indicators. A potentially useful alternative approach is to estimate an efficiency frontier (Farrell 1957; Charnes *et al.* 1978; Tomkins and Green 1988; Barrow 1990) using *data envelopment analysis*. This allows individual accounting units (such as cost centres) to be compared with the 'best practice' units within any given system (having taken into account all quantifiable inputs). It would be interesting and potentially valuable to compare the results of the regression approach with those obtained using data envelopment analysis.

Fifth, only a very limited range of performance indicators has been investigated in this book. Future research needs to consider a much wider range of university activities. For example, we suggest that detailed statistical investigations are needed of inter-university variations in the following variables:

1. the completion rate of postgraduate students
2. the first destination of postgraduates
3. the extent to which universities are catering for students with non-standard qualifications
4. the involvement of universities in contract research and consultancy
5. the interaction between universities and their local and regional communities
6. the responsiveness of universities to changing circumstances such as the introduction of a credit transfer system; setting up new courses and new degrees; and providing short courses and part-time courses for mature students and for workers extending their range of skills.

Another potentially important issue which we have not examined in this book relates to the *joint production* of different types of outputs. Outputs have been treated as if they are completely independent of each other even though it is very clearly the case that the teaching, research and administrative tasks undertaken by academic staff are often very difficult to separate. Research and teaching are often very closely intertwined and treating these as separate activities is inevitably artificial and potentially misleading. Future research must address this issue if acceptable performance indicators are to be constructed.

The final problem which we believe requires attention is the dearth of information about the career paths of graduates (and perhaps even non-graduates). The First Destination Record provides virtually worthless information about the labour market prospects of graduates from different universities and it would be far more valuable to collect data which described the career path of each university's graduates over (say) their first five years in the labour market. If such an exercise were undertaken only once every three years for a sample of graduates, it would provide far more valuable information than is currently obtainable from the First Destination Record.

Conclusion

Perhaps the only safe way to measure performance is to take an extremely broad view of what universities do and the processes they use to achieve their ultimate objectives. This would avoid undue reliance being placed upon an excessively narrow range of *quantifiable* performance indicators. In the last resort, decisions will have to be made about the weight to be attached to each *available* indicator of performance. A consensus will ultimately have to be reached within the higher education sector about which indicators are acceptable and the extent to which they should be used in the allocation of resources both within and between institutions.

Our final word is one of warning. No one has yet devised even a *single* indicator of performance which commands wide support amongst the academic community. Performance measurement is still very much in its infancy and those using performance indicators, whether they refer to teaching or research activities, should use them with great caution and considerable humility. They would do well to heed the warning issued annually in *University Management Statistics and Performance Indicators*: 'uncritical use of these indicators may seriously damage the health of your university' (Committee of Vice-Chancellors and Principals).

References

ABRC (Advisory Board for the Research Councils) (1987). *A Strategy for the Science Base*, London, HMSO.

ABRC/UGC (Advisory Board for the Research Councils/University Grants Committee) (1982). *Report of a Joint Working Party on the Support of University Scientific Research* (Merrison Report), Cmnd. 8567, London, HMSO.

Aleamoni, L. M. and Yimer, M. (1973). 'An investigation of the relationship between colleague rating, student rating, research productivity and academic rank in rating instructional effectiveness', *Journal of Educational Psychology*, 64, 3: 274–7.

Anderson, R. C., Narin, F. and McAllister, P. (1978). 'Publication ratings versus peer ratings of universities', *Journal of the American Society for Information Science*, 29: 91–103.

Anderson Report (1960). *Grants to Students*, Report of a committee appointed by the Minister of Education and the Secretary of State for Scotland in June 1958, Cmnd. 1051, London, HMSO.

Astin, A. W. (1975). *Preventing Students from Dropping Out*, San Francisco, Jossey-Bass.

Astin, A. W., Korin, W. and Green, K. (1987). 'Retaining and satisfying students', *Educational Record*, 68, 1: 36–42.

Barrow, M. M. (1990). 'Techniques in efficiency measurement in the public sector', in M. Cave, M. Kogan and R. Smith (eds) *Output and Performance Measurement in Government: The State of the Art*, London, Jessica Kingsley Publishers.

Bayer, A. E. and Folger, J. (1966). 'Some correlates of a citation measure of productivity in science', *Sociology of Education*, 39: 381–90.

Bee, M. and Dolton, P. (1985). 'Degree class and pass rates: an inter-university comparison', *Higher Education Review*, 17: 45–52.

Bell, J. G. and Seater, J. J. (1978). 'Publishing performance: departmental and individual', *Economic Inquiry*, 16: 599–615.

Bentham, G. (1987). 'An evaluation of the UGC's ratings of the research of British university geography departments', *Area*, 19:147–54.

Berdahl, R. (1983). 'Coordinating structures: the UGC and US state coordinating agencies', in M. Shattock (ed.) *The Structure and Governance of Higher Education*, Surrey, SRHE.

Blaug, M. (1968). 'The productivity of universities', in M. Blaug (ed.) *Economics of Education*, vol. 2, Harmondsworth, Penguin.

Bowen, H. R. (1980). *The Costs of Higher Education: How Much do Colleges and*

Universities Spend per Student and How Much Should they Spend?, San Francisco, Jossey-Bass.

Brandl, J. E. (1970). 'Public service outputs of higher education: an explanatory essay', in B. Lawrence, G. Weathersby and V. W. Patterson (eds) *The Outputs of Higher Education*, Colorado, WICHE.

Cave, M. and Hanney, S. (1990). 'Performance indicators in higher education and research', in M. Cave, M. Kogan and R. Smith, *Output and Performance Measures in Government: The State of the Art*, London, Jessica Kingsley Publishers.

—— (1991). 'Performance indicators in higher education: an international survey', in *The Encyclopaedia of Higher Education*, edited by B. R. Clark and G. Neave, Oxford, Pergamon Press.

Cave, M., Hanney, S., Kogan, M. and Trevett, G. (1988). *The Use of Performance Indicators in Higher Education: A Critical Analysis of Developing Practice*, London, Jessica Kingsley Publishers.

Charnes, A., Cooper, W. W. and Rhodes, E. (1978). 'Measuring the efficiency of decision-making units', *European Journal of Operational Research*, 2, 6: 429–44.

Chickering, A. W. and Kuper, E. (1971). 'Educational outcomes for commuters and residents', *Educational Record*, 52: 255–61.

Clayton, K. M. (1988). 'Recent developments in the funding of university research', *Higher Education Quarterly*, 42: 20–37.

Cole, J. R. and Cole, S. (1972). 'The Ortega hypothesis', *Science*, 178: 368–75.

—— (1974). 'Citation analysis', *Science*, 183: 32–3.

Cole, S. and Cole, J. R. (1967). 'Scientific output and recognition: a study in the operation of the reward system of science', *American Sociological Review*, 32: 377–90.

CVCP (Committee of Vice-Chancellors and Principals) (1987). *University Management Statistics and Performance Indicators, UK Universities*, London.

—— (1988). *University Management Statistics and Performance Indicators, UK Universities*, London.

—— (1989). *University Management Statistics and Performance Indicators, UK Universities*, London.

Crane, D. (1965). 'Scientists at major and minor universities: a study of productivity and recognition', *American Sociological Review*, 30: 699–714.

Croom, D. L. (1970). 'Dangers in the use of the Science Citation Index', *Nature*, 227: 1173.

Crum, R. and Parikh, A. (1983). 'Headmasters' reports, admissions and academic performance in Social Sciences', *Educational Studies*, 9: 169–84.

Davis, P. and Papanek, G. F. (1984). 'Faculty ratings of major economics departments by citations', *American Economic Review*, 74: 225–30.

De Rome, E. and Lewin, T. (1984). 'Predicting persistence at university from information obtained at intake', *Higher Education*, 13:49–66.

Dean, J. W. (1976). 'An alternative rating system for university economics departments', *Economic Inquiry*, 14: 146–53.

Dent, P. L. and Lewis, D. J. (1976). 'The relationship between teaching effectiveness and measures of research quality', *Educational Research Quarterly*, 1, 3: 3–16.

Department of Education and Science (1972). *Education: A Framework for Expansion*, Cmnd. 5174, London, HMSO.

—— (1978). *Higher Education into the 1990s*, London, HMSO.

—— (1985). *The Development of Higher Education into the 1990s*, Cmnd. 9524, London, HMSO.

—— (1987a). 'Changes in structure and national planning of higher education:

contracts between the funding bodies and higher education institutions', Consultative document, London.
—— (1987b). *Higher Education: Meeting the Challenge*, Cmnd. 114, London, HMSO.
—— (1987c). *Review of the University Grants Committee* (Croham Report), Cmnd. 81, London, HMSO.
—— (1989). 'Shifting the balance of public funding of higher education to fees', Consultative Paper, London.
Dixon, M. (1982). 'Need for inquiry', *Financial Times*, 21 January: 14.
—— (1984). 'How universities fared in the job market', *Financial Times*, 26 January: 10.
—— (1985a). 'Worsening freeze on supply of key workers', *Financial Times*, 17 January: 33.
—— (1985b). 'What happened to universities' graduates?', *Financial Times*, 14 November: 15.
—— (1987). 'How graduates fared', *Financial Times*, 9 September: 15.
Entwistle, N. J. and Wilson, J. D. (1977). *Degrees of Excellence: The Academic Achievement Game*, London, Hodder and Stoughton.
Farrell, M. J. (1957). 'The measurement of productive efficiency', *Journal of the Royal Statistical Society, Series A*, 120, 2: 253–90.
Freeman, P. R. (1970). 'A multivariate study of students' performance in the university examinations', *Journal of the Royal Statistical Society, Series A*, 133: 38–55.
Garfield, E. (1970). 'Citation indexing for studying science', *Nature*, 227: 669–71.
Gillett, R. (1987a). 'Serious anomalies in the UGC comparative evaluation of the research performance of psychology departments', *Bulletin of the British Psychological Society*, 40: 42–9.
—— (1987b). 'No way to assess research', *New Scientist*, 115 (1571): 59–60.
Gillett, R. and Aitkenhead, M. (1987). 'Rank injustice in academic research', *Nature*, 327, 6,121: 381–2.
Gleave, M. B., Harrison, C. and Moss, R. P. (1987). 'UGC research ratings: the bigger the better?', *Area*, 19:163–6.
Goudsmit, S. A. (1974). 'Citation analysis', *Science*, 183: 28.
Graves, P. E., Marchand, J. R. and Thompson, R. (1982). 'Economics departmental rankings: research incentives, constraints and efficiency', *American Economic Review*, 72: 1131–41.
—— (1984). 'Economics departmental rankings: reply and errata', *American Economic Review*, 74: 834–6.
Hammond, P. E., Meyer, J. W. and Miller, D. (1969). 'Teaching versus research: sources of misperceptions', *Journal of Higher Education*, 40: 682–90.
Hare, P. and Wyatt, G. (1988). 'Modelling the determination of research output in British universities', *Research Policy*, 17: 315–28.
Harris, G. (1988). 'Research performance indicators in Australian university economics departments', presented at the Australia Association for Research in Education Conference, University of New England.
—— (1989). 'Research output in Australian university research centres in economics', *Higher Education*, 18, 4: 397–409.
Harry, J. and Goldner, N. S. (1972). 'The null relationship between teaching and research', *Sociology of Education*, 45: 47–60.
Hayes, J. R. (1971). 'Research, teaching and faculty fate', *Science*, 172: 227–30.
Hirsch, B. T., Austin, R., Brooks, J. and Moore, J. B. (1984). 'Economics departmental rankings: comment', *American Economic Review*, 74: 822–6.

Hogan, T. D. (1984). 'Economics departmental rankings: comment', *American Economic Review*, 74: 827–33.

House, D. R. and Yeager, J. H. (1978). 'The distribution of publication success within and among top economics departments: a disaggregative view of recent evidence', *Economic Inquiry*, 16: 593–8.

House of Commons (1987). *Education Reform Bill*, Bill 53, Session 1987/88.

Janke, N. C. (1967). 'Abuses of citation indexing', *Science* 156: 892.

Jarratt Report (1985). *Report of the Steering Committee for Efficiency Studies in Universities*, London, Committee of Vice Chancellors and Principals.

Johnes, G. (1988). 'Determinants of research output in economic departments in British universities', *Research Policy*, 17: 171–8.

—— (1989). 'Ranking university departments: problems and opportunities', *Politics*, 9, 2: 16–22.

—— (1990). 'Measures of research output: university departments of economics in the UK, 1983–88', *Economic Journal*, 100: 556–60.

Johnes, G., Taylor, J. and Ferguson, G. (1987). 'The employability of new graduates: a study of differences between UK universities', *Applied Economics*, 19: 695–710.

Johnes, J. (1990a). 'Determinants of student wastage in higher education', *Studies in Higher Education*, 15, 1: 87–99.

—— (1990b). 'Unit costs: some explanations of the differences between UK universities', *Applied Economics*, 22: 853–62.

Johnes, J. and Taylor, J. (1987). 'Degree quality: an investigation into differences between UK universities, *Higher Education*, 16: 581–602.

—— (1989a). 'Undergraduate non-completion rates: differences between UK universities', *Higher Education*, 16: 209–25.

—— (1989b). 'The first destination of new graduates: comparisons between universities', *Applied Economics*, 21: 357–73.

—— (1990). 'Undergraduate non-completion rates; a reply', *Higher Education*, 19: 385–90.

Jones, C. L., McMichael, P. M. and McPherson, A. F. (1973). 'Residence and the first year student', *Universities Quarterly*, 28: 111–22.

Jones, P. K. (1989). *Report on the 1989 Research Assessment Exercise*, London, Universities Funding Council.

Kapur, R. L. (1972). 'Student wastage at Edinburgh University', *Universities Quarterly*, 26: 353–77 and 483–96.

King, J. (1987). 'A review of bibliometric and other science indicators and their role in research evaluation', *Journal of Information Science*, 13: 261–76.

Krishnan, K. S. and Clelland, R. C. (1973). 'Selection of undergraduate freshmen using discriminant analysis', *Journal of Experimental Education*, 41, 3: 28–36.

Lawani, S. M. (1977). 'Citation analysis and the quality of scientific productivity', *Bioscience*, 27: 26–31.

Layard, R. and Verry, D. (1975). 'Cost functions for university teaching and research', *Economic Journal*, 85: 55–74.

Lindsey, D. (1980). 'Production and citation measures in the sociology of science', *Social Studies of Science*, 10: 145–62.

Linsky, A. S. and Straus, M. A. (1975). 'Student evaluations, research productivity, and eminence of college faculty', *Journal of Higher Education*, 46: 89–102.

Lloyd, C. H. (1987). 'The research productivity of UK dental schools in the years 1980–85', *Medical Science Research*, 15, 7: 349–53.

McGervey, J. D. (1974). 'Citation analysis', *Science*, 183: 28–31.

McPherson, A. and Paterson, L. (1990). 'Undergraduate non-completion rates: a comment', *Higher Education*, 19: 377–83.

MacRoberts, M. H. and MacRoberts, B. R. (1984). 'The negational reference: or the art of dissembling', *Social Studies of Science*, 14: 91–4.

—— (1987a). 'Quantitative measures of communication in science; a study of the formal level', *Social Studies of Science*, 16: 151–72.

—— (1987b). 'Another test of the normative theory of citing', *Journal of the American Society of Information Science*, December.

Manis, J. G. (1951). 'Some academic influences upon publication and productivity', *Social Forces*, 29: 267–72.

Margolis, J. (1967). 'Citation indexing and evaluation of scientific papers', *Science*, 155: 1213–19.

Marsh, L. M. (1966). 'College dropouts: a review', *Personnel and Guidance Journal*, 44: 475–80.

Martin, B. R. and Irvine, J. (1983). 'Assessing basic research', *Research Policy*, 12: 61–90.

May, K. O. (1967). 'Abuses of citation indexing', *Science*, 156: 890–2.

Meltzer, B. N. (1949). 'The productivity of social scientists', *American Journal of Sociology*, 55: 25–9.

Miller, G. W. (1970). *Success, Failure and Wastage in Higher Education*, London, Harrap.

Moore, P. G. (1987). 'University financing 1979–86', *Higher Education Quarterly*, 41: 25–42.

Moravcsik, M. J. (1973). 'Measures of scientific growth', *Research Policy*, 2: 266–75.

Nevin, E. (1972). 'How not to get a first', *Economic Journal*, 82: 658–73.

—— (1985). 'The finance of university academic departments', *Applied Economics*, 17: 761–79.

Niemi, A. W. (1975). 'Journal publication performance during 1970–74: the relative output of Southern Economics Departments', *Southern Economic Journal*, 42: 97–106.

Panos, R. J. and Astin, A. W. (1968). 'Attrition among college students', *American Educational Research Journal*, 5: 57–72.

Phillimore, A. J. (1989). 'University research performance indicators in practice: the UGC's evaluation of British universities 1985/86', *Research Policy*, 18: 255–71.

Porter, A. L. (1977). 'Citation analysis: queries and caveats', *Social Studies of Science*, 7: 257–67.

Powell, J. L. (1973). 'Ability no measure of success', *The Times Higher Education Supplement*, 23 March: 10.

Robbins Report (1963). *Higher Education*, Cmnd. 2154, London, HMSO.

Sear, K. (1983). 'The correlation between A level grades and degree results in England and Wales', *Higher Education*, 12: 609–19.

Shattock, M. L. and Berdahl, R. O. (1984). 'The UGC idea in international perspective', *Higher Education*, 13: 613–18.

Sizer, J. (1988). 'In search of excellence – performance assessment in the UK', *Higher Education Quarterly*, 42: 152–61.

Smith, D. M. (1986). 'UGC research ratings: pass or fail?', *Area*, 18: 247–50.

Smith, R. and Fielder, F. (1971). 'The measurement of scholarly work: a critical review of the literature', *Educational Record*, 52: 225–32.

Smith, T. (1987). 'The UGC's research rankings exercise', *Higher Education Quarterly*, 41: 303–16.

Summerskill, T. (1962). 'Dropouts from college', in N. Sanford (ed.) *The American College*, New York, Wiley.

Tarsh, J. (1982). 'The labour market for new graduates', *Employment Gazette*, 90: 205–15.

Taylor, J. (1986a). 'The employability of graduates: differences between universities', *Studies in Higher Education*, 11: 17–27.

—— (1986b). 'Comparing universities: some observations on the first destination of new graduates', *Higher Education Review*, Autumn: 33–43.

Taylor, J. and Johnes, J. (1989). 'An evaluation of performance indicators based upon the first destination of university graduates', *Studies in Higher Education*, 14: 219–35.

Tinto, V. (1982). 'Defining dropout: a matter of perspective', in E. T. Pascarella (ed.) *Studying Student Attrition*, San Francisco, Jossey-Bass.

Tomkins, C. and Green, R. (1988). 'An experiment in the use of data envelopment analysis for evaluating the efficiency of UK university departments of accounting', *Financial Accountability and Management*, 4, 2: 147–64.

Universities of Scotland (1989). *Student Non-Completion Rates*, Standing Conference of the Universities of Scotland, University of Strathclyde.

UFC (Universities Funding Council) (1989a). 'Funding and planning: 1991/92 to 1994/95', Circular letter 39/89, London, UFC.

—— (1989b). 'Funding and planning: 1991/92 to 1994/95', Circular letter 20/89, London, UFC.

—— (1989c). 'Research selectivity exercise 1989: the outcome', Circular letter 27/89, London, UFC.

UGC (University Grants Committee) (1968). *Enquiry into Student Progress*, London, HMSO.

—— (1982). *Annual Survey, Academic Year 1980/81*, Cmnd. 8663, London, HMSO.

—— (1984). *A Strategy for Higher Education into the 1990s*, London, HMSO.

Voeks, V. W. (1962). 'Publications and teaching effectiveness', *Journal of Higher Education*, 33: 212–18.

Wade, N. (1975). 'Citation analysis: a new tool for science administrators', *Science*, 188: 429–32.

Wallmark, J. T. and Sedig, K. G. (1986). 'Quality of research measured by citation method and peer review – comparison', *IEEE Transactions on Engineering Management*, EM-33: 218–22.

Wankowski, J. (1972). 'Student wastage: the Birmingham experience', in H. J. Butcher and E. Rudd (eds) *Contemporary Problems in Higher Education*, Maidenhead, McGraw-Hill.

Webster, D. S. (1981). 'Methods of assessing quality', *Change*, 13, 7: 20–4.

Whitley, R. and Frost, P. A. (1971). 'The measurement of performance in research', *Human Relations*, 24, 2: 161–78.

Yaes, R. J. (1974). 'Citation analysis', *Science*, 183: 31–2.

Author Index

Subject Index

The Society for Research into Higher Education

The Society exists both to encourage and coordinate research and development into all aspects of higher education, including academic, organizational and policy issues; and also to provide a forum for debate – verbal and printed.

The Society's income derives from subscriptions, book sales, conference fees, and grants. It receives no subsidies and is wholly independent. Its corporate members are institutions of higher education, research institutions and professional, industrial, and governmental bodies. Its individual members include teachers and researchers, administrators and students. Members are found in all parts of the world and the Society regards its international work as amongst its most important activities.

The Society is opposed to discrimination in higher education on grounds of belief, race etc.

The Society discusses and comments on policy, organizes conferences, and encourages research. Under the imprint SRHE & OPEN UNIVERSITY PRESS, it is a specialist publisher of research, having some 40 titles in print. It also publishes *Studies in Higher Education* (three times a year) which is mainly concerned with academic issues; *Higher Education Quarterly* (formerly *Universities Quarterly*) mainly concerned with policy issues; *Abstracts* (three times a year); an *International Newsletter* (twice a year) and *SRHE News* (four times a year).

The Society's committees, study groups and branches are run by members (with help from a small secretariat at Guildford). The groups at present include a Teacher Education Study Group, a Staff Development Group, and a Continuing Education Group and a Women in Higher Education Group. The groups may have their own organization, subscriptions, or publications (e.g. the *Staff Development Newsletter*). A further *Questions of Quality* Group has organized a series of Anglo-American seminars in the USA and the UK.

The Society's annual conferences are held jointly; 'Access and Institutional Change' (1989, with the Polytechnic of North London). In 1990, the topic will be 'Industry and Higher Education' (with the University of Surrey). In 1991, the topic will be 'Research and Higher Education', with the University of Leicester; in 1992, it will be 'Learning and Teaching' (with Nottingham Polytechnic). Other conferences have considered 'HE After the Election' (1987) and 'After the Reform Act' (July 1988).

The Editorial Board of the Society's imprint seeks authoritative research or study in the field. It offers competitive royalties, a highly recognizable format in both hardback and paperback and the world-wide reputation of the Open University Press.

Members receive free of charge the Society's *Abstracts*, annual conference Proceedings (or *Precedings*), *SRHE News* and *International Newsletter*. They may buy SRHE & Open University Press books at discount, and *Higher Education Quarterly* on special terms. Corporate members also receive the Society's journal *Studies in Higher Education* free (individuals on special terms). Members may also obtain certain other journals at a discount, including the NFER *Register of Educational Research*. There is a substantial discount to members, and to staff of corporate members, on annual and some other conference fees.

Further Information: SRHE at the University, Guildford GU2 5XH, UK (0483) 39003.